D0729460

Regulating Wall Street:
CHOICE Act vs. Dodd-Frank

Regulating Wall Street: CHOICE Act vs. Dodd-Frank

Editors

Matthew P. Richardson
Kermit L. Schoenholtz
Bruce Tuckman
Lawrence J. White

Contributing Authors

Barry E. Adler
Thomas F. Cooley
Yiwei Dou
Ralph S. J. Koijen
Thomas Philippon
Matthew P. Richardson
Stephen G. Ryan
Kermit L. Schoenholtz
Philipp Schnabl
Marti G. Subrahmanyam
Bruce Tuckman
Stijn van Nieuwerburgh
Laura L. Veldkamp
Paul A. Wachtel
Ingo Walter
Lawrence J. White

This report has been prepared by faculty members of the NYU Stern School of Business and the NYU School of Law. We thank Judy DiClemente for her excellent editorial support and RFB Orange for their work in designing the cover. We also thank our colleagues at Stern and the Law School for very helpful conversations and guidance. This White Paper reflects the opinions of the editors and authors, not of NYU Stern or the Law School.

This document was created by a team of faculty from the NYU Stern School of Business and the NYU School of Law. This version was completed on March 1, 2017.

Foreword

This White Paper is the joint work of more than a dozen faculty members of the NYU Stern School of Business and the NYU School of Law. Stern and Law School faculty have published several books in recent years on regulatory reform, including a comprehensive assessment of the Dodd-Frank Act.[1]

The goal of the authors remains to contribute thoughtfully to the public discussion about ensuring a safe and efficient financial system. This White Paper, which builds on earlier Stern faculty publications, assesses the strengths and weaknesses of the Financial CHOICE Act proposed by the House Financial Services Committee. The CHOICE Act is the most comprehensive proposal for financial reform since Dodd-Frank and would, if enacted, dramatically alter the regulatory regime established by Dodd-Frank.

---

[1] Acharya, Viral, Thomas F. Cooley, Matthew P. Richardson, and Ingo Walter, eds., *Regulating Wall Street: The Dodd-Frank Act and the New Architecture of Global Finance*, Wiley, November 2010.

—

Table of Contents

Linkages among the White Paper, the CHOICE Act and Dodd-Frank

Section of this White Paper	CHOICE Act	Dodd-Frank Act
Bank Capital Regulation and the Off-Ramp	Title I	Title I, Subtitle C
Resolution Authority Redux	Title I, Title II	Title I, Title II
The Volcker Rule and Regulations of Scope	Title IX	Section 619
Regulating Insurance Companies and the FSOC Designation of SIFIs	Title II, Subtitle A; Title V	Title I, Subtitle A; Title V
Don't Forget the Plumbing: Payment, Clearing, and Settlement Companies in the Dodd-Frank and Financial CHOICE Acts	Title II, Subtitle E	Title VIII
Monetary Policy and the Financial CHOICE Act	Title VII	Title XI
Rebalancing Consumer Protection in the Trump Era	Title III	Title X
Credit Rating Agencies and the Financial CHOICE Act	Title IV, Subtitle B	Title IX, Subtitle C
Evaluation of Accounting-Related Proposals in the Financial CHOICE Act	Title I; Title IV, Subtitles A, B; Title VI, Subtitle A; Title XI, Subtitle N	Title IX, Subtitle D

Reining in the Regulators: Title VI of the Financial CHOICE Act	Title VI	Not addressed in the Act
Streamlining the Regulatory Apparatus	Not addressed in the Act	Not addressed in the Act
De Facto Banking Activities	Not addressed in the Act	Not addressed in the Act
What To Do About the GSEs?	Not addressed in the Act	Not addressed in the Act

Executive Summary

By Matthew P. Richardson, Kermit L. Schoenholtz, Bruce Tuckman, and Lawrence J. White

When a large part of the financial sector is funded with fragile, short-term debt and is hit by a common shock to its long-term assets, there can be en masse failures of financial firms and disruption of intermediation to households and firms. This occurred in the fall and winter of 2008–2009, following the collapse (or near collapse) of many of the largest financial institutions. Over the next six months, the economy and financial markets worldwide tumbled.

In the aftermath of this disaster, governments and regulators cast about for ways to prevent—or render less likely—its recurrence. The existing regulatory framework was wholly unsuited to deal with *systemic risk*: the widespread failure of financial institutions and freezing up of capital markets that impair financial intermediation. In the United States, this recognition led to the Dodd-Frank Wall Street Reform and Consumer Protection Act of 2010.

In an earlier book, *Regulating Wall Street: The Dodd-Frank Act and the New Architecture of Global Finance*, faculty at the NYU Stern School of Business and the NYU School of Law provided a detailed analysis of the strengths and weaknesses of Dodd-Frank.

On the positive side, Dodd-Frank aimed to reduce systemic risk. It called for higher capital and liquidity requirements for banks; the establishment of the Financial Stability Oversight Council (FSOC) to focus regulatory attention on monitoring and containing systemic risk, including designation of new entities called *systemically important financial intermediaries* (SIFIs); the creation of a resolution authority for failing SIFIs; and the formation of the

—
3

Consumer Finance Protection Bureau (CFPB), among numerous other regulations.

On one level, Dodd-Frank has been successful. The NYU Stern Volatility Lab produces systemic risk rankings of financial firms and sectors worldwide (see https://vlab.stern.nyu.edu/en/welcome/risk/). The evidence clearly points not only to much lower systemic risk in the U.S. financial system today relative to the crisis, but also relative to other regions in the world, especially the large countries (and their financial systems) in Europe and Asia. This improvement in safety has been associated with (rather than prevented) relatively good business performance of U.S. banks compared with others.

On the negative side, for all its good intentions, Dodd-Frank arguably does not fully address either the emergence or full-blown onset of systemic risk, suggesting the need to rethink the legislation. Moreover, Dodd-Frank's approach to regulation is more burdensome than necessary for containing systemic risk. In effect, Dodd-Frank threw the proverbial kitchen sink at the financial system. In trying to address problem areas, Dodd-Frank offers multiple regulations, with accumulating costs matched against the same benefit.

Against this background, and with the change in power in Washington, DC, both Congress and the Administration seek to repeal parts of Dodd-Frank, streamline regulation, and reduce compliance costs. The goal of this White Paper is to comment on these potential changes, and, by doing so, promote regulatory changes that make the financial system *both safer and more efficient*. With this in mind, the authors of the essays that follow assessed the strengths and weaknesses of the most complete alternative proposed to Dodd-Frank—namely, the Financial CHOICE Act—by comparing it section by section to the current regulatory regime of Dodd-Frank.

—

In brief, while many aspects of the CHOICE Act are consistent with improving efficiency, in our judgment the CHOICE Act would make the financial system notably less safe, because it does not properly address systemic risk. Some of the main highlights are:

- The CHOICE Act's "off-ramp" provision trades off higher capital requirements against an exemption from much of the Dodd-Frank regulation. We applaud the push toward higher capital and away from Dodd-Frank's regulatory burdens. Nevertheless, while this off-ramp should be available for more than 99% of the banks, up to a few dozen large, complex, and highly interconnected intermediaries should still be subject to the key systemic risk regulations of Dodd-Frank. Otherwise, the financial system will be significantly less safe:

  o In conjunction with the heightened leverage ratio (the CHOICE Act's proposal of 10% is at the low end to be considered), there should also be a risk-weighted capital requirement to control excess risk-taking. In addition, banks' off-balance sheet positions need to be incorporated into both capital ratios.

  o The only true systemic risk assessment tool included in Dodd-Frank is the annual stress test that is applied to SIFIs. Since stress tests can reveal what happens to the system when all large banks and other SIFIs are simultaneously under duress, reducing their frequency would make the financial system substantially less safe. Eliminating them could be catastrophic.

  o Whether the "Orderly Liquidation Authority" (OLA) of Dodd-Frank or the CHOICE Act's alternative bankruptcy procedure is employed when a SIFI fails, it is crucial that these SIFIs have supplied credible resolution plans ("Living Wills") to the regulatory bodies. This way, the failure of the SIFI can be better managed, reducing the likelihood of any bailout and helping to bring back market discipline. Authority for federal funding also would be needed under either alternative (for example, to provide debtor-in-possession finance in a bankruptcy procedure).

- General market conditions will encourage regulatory circumvention, for example, by incentivizing nonbanks to perform *de facto* banking activities, exacerbated further by higher capital requirements on banks. The CHOICE Act eliminates the authority of the FSOC to designate SIFIs, thus worsening the tendency (already evident in Dodd-Frank) to regulate by legal form, rather than by economic function. For example, had the CHOICE Act been in place prior to the last crisis, the very large investment banks such as Bear Stearns, Goldman Sachs, Lehman Brothers, Merrill Lynch, and Morgan Stanley would not have been subject to enhanced prudential supervision. Given their large-scale financial intermediation activities and very high leverage, it is not clear why these nonbanks should be regulated less rigorously than the large, complex, and interconnected banks. Rather, they (and other systemic nonbanks) should be subject to minimum capital requirements, stress tests, and Living Wills, and should be put through a credible resolution process if failing.

- Dodd-Frank imposes a range of new and complex rules on the regulation of banks and financial products, many of which have little to do with the management of systemic risk. Along with the costs of compliance, these rules tend to reduce competition and restrict innovation. Some of these new rules impact "Main Street" banks by drawing them into the regulation net. The CHOICE Act takes aim at many of these regulations. Some examples are:

- o Requiring cost-benefit analyses in financial regulation. We argue that a more effective cost-benefit approach would be a targeted one that requires such analyses only in specific areas that are most likely to be amenable. The goal should be to promote a culture of analysis within the agencies rather than to throw sand in the gears of the regulatory system.

- o Repeal of a number of regulations, most notably, the Volcker Rule. We share the view that systemic risk reduction resulting from the Volcker Rule does not warrant the costs that it imposes.

- o Restructuring the CFPB to be a more accountable agency, focused on economic efficiency, enforcement and financial literacy, rather than approval and/or banning of financial products. We offer a nuanced assessment of this proposal.

Importantly, this summary reflects just a portion of the findings of the essays that follow. In addition to comparing aspects of the CHOICE Act with the Dodd-Frank regime, a sizable part of the White Paper focuses on key financial areas addressed by neither, including the government-sponsored enterprises (GSEs), the burdensome and ineffective complexity of the U.S. regulatory structure, and nonbanks' *de facto* ("shadow") banking activities.

White Paper Highlights

Financial CHOICE Act	Dodd-Frank	NYU Stern & Law
Off-Ramp: Banks with capital greater than 10% of assets may take an off-ramp to avoid the heightened scrutiny of Dodd-Frank.	In addition to regulations and capital requirements, big banks must pass *stress tests* and prepare *Living Wills* to expedite their resolution.	For large, systemic firms, more capital, Living Wills, and stress tests are needed to make the system safe. Compliance burdens can be lowered for most other banks.
SIFIs and FMUs: Eliminate the designations of Systemically Important Financial Institutions and Financial Market Utilities.	The Financial Stability Oversight Council (FSOC) may designate nonbanks as SIFIs or FMUs and impose stricter oversight.	Systemic firms merit strict scrutiny (banks or nonbanks). FMUs need resolution plans, too, and their designations should not limit competition.
Bankruptcy for Large, Failing Financial Institutions: Permit no access to public funds.	Orderly Liquidation Authority imposes losses on investors. Public funds can be used temporarily to facilitate resolution.	For a resolution plan to be optimal and credible, even under a new bankruptcy code, temporary access to public funds is needed.
The Volcker Rule: Repeal it.	The Volcker Rule: Prohibit bank proprietary trading and other activities to contain risk.	The Volcker Rule is too inefficient in controlling systemic risk to justify its high compliance costs.
Monetary Policy: The Federal Reserve should have to defend deviations from a simple monetary policy rule.		Fed independence, key to good economic performance, would be overly curtailed by the CHOICE Act's mix of rules and audits.

CFPB: Reform the Consumer Financial Protection Bureau: increase accountability; require cost-benefit analysis; restrict power to ban products and services.	Set up the CFBP to regulate financial products and services.	The CFBP should be more accountable and should move away from product bans, but needs authority to protect consumers.
		U.S. Financial Regulators: Streamline the structure.
		GSEs and U.S. Housing Finance: Move toward a private system, with any guarantees market priced.
		De Facto **(Shadow) Banking:** Contain the systemic risks.

Introduction

By Thomas F. Cooley

The financial crisis of 2007-2009 and the accompanying contraction in the global economy made it clear that the safety and soundness of the world financial system was seriously impaired and required attention. For the United States, this was a wake up call. The regulatory framework that had functioned well enough since the 1930s had failed.

In response, the United States was the first mover among the world's leading economies in outlining a new regulatory architecture for financial markets. The result was the Dodd-Frank Wall Street Reform and Consumer Financial Protection Act of 2010, the most comprehensive regulatory plan for financial markets since the 1930s. The Dodd-Frank Act was not a fully formed set of rules or even a coherent new regulatory architecture for the United States. Rather it was an attempt to create some common mechanisms for communication and collaboration within the existing regulatory system through a newly created multi-agency organization—the Financial Stability Oversight Council (FSOC)—and a roadmap for rulemaking to address the obvious flaws in the system. It outlined a path for addressing the flaws in the existing regulatory architecture.

The scope of Dodd-Frank is vast, covering everything from consumer financial protection to executive compensation in the financial sector, to the origins of "conflict minerals." It outlined 390 rulemaking requirements, of which roughly 80% have been met. The resulting increase in regulatory complexity, compliance costs for financial institutions and coordination costs for the regulators has, not surprisingly, led to a backlash against the excesses of the Dodd-Frank regulations.

This backlash is manifest most clearly in President Trump's Executive Order of February 3, 2017, outlining "core principles" that are to guide financial regulation in the United States and directing the Treasury Secretary and the FSOC to report on how current regulations fit those core principles. That order is a shot across the bow for financial regulators. More direct is the draft legislation that has been proposed by the House Committee on Financial Services: The Financial CHOICE Act. This broad-based legislation is seemingly aimed at dismembering much of the regulation that resulted from the Dodd-Frank Act and it offers financial market participants an enticing path to escape the more onerous aspects of Dodd-Frank.

Faculty at the NYU Stern School of Business and the NYU School of Law have collaborated on two previous books about the Dodd-Frank Act, as well as books about housing finance and regulation of the insurance industry, all topics that were ripe for examination in the aftermath of the financial crisis.[2] In this White Paper, we offer a critical assessment of the Financial CHOICE Act, discuss its strengths and weaknesses, and analyze whether it represents a step in the right direction for financial regulation, an improvement in regulatory architecture, and a constructive amendment to Dodd-Frank.

Our early assessments of Dodd-Frank found much to criticize in the legislation, but we viewed it as an important step in the direction of making the financial system less risky. It was important because it correctly identified the overarching threat to financial stability and the root cause of the 2008 crisis as the accumulation of systemic risk—risk of collapse because of the interconnected financial risks—in the financial system.

An objective of Dodd-Frank was to identify sources of systemic risk, identify systemically risky institutions, establish ways of monitoring

---

[2] Acharya et al., eds., *Regulating Wall Street:* The Dodd Frank Act and the New Architecture of Global Finance, Wiley, 2011. Acharya et al, *Dodd-Frank One Year On,* VoxEu 2012. Acharya et al., *Guaranteed to Fail,* Princeton University Press, 2011, Biggs, John and M. Richardson, eds., *Modernizing Insurance Regulation,* Wiley 2014.

---

systemic risk in the financial system, limit excessive risk-taking by financial institutions, and provide a roadmap for resolving insolvent institutions. To achieve these goals, Dodd-Frank created the FSOC to monitor systemic risk and identify "systemically important financial institutions" (SIFIs). The legislation required annual stress tests to monitor the adequacy of bank capital in volatile markets. It increased capital requirements (with additional requirements imposed on SIFIs) and required them to conduct regular stress tests to assess the robustness of bank capital in a crisis. It tried to limit the accumulation of systemic risk via the Volcker Rule. It required firms to file resolution plans (Living Wills) and outlined an Orderly Liquidation Authority (OLA) to provide a roadmap and a mechanism for unwinding insolvent firms with minimal disruption to the system.

But the shortcomings of Dodd-Frank were many, and they are at the root of the current backlash. The strengths and weaknesses as we viewed them at the time are discussed in detail in our earlier books.

With nearly seven years of additional perspective, the weaknesses are clearer. Dodd-Frank missed a golden opportunity to simplify and rationalize the very balkanized U.S. regulatory architecture, where responsibility is spread across many institutions, some with overlapping authority. Dodd-Frank did not sufficiently address the issue of the capital adequacy of financial institutions. Its proposals for the orderly liquidation of insolvent institutions were questionable. The proposed Volcker Rule was complicated and difficult to implement, and it became clear that proprietary trading and investing activities were not at the root of the financial crisis. Dodd-Frank did not address the problems of the Government-Sponsored Enterprises (GSEs) or housing finance. It did not address the problem of pricing government guarantees (deposit insurance, lender of last resort access, too-big-to-fail guarantees). It limited the lender of last resort (LOLR) authority of the Fed, constraining its ability to respond in a crisis. The result of the regulatory reform process that Dodd-Frank initiated, to date, has been a vastly more complicated regulatory structure that many doubt is adequate to forestall the next crisis and that some blame for the demise of many small community banks (institutions that are not viewed as part of the systemic problem) and a decline in bank lending.

Given these concerns, the time was ripe for a challenge, and the CHOICE Act does exactly that. In the following essays, we offer an assessment of the components of the CHOICE Act and consider whether they will lead to a safer, more functional financial system.

The essays find constructive elements in the CHOICE Act, and in places we agree with its conclusions and policy recommendations. We also agree with the need to streamline and prune the overly complex regulations that have emerged in the wake of Dodd-Frank.[3] However, the most glaring shortcoming of the CHOICE Act is that it does not recognize the central role of systemic risk. In the end, the CHOICE Act would exacerbate the too-big-to-fail problem by eliminating both the designation of SIFIs and financial market utilities (FMUs), and by prohibiting temporary government lending for resolving failed SIFIs.

Among the Act's false premises are that: (1) SIFIs exist solely because of the implicit government guarantees associated with designating them; and (2) eliminating SIFI designation means that the government will not bail out the creditors of a systemic intermediary in a crisis even if that would induce another economic collapse. Other parts of the Act are overreaching. For example, it would not only restrict the power of the Fed to respond to crises, but also would undercut its ability to conduct monetary policy independently in response to the needs of the economy. It would not only reform the structure and financing of the Consumer Financial Protection Bureau (CFPB) but also would undercut its core

---

[3] Nowhere is this more evident than in the set of rules deemed necessary to implement the Volcker Rule.

mission to encourage educated consumers, promote transparency of financial products and handle consumer complaints.

Of at least equal concern are the issues that the CHOICE Act does not touch: housing finance, *de facto* (shadow) banking, the complex structure of U.S. regulators, and cross-border regulatory issues.

In the end, one has to evaluate the CHOICE Act by asking whether the future of the financial system would be safer and more stable under it or with Dodd-Frank—even in its current form. We think the CHOICE Act would <u>increase</u> the riskiness of our financial system.

Bank Capital

The CHOICE Act begins with a premise that we endorse: Financial institutions that are well capitalized relative to their risk exposure pose less risk to the financial system and make the possibility of a systemic crisis much smaller. It is widely agreed that the financial system was undercapitalized prior to 2008. But Dodd-Frank did not directly address the idea of ensuring financial stability directly through capital requirements, or at least it did not do it very well. The CHOICE Act offers a very enticing prospect: Financial institutions that are "well managed and well capitalized—those with a simple leverage ratio of greater than 10%" would be offered an "off-ramp" from the Dodd-Frank regulations.

The CHOICE Act offers an extensive argument in favor of a simple leverage ratio as a measure of capital adequacy and a critique of the Basel risk-based capital approach. We generally support these arguments. The Act also offers a defense of the estimate of 10% as an adequate "safe" level. The essays in this White Paper address this issue in detail. The relevant empirical and quantitative evidence suggest that 10% is at the <u>very</u> low end of what might be an adequate level of capital to forestall a crisis. An indicator of how far off it may be is the "Minneapolis Plan."[4] This alternative proposal for ending Too-Big-To-Fail—based largely on higher capital cushions—envisions leverage ratios more than twice the CHOICE Act's 10%.

There is also an issue with how the CHOICE Act measures the leverage ratio. It uses Generally Accepted Accounting Principles (GAAP). Under GAAP, the average leverage ratio of the U.S. globally systemically important banks (G-SIBs) already is 8.24%. But, under International Financial Reporting Standards (IFRS), which do not net out derivative positions but use gross derivatives positions, their average leverage ratio is 5.75%. For systemic risk, the latter measurement system is more appropriate, because netting of offsetting derivatives positions may not be feasible in a crisis.

There is a deeper problem than just having the level of capital wrong. The CHOICE Act does not address the critical issue of what happens to the value of that capital when the economy and capital markets are in distress. It simply fails to recognize the nature and importance of systemic risk.

The CHOICE Act argues that the regulatory burdens and the costs of compliance with Dodd-Frank fall most heavily on small community banks that provide much of the funding for small business in the United States. This argument is misplaced. Small banks are exempt from stress tests, systemic capital surcharges, Living Wills and other aspects of Dodd-Frank that apply to the few large, systemically important banks. But the fixed costs of basic regulatory compliance do pose a higher *proportional* burden on small banks relative to their size. The CHOICE Act argues that the regulatory burden on small banks has led a decline in the number of banks, in funding for small firms and a rise in the cost of credit for small business. These assertions require some scrutiny, but the notion that the increased

---

[4] https://www.minneapolisfed.org/publications/special-studies/endingtbtf/the-minneapolis-plan-to-end-too-big-to-fail

---

cost of compliance is a burden for small banks is not in dispute. So, the idea of an off-ramp for small banks is appealing.[5]

What about big banks? The CHOICE Act thinks the same logic applies to big banks. It does a good job of disputing the notion that higher capital requirements will lead to less lending. It also takes on the arguments that "equity is expensive." However, because the Act misunderstands the nature of systemic risk, it understates the necessity for large banks to have sufficient capital to withstand systemic problems, and it ignores the role that stress tests can play in identifying those systemic problems.

Systemic Risk

The CHOICE Act is plagued by a problem that beleaguered the Dodd-Frank drafters: It confuses legal form and economic function and, in the process, shows a lack of understanding of the sources of the crisis. One of the more strident sections of the Act would repeal the authority of the FSOC to designate financial institutions as SIFIs and payments, clearing, and settlements companies as FMUs. It would also abolish the research arm of the Treasury (Office of Financial Research, OFR) that supports the FSOC's work. The framers of the CHOICE Act view the FSOC's authority as regulatory overreach that uses arbitrary and capricious standards and that enshrines the firms designated as too-big-to-fail.

However, it is not the designation that makes firms risky; it is their activities. As a result, it is critical to monitor that risk. A key part of that monitoring is to know exactly the nature of a firm's capital and liabilities and to understand how a firm's capital and liquidity will

---

[5] The suggestion that Dodd-Frank is responsible for a decline in the number of banks or the decline in lending is open to debate. See Cecchetti and Schoenholtz: http://www.moneyandbanking.com/commentary/2016/12/12/dodd-frank-the-choice-act-and-small-banks

perform in a crisis. That is what systemic risk monitoring is all about, and that is the role of the FSOC and SIFI designation.[6]

The CHOICE Act is completely misguided in wanting to eliminate the oversight of systemic risk and the use of stress tests to understand how capital holds up in a crisis. The Act legitimately decries the "form" of the FSOC. But, that is a legacy of the complex regulatory system that we still have. The inelegant form does not undercut the importance of the function of the FSOC, or its OFR research arm, which is to monitor system risk and the institutions, practices and mechanisms that make the financial system vulnerable.

Stress tests are the critical means to ensure that the capital requirements are enforced and not circumvented (say, through off-balance sheet or derivatives exposure). They allow better insight into the banks' own risk models and management to see where the system as a whole may be vulnerable. They are the only mechanism for examining the well-being of a systemic intermediary when the financial system as a whole may be in distress. Offering an off-ramp from stress tests would seriously undermine the effectiveness of capital regulation for the most systemic intermediaries.

The CHOICE Act also attacks the FSOC for concerning itself with the migration of risk to the "shadow banking system"—what we refer to as *de facto banking activities*—activities that involve transformations of liquidity, maturity, and credit that "take place without direct and explicit access to public sources of liquidity or credit backstops." Instead, the Act's drafters should applaud this focus. Perhaps the view is that, since shadow banking is often the result of regulatory arbitrage, in a "regulation lite" world, it will not be a problem. Dodd-Frank did not concern itself enough with the shadow banking system—again focusing on form rather than

---

[6] It is also why we at Stern have pioneered the development of systemic risk measures.

---

function—even though much of the financial crisis first showed up in the shadow banking system.

Dodd-Frank also sought to limit the possibilities for the buildup of systemic risks by incorporating the Volcker Rule. The rule prohibits bank holding companies or their subsidiaries from engaging in proprietary trading and sponsoring hedge funds or private equity funds. The rule was intended to limit the accumulation of difficult-to-assess risk on banks' books through these activities.

The Volcker Rule, although simply stated at the outset, turned into many pages of regulations and, in the end, seems wholly impractical. Compliance is a nightmare for many institutions. There is also little evidence that proprietary trading or banks' relationships with hedge funds played a significant role in the financial crisis. There is also some evidence that liquidity provision has fallen and that the Volcker Rule could be one of the reasons.

For these reasons, this is a case where we agree with the conclusion of the CHOICE Act that the Volcker Rule should be scrapped.

Resolution

The key goal of Dodd-Frank was to end the notion of too-big-to-fail—to save future regulators from facing the terrible choice of bailing out insolvent institutions or letting them collapse in a disorderly way with lots of collateral damage, as with Lehman Brothers. The Dodd-Frank solution was to require banks to provide Living Wills specifying exactly how they will be restructured in the event of failure and to create an OLA within the FDIC for insolvent firms. The Dodd-Frank architects envisioned the OLA as a way of replacing taxpayer-funded bailouts by laying out a procedure for the FDIC, an institution with a long history of resolving and restructuring insolvent institutions, to restructure large systemic institutions.

Many have expressed doubts about whether the OLA framework is the right conceptual framework for resolving systemically important firms. The CHOICE Act cites our previous critique[7] of the plan. Conceptual gaps and distorted incentives in the design of Dodd-Frank's OLA raise concerns that—in the next financial crisis, as in the last—regulatory discretion and forbearance might take hold as the preferred route of crisis resolution.

The CHOICE Act argues that insolvent institutions should be addressed instead using the Federal Bankruptcy Code. This is a position that has been the subject of lively debate in the academic and legal literature. Of course, this would require a new Chapter of the Bankruptcy Code to address the unique problems of large systemic financial institutions. Advocates of the bankruptcy approach argue that: it is administered through the judicial system and is less subject to regulatory discretion; it provides more certainty about how creditors will be treated in bankruptcy; and it does not require taxpayer funds to reorganize or liquidate a failed institution. These are all valid points. However, some of these may seem like a distinction without a difference, as the OLA was always intended to adhere as closely as possible to the Bankruptcy Code. It is also the case that in bankruptcy, someone has to provide debtor-in-possession financing, and this is not spelled out by the CHOICE Act. Further, bankruptcy can be a slow, grinding process, which can create extended value-destroying uncertainty for the liability holders who may have claims on a beleaguered financial institution that total in the hundreds of billions of dollars.[8]

The alternative route to resolving insolvent institutions—not addressed by the CHOICE Act—is to build rule-based recapitalization directly into the capital structure, as well as imposing upfront capital requirements that are tied to systemic risk. This alternative uses bail-in-able debt that can be converted to

---

[7] Acharya et al., *Regulating Wall Street*.

[8] This was all-too-well illustrated in the case of the Lehman bankruptcy.

equity if a firm becomes insolvent. Bail-in-able debt has been enthusiastically embraced in Europe in the form of contingent-convertible (Co-Co) bonds and total loss absorbing capacity (TLAC) debt. There are many issues raised by this approach as well, including triggers for conversion, accounting standards for the assessment of equity, and valuations in a distressed environment. The first line of defense against insolvency is always higher equity. But the appeal of automatic recapitalization is that it relies less on external funding and administrative discretion.

Whether any of these different approaches to resolution can effectively deal with a systemic crisis or not will be known only the next time we do have a crisis.

The Federal Reserve

Many observers were concerned about the role of the Federal Reserve in the financial crisis. The Fed made liberal use of its authority under section 13(3) of Federal Reserve Act to lend to "any individual, partnership or corporation" under unusual and exigent circumstances.

Critics of some of the choices made by the Fed at the time of the crisis argued that the Fed had overreached and, by extending its lender of last resort facility to so many actors, had increased moral hazard. Dodd-Frank responded by limiting the ability of the Fed to use its 13(3) authority, for example by prohibiting loans to individual nonbanks outside of a pre-approved program of broad access. In our earlier books, we expressed concern that this limited the ability of the Fed to respond in a crisis.

The CHOICE Act seeks to limit the Fed's role even further by restricting how the Fed conducts its monetary policy, how it functions as the LOLR, and how it exercises its regulatory responsibilities.

The Act's calls to constrain monetary policy ignore a large and persuasive body of evidence that supports the importance of independent central banks and monetary policy. This is discussed in detail in these essays. Aside from that blind spot, the CHOICE Act's limitations on LOLR lending and attacks on the Fed's stress testing and other regulatory functions again displays a failure to understand the critical role of systemic risk.

The Federal Reserve played a critical role in the financial crisis and its aftermath. If anything, the experience of the past decade underscores how important it is to have an independent and agile central bank. In the aftermath of the crisis, we have a better understanding of the extent of systemic risk and the important role it plays in financial stability.

The difficult choice for Fed policy is how it deploys its LOLR facility in a crisis. The CHOICE Act deploys a lot of rhetoric about how the Fed should adhere to Bagehot's dictums to lend only to solvent borrowers, on good collateral, at penalty rates. Clearly the Fed should be open to all systemic institutions and lend only to those that are solvent. To lend knowingly to insolvent institutions would vastly increase the moral hazard in the financial system. It would also undermine the LOLR role—which requires lending broadly to solvent, but illiquid firms—because any firm that "went to the window" would have a potential stigma. Lending to an insolvent firm also would subordinate private creditors in the ultimate bankruptcy process.

But deciding who is solvent or insolvent in a crisis is extremely difficult. That was the great quandary surrounding Lehman Brothers in September of 2008. And that is exactly why the institutions that Dodd-Frank put in place to assess systemic risk—institutions that the CHOICE Act would dismantle—are so important.

Consumer Financial Protection

The Consumer Financial Protection Bureau (CFPB) has been controversial since its inception. The framers of Dodd-Frank did not do the CFPB a service by giving it the unique structure that the agency has within the regulatory bureaucracy. The CFPB is governed by a single director, appointed by the President and confirmed by Congress, who serves a five-year term. Once appointed, the director cannot be removed except for cause. The CFPB is funded directly from the Federal Reserve. The CFPB need only submit a budget to the Fed certifying what it needs to finance operations. This structure is unorthodox to say the least. Funding any government agency directly from the profits of the Fed is a bad idea because it undermines the independence of the Fed and it can hinder appropriate oversight by elected officials. Most of the other regulatory agencies are funded from fees related to their regulatory functions (e.g., examination fees) and/or Congressional appropriations.

The original remit of the CFPB was to help consumers understand and use relevant information about financial products. It aimed to shield them from abuse, deception, and fraud by ensuring that disclosures for financial products are accurate and easy to understand. The CFPB has adopted a broad interpretation of that mandate.

The CHOICE Act proposes to overhaul the structure and financing of the CFPB to bring it more in line with other regulatory institutions. It also would restrict the authority of the CFPB to limit consumers' access to products that it deemed "abusive" and would require that product safety regulations be justified by a cost-benefit analysis. It is encouraging that the CHOICE Act does not recommend abolishing the CFPB. That is implicit recognition that there are "product safety" issues with financial products and thus the need for education, standards and transparency. At the same time, the CHOICE Act seems determined to limit the flow and public dissemination of information from consumers about their issues with financial products.

Some Gaping Holes in the Financial CHOICE Act

The CHOICE Act is notable for the issues it did not touch. Like Dodd-Frank, it does not address the problems of the GSEs—Fannie Mae and Freddie Mac—that remain at the heart of the U.S. mortgage market. The GSEs are not a regulatory priority because they remain in conservatorship, are currently profitable and have limited their downside risk. Any attempt to reform them and limit the government's exposure from guarantees would raise the cost of mortgage finance—something that is politically unpalatable. Nevertheless, reform of housing finance is both feasible and desirable.

Another important gap is the neglect of the "shadow banking" sector. Neither Dodd-Frank nor the CHOICE Act addresses the systemic risks arising from *de facto banking activities* per se. But this sector was hugely important in the crisis. The growth of the "shadow banking" system permitted financial institutions to engage in maturity transformation with too little transparency, capital, or oversight. Large, short-term funded, substantially interconnected financial firms came to dominate key credit markets. Huge amounts of risk moved outside the more regulated parts of the banking system to where it was easier to increase leverage. Legal loopholes allowed large parts of the financial industry to operate without oversight or transparency. Entities that perform the same market functions as banks escaped meaningful regulation solely because of their corporate form.

Yet by focusing on measuring and monitoring systemic risk, by designating systemically risky institutions, and by insisting on stress tests, Dodd-Frank at least has a foot in the door of addressing the problems that can arise from these *de facto* banks. And the FSOC has been actively engaged in the debate over how to regulate them.

The CHOICE Act has nothing to say about this important sector of the financial system.

Conclusion

Dodd-Frank was not the perfect remedy for all of the problems of the U.S. financial sector that came together to form the "perfect storm" of the financial crisis of 2007-2009. Many faculty authors at Stern have previously criticized the shortcomings of the Dodd-Frank, and in this White Paper we again criticize many of these shortcomings with the advantage of a few more years of experience. But, to its credit, the Dodd-Frank did recognize the importance and pernicious nature of systemic risk in the U.S. financial system and created prudential regulatory institutions and procedures to address and reduce that risk. Again, those institutions and procedures are far from perfect and could surely be made better. But, on balance, Dodd-Frank represented a positive step in lessening the risk in our financial system.

The Financial CHOICE Act espouses some principles that we heartily endorse. Chief among them is that the more well-capitalized institutions are, the less threat they pose to financial stability. And we endorse removing many inefficient parts of the Dodd-Frank. But at the end of the day, the CHOICE Act is fatally flawed by a failure to recognize systemic risk and to understand the dangers that it poses for the financial system and thus for the healthy functioning of the U.S. economy. Because of this failure, the CHOICE Act represents a potential step backward in the establishment of a prudential regulatory system that would ensure a safer and better functioning financial sector for the U.S. economy.

Because the Financial CHOICE Act is still at the stage of proposed legislation, there is adequate time and opportunity for its drafters to reach a better understanding of these issues. We hope that the chapters in this White Paper will help in this process.

Managing Systemic Risk:
The Core of the Financial CHOICE Act

Bank Capital Regulation and the Off-Ramp

By Philipp Schnabl[9]

Bank Capital and Systemic Risk

One of the important lessons from the 2007-2009 financial crisis has been that failures of large financial institutions can impose costs on the entire system (referred to as systemic risk). The failure of "systemically important financial institutions" (SIFIs) invariably puts regulators in a compromised situation since, absent a credible bankruptcy regime, they are forced to rescue the failed institutions to preserve a functioning financial system and avert a credit crunch. In the most recent financial crisis, this involved protecting not just insured creditors, but also sometimes uninsured creditors and even shareholders. The anticipation that these bailouts will occur compromises market discipline in good times, encouraging excessive leverage and risk taking. This reinforces the systemic risk in the system and creates the need for bank regulation to contain systemic risk.[10]

Capital requirements play an important role in limiting systemic risk. Banks have an incentive to issue too little capital relative to their size because they do not take into account the cost of a systemic crisis. Bank capital regulation ensures that banks have a specified minimum amount of capital relative to their risk exposures. If the banking system is sufficiently capitalized, the likelihood of a systemic crisis is low. In the extreme case, if all banks

[9] The author is an Associate Professor at New York University, Stern School of Business, and affiliated with the National Bureau of Economic Research (NBER) and the Center for Economic Performance (CEPR). This draft was partially written while the author was an unpaid Visiting Scholar at the New York Federal Reserve (January to June 2017). I thank Viral Acharya, Matthew P. Richardson, Bruce Tuckman, Kermit L. Schoenholtz, and Larry White for helpful comments on the draft. I thank Patrick Farrell for research assistance. All errors are my own.
[10] See Chapters 5 and 6 of Acharya et al. (2011).

are financed with 100% equity, there is no risk of a bank failure, and there is no risk of a systemic crisis.[11] Hence, bank capital regulation can ensure that banks have sufficient capital to withstand a crisis.

The need for bank capital requirements must be weighed against the direct and indirect costs of capital regulation. The direct costs are expenses paid by regulators and banks in order to implement capital regulation. There will also be recurring expenses, because regulations have to be updated as the banking industry evolves. Some of these costs may be offset by better bank risk management if banks benefit from interacting with regulators. Such benefits may arise if regulators collect and distribute information that improves the efficiency of the system but cannot be accessed by individual banks (e.g., information on system-wide exposures).

The indirect costs are inefficiencies in the banking system due to capital regulation. Some argue that, at least theoretically, high capital requirements may distort incentives for bank management. Specifically, higher capital requirements may reduce monitoring by debt holders and depositors and lead to a less efficient banking system. It has also been argued that higher capital requirements may impair lending. Specifically, if bank equity is costly due to informational frictions, then requiring more capital can lead to a decrease in credit supplied by the banking system. This reduction in lending is inefficient if potential projects have a positive net present value and firms cannot access other sources of financing (e.g., Calomiris and Kahn (1991), Diamond and Rajan (2000)).[12]

---

[11] A 100% equity-financed banking system is considered extreme because a significant part of a bank's business is the issuance of money-like securities such as deposits or wholesale funding (e.g., repos, commercial paper, etc.). These money-like securities provide liquidity benefits that are part of a bank's business model.

[12] Bank capital requirements may reduce lending because higher capital requirements reduce the expected value of FDIC insurance and too-big-to-fail guarantees. In this case, the decline in lending is optimal because lending is excessive because of government guarantees.

There is a large empirical literature on the benefits and cost of bank capital. Considerable evidence exists that having banks with higher capital levels is beneficial during a crisis. Banks with more capital are generally better able to withstand crisis and lend more if there is a negative shock (e.g., Peek and Rosengren (2000), Ivashina and Scharfstein (2010), Cornett et al. (2011), Schnabl (2012), Paravisini et al. (2015)). However, there is some uncertainty as to whether there are significant costs of requiring higher capital ratios. Some argue that higher capital requirements decrease lending during normal times, although there is considerable disagreement regarding the economic magnitude of these effects.[13]

Any regulatory framework therefore needs to strike a balance between keeping systemic risk at an acceptable level, while making sure that the costs of regulation are adequate relative to the risk.[14] A general lesson of the 2007-2009 financial crisis was that bank regulation paid insufficient attention to the risk of systemic crisis. Bank regulation was focused primarily on preventing individual bank failures, without paying much attention to preventing a large-scale systemic crisis involving many failures. It turned out that the banking system entered the financial crisis with too little capital, and many banks became distressed once the crisis intensified in October 2008. In order to maintain a functioning financial system, the U.S. Government decided to bail out many banks—including some of the largest ones—which exposed taxpayers to significant credit risk.[15] The government also provided large subsidies to nonbanks that did not fit the regulatory definition of a bank but effectively provided banking services, such as lending, market making, and securitization.

---

[13] Admati and Hellwig (2013) argue that the costs of high bank capital requirements are negligible. Calomiris (2012) argues that the costs can be substantial.

[14] Regulators also need to recognize that higher capital requirements increase incentives for nonbanks to arbitrage regulation. Regulation should therefore focus on economic function rather than institutional characteristics.

[15] Optimal Bailouts minimize the cost to taxpayers by providing subsidies only to debt holders and not equity holders (Philippon and Schnabl (2012)).

To ensure that such bailouts are less likely going forward and to minimize the expected cost to taxpayers, many observers have argued that regulation needs to monitor systemic risk and keep it at an acceptable level. The Dodd-Frank Act was an attempt to strike the right balance between the costs and benefits of bank regulation with a special focus on SIFIs.[16]

How the Dodd-Frank Act Addresses Systemic Risk

In June 2010, Congress passed the Dodd-Frank Act. Broadly speaking, the Dodd-Frank Act imposes regulatory constraints on large banks that reduce the likelihood of another systemic crisis. Many features of the Dodd-Frank Act are sensible and conform to the recommendations of the first NYU Stern Book, *Restoring Financial Stability* (2009). Other features of Dodd-Frank, however, are problematic for the financial system, and many are left to the implementation of various regulatory bodies. For an overview of the main issues, see the second NYU Stern Book, *Regulating Wall Street: The Dodd–Frank Act and the New Architecture of Global Finance* (2011). It is beyond the scope of this chapter to review all aspects of how the Dodd-Frank Act addresses systemic risk. But a brief description of the main elements will serve as an introduction to the proposed changes under the Financial CHOICE Act.

The Dodd-Frank Act focuses on systemic risk. It establishes a Financial Stability Oversight Council (FSOC), which is chaired by the

---

[16] It is important to distinguish the reasoning for regulating systemic risk from the traditional reasoning of regulating banks. The traditional argument focuses on the liabilities structure of banks and banks' role as providers of risk-free deposits. To guarantee the safety of deposits, the U.S. Government provides deposit insurance through the Federal Deposit Insurance Corporation (FDIC) on deposits below a certain limit. In turn, the provision of deposit insurance exposes the U.S. Government to the risk of bank failures and therefore requires regulation (see, for example, Dewatripont and Tirole (1994)). In addition, bank financing may be biased towards debt because debt financing has tax advantages relative to equity. This bias towards debt financing can be eliminated by giving equal tax treatment to debt and equity.

Secretary of the Treasury and consists of the top financial officers from various governmental and regulatory agencies. The chief role of the FSOC is to identify systemic risks wherever they arise and to recommend policies to regulatory bodies. As a quick rule of thumb, financial institutions that have a huge concentration in volume of one or more product areas are likely candidates to be systemically risky institutions. These entities are likely to be making markets in that product and are likely to be systemic in that their failures would impose significant counterparty risk and disruptions on other financial institutions.

The Dodd-Frank Act leaves significant leeway to regulators regarding the specific policies to reduce systemic risk. Capital regulation through risk-based capital requirements and leverage limits plays an important role. In addition, Dodd-Frank also mentions the following policies:

- Liquidity requirements;
- Resolution plan and credit exposure report requirements;
- Concentration limits;
- Contingent capital requirements;
- Enhanced public disclosures;
- Short-term debt limits; and
- Risk management requirements.

Since the implementation of the Dodd-Frank Act, it has become clear that all banks with at least $50 billion in assets receive considerable scrutiny under the new regulation. These banks have become the focus of regulators and should be considered the core of banks designated as SIFIs.

SIFIs have to undergo annual stress tests that evaluate whether a bank has sufficient capital to withstand a large-scale crisis. Given that stress tests focus on crisis scenarios, they are particularly well suited for addressing systemic risk.[17] The stress tests are conducted by bank regulators and require banks to submit detailed plans and documentation for stress scenarios. The submissions are evaluated and verified by bank regulators. If regulators deem a submission unsatisfactory, regulators can require a bank to raise more capital. Regulators have exercised these powers several times over the past few years.

How the Financial CHOICE Act Addresses Systemic Risk

The CHOICE Act argues that banks should be exempt from Dodd-Frank if they have sufficient capital, referring to this opt-out option as the "Dodd-Frank Off-Ramp for Strongly-Capitalized, Well-Managed Banking Organizations." The CHOICE Act proposes using a simple capital ratio of 10% as the threshold for the "off-ramp." If a bank's capital ratio exceeds 10%, the bank should be considered sufficiently capitalized and would not need to follow the regulations of the Dodd-Frank Act. The capital ratio under the Financial CHOICE Act treats all asset risk equally, assigning a risk weight of one to all assets. The Financial CHOICE Act also requires that banks maintain an acceptable risk rating from regulators, which adds an additional layer of security.[18]

The logic behind the Financial CHOICE Act is straightforward: It argues that banks with sufficient capital do not require the supervision imposed by Dodd-Frank. The reason is that banks with sufficient capital have the appropriate incentives for risk taking, because equity holders ultimately bear any cost of excessive risk taking, and there is no scope for moral hazard. Hence, as long as there is sufficient capital, there is no need to be concerned about financial risk-taking leading to financial crisis.

---

[17] Most other policies reduce the individual likelihood of failure of SIFIs. These policies will generally reduce systemic risk, but they are not well suited to evaluate and address systemic risk directly.

[18] Banks have to maintain a CAMELS (Capital adequacy, Assets, Management capability, Earnings, Liquidity, Sensitivity to market risk) rating of 1 or 2.

The main benefit of the proposal is that well-capitalized banks would not need to spend resources to comply with the regulations imposed under Dodd-Frank. Presumably, less regulation would reduce the cost of compliance and make banks more efficient. It may also reduce the fixed cost of running a bank, thus promoting bank entry and helping small banks, which find it difficult to cover the fixed costs of complying with bank regulation.

Overall Assessment of the Off-Ramp under the Financial CHOICE Act

The overall logic of the CHOICE Act is sensible. There is a trade-off between the benefits and costs of bank capital regulation. If a bank is highly capitalized, the benefits of regulation are smaller, because moral hazard concerns are less important and bank equity holders are more likely to make efficient lending decisions. Holding everything else equal, it therefore makes sense to reduce regulation as banks hold more equity.

There are two important caveats to this argument: First, banks react to changes in thresholds. If a threshold of 10% provides an opportunity to avoid regulation, banks may choose to structure their balance sheets in a way that satisfies this requirement without necessarily reducing risk. The history of bank regulation has observed this dynamic so many times that it has been coined Goodhart's Law: "When a measure becomes a target, it ceases to be a good measure."[19] As discussed below in more detail, the "off-ramp," therefore, needs to take into account a bank's incentive to adjust its balance sheet in response to the threshold. Banks have a number of ways to achieve a higher capital ratio without reducing their risks, and regulation needs to take these incentives into account.

---

[19] The principle is also known as the "Lucas critique."

Second, the level of the threshold is important. At a capital ratio of 10%, banks can still finance 90% of their balance sheet with debt, and thus remain highly levered. Importantly, the ratio proposed under the Financial CHOICE Act is measured during regular times when the economy is doing well. However, from a systemic risk point of view, the question is whether banks have sufficient capital during a crisis.[20] As discussed below, it is therefore important to consider both the level of the threshold and how to measure the capital ratio.

The remainder of this assessment discusses policies that need to be in place in order to allow for a safe off-ramp. In practice, these regulations will require keeping significant elements of the Dodd-Frank Act in order to ensure proper monitoring and regulation of banks choosing the off-ramp. The following discussion focuses on banks that are systemically important—namely the ones with at least $50 billion in assets. The off-ramp is more defensible and easier to implement for small banks, although some regulation may also be necessary for small banks.[21]

Considerations for the Off-Ramp Proposal

The Role of Stress Tests

Stress tests evaluate capital levels during a crisis. Banks have long conducted internal stress tests to evaluate their exposure to sudden changes in the economic environment. Dodd-Frank introduced stress tests as an important tool for regulators, and it standardized the use of stress tests across banks. Stress tests are now considered an essential tool to understand bank capital levels in stressed scenarios.

---

[20] The Volatility Institute at NYU Stern provides estimates of bank systemic risk exposure and systemic risk ranking. The estimates are updated daily and can be accessed at https://vlab.stern.nyu.edu/welcome/risk/.

[21] See Dou and Ryan (2017), in this White paper, for a discussion of the off-ramp for medium-sized and small banks.

The CHOICE Act proposes to exclude banks from stress tests if they exceed a capital requirement of 10%. This proposal fundamentally misunderstands the purpose of systemic risk regulation. The objective of systemic risk regulation is to ensure that a bank has sufficient capital during a crisis. Holding everything else equal, a bank with a high level of capital during normal times is also likely to have more capital during a crisis. However, if the bank is also more exposed to a systemic crisis—e.g., by investing in illiquid assets that are likely to decline in value during a systemic crisis—it is not sufficient to have high capital during normal times. In fact, regulation based on a simple leverage ratio provides incentives for banks to increase their exposure to systemic risk.[22] At a minimum, the off-ramp would need to be based on the expected capital ratio during a crisis rather than capital during regular times.

Stress tests are successful if they provide a good measure of expected capital during a crisis. This goal can only be achieved if stress tests are credible in the sense that the results cannot be manipulated by participating institutions. The CHOICE Act proposes to publish all scenarios and models used in stress tests in advance. The underlying idea is that this would make the stress tests more transparent. Even though transparency is a laudable objective, in our view publishing all the information upfront is not recommended. To make a simple comparison, publishing the stress test scenarios in advance is like giving students their exam prior to the exam date. If banks know the scenarios upfront, the test is subject to gaming, and some banks may tailor their submission to pass the test. Hence, in order to minimize gaming against the tests, it is important to keep an element of surprise. Alternatively, regulators would need to ask banks to submit expected capital levels under a much larger number of scenarios than currently used.

---

[22] Farhi and Tirole (2012).

This alternative would reduce gaming but may lead to even larger cost for complying with the stress tests.[23]

This is not to say that bank stress tests necessarily have been conducted optimally. Regulators are still learning about this new approach to regulation, and some of the modeling and regulatory choices may appear arbitrary. There is room for streamlining the tests and scope for increasing the transparency. However, given the benefits of the tests, it seems sensible to maintain the current approach and improve the test rather than abandoning it altogether. To continue with the example from above, if a professor gives a badly written exam, the objective should be improving the content of the exam, rather than abandoning exams altogether.[24]

It is also important to be clear about the costs of bank stress tests, which can be separated into a social cost and a private cost. The main penalty for failing a stress test is the requirement to raise more equity—usually through lowering payouts to shareholders. Even though such a penalty may be perceived as costly by banks, it may not be costly from a social perspective. The reduction in payouts simply means that shareholders' equity is increased by the same amount. To the extent that the increase in bank equity is lower than the payouts, the difference can come from decreasing the expected government subsidy. As discussed above, higher equity required under the stress tests is only socially costly to the extent that it distorts bank management and reduces lending to

---

[23] A cautionary tale is the failure of stress testing for Government-Sponsored Enterprises (GSEs). GSEs had to undergo stress tests before the 2008 financial crisis, but never experienced meaningful capital shortfalls. A subsequent analysis of these stress tests suggests that the GSEs gamed the tests because the stress test models were fully disclosed prior to the tests (Frame, Gerardi and Willen (2015)).

[24] Acharya, Pedersen, Richardson, and Philippon (2017) find that the bank stress tests deliver similar results to systemic risk measures based on publicly available market data. This finding provides some external validity to results of the stress tests. It also suggests that the results are consistent with information on systemic risk embedded in security prices.

---

socially optimal projects. Hence, penalties under stress tests do not necessarily represent a social cost and may even improve the safety of the financial system.

Market versus Book Values

The capital ratio is based on a simple leverage ratio. Our understanding of the Financial CHOICE Act is that the capital ratio is computed using book values instead of market values. Yet, book values tend to be uninformative about a bank's capital position— especially in the midst of a crisis. This is because banks have strong incentives to delay the recognition of losses. This delay is partly to avoid attention by regulators and investors but also to avoid triggering bank runs that can lead to bank failure.

The U.S. financial crisis provides plenty of examples of banks that were well-capitalized based on book measure of leverage immediately prior to going bankrupt. Among broker-dealers, Lehman Brothers had a Tier 1 capital ratio of 11% in the week prior to its failure. Among deposit-taking institutions, Washington Mutual was considered sufficiently capitalized with a Tier 1 capital ratio of 7% prior to its failure.

Hence, it is likely that book values become uninformative during a crisis. It is therefore advisable to include information on market values when evaluating bank capital. To be clear, we do not necessarily advocate replacing book values with market values. A reasonable case can be made that market values can overstate the decline in equity value during a crisis. Hence, it is sensible to incorporate market values in the evaluation of capital levels in addition to using book values.[25]

---

[25] Acharya, Engle, and Pierret (2014) examine the role of using market versus book values in the context of the European sovereign debt crisis.

Off-Balance Sheet Exposures

Many financial intuitions have off-balance sheet exposures that can add to a bank's liabilities during a systemic crisis. The Financial CHOICE Act acknowledges such exposures and mentions that some off-balance sheet exposures will be included in the computation of capital ratios. This is sensible but does not go far enough. Banks that want to circumvent capital requirements tend to find ways to structure risk such that they remain off-balance sheet. For example, prior to 2008, many banks sponsored asset-backed commercial paper (ABCP) conduits. The conduits were considered off-balance sheet for regulatory purposes and only triggered small capital charges. Yet, liquidity guarantees were structured to avoid capital requirements, while providing full insurance to outside investors. Once there was turmoil in money market in August 2007, most banks were contractually obligated to purchase the assets in ABCP conduits or finance them otherwise (Acharya, Suarez, and Schnabl (2013)). Given that conduits effectively had no equity, conduit assets increased bank leverage in the midst of a crisis and should have been included in the computation of capital ratios before the crisis.

There are other examples of such regulatory arbitrage. Recent work using data on internal risk models has found that banks with less capital tend to assign lower probabilities of default even for similar loans (Plosser and Santos, 2015). Other research has shown that banks became more optimistic about risk when risk assessments were used for capital regulation, and this effect was larger for less capitalized banks (Behn, Haselmann, and Vig (2014)). There is also work showing that banks assign a lower "Value at Risk" to their security holdings if they are capital constrained (Begley, Purnanandam, and Zheng (2016)).

Post-crisis bank regulation addresses many of the known loopholes for regulatory arbitrage. However, it should be expected that some banks may find new ways to reduce reported leverage ratios by putting assets off-balance sheet. In many instances, such off-balance sheet exposures are justified by a clear economic rationale, but sometimes they are not. It is important that bank regulators monitor off-balance sheet activities and decide whether to include them in the computation of capital ratios. In combination with stress tests, the proper monitoring of off-balance sheet activities can go a long way toward ensuring that banks have sufficient capital during a crisis.

Measuring Leverage

Measuring leverage is difficult. Setting aside the issue of off-balance sheet vehicles, there are many other choices that can materially affect measured leverage. One way to illustrate this is by comparing leverage under different accounting systems.

U.S. banks generally use Generally Accepted Accounting Principles (GAAP), while European banks use International Financial Reporting Standards (IFRS). One important difference between the two accounting systems is the treatment of derivatives. Under GAAP, banks can net out derivatives exposures on the asset and liabilities sides. Given that derivatives exposures on the liabilities side are debt, the netting generally decreases reported leverage. In contrast, IFRS does not allow netting given that derivatives exposures create liabilities in bankruptcy. Both accounting systems have their merits, but it is important to note that technical decisions regarding derivative exposure can have large effects on measured leverage.[26]

For example, as of the second quarter of 2016, almost all large U.S. banks have capital ratios that are significantly lower than 10%, ranging from 4.93% (Bank of New York Mellon) to 8.97% (Citigroup) using GAAP. Capital ratios are even lower when using IFRS

---

[26] For a discussion of the issue of derivatives in measuring leverage, see a blog post by Cecchetti and Schoenholtz (2016) that can be accessed here: http://www.moneyandbanking.com/commentary/2016/5/2/leverage-and-risk.

accounting. For large U.S. banks, they range from 4.14% (Goldman Sachs) to 8.01% (Wells Fargo).[27]

The Role of Risk Weights

The Financial CHOICE Act argues that risk-weighted capital ratios such as the Tier 1 ratio have failed. It argues in favor of a simple leverage ratio that does not use risk weights. The underlying logic for this decision is that risk weighting can be manipulated.

The CHOICE Act correctly points out that risk-weighted ratios can be manipulated and performed worse than expected during the U.S. financial crisis. However, the use of a simple leverage ratio does not solve this problem—it simply sets the risk weight equal to 1 for all assets. Even a simple leverage ratio still uses risk weights and therefore provides incentives for banks to adjust their balance sheets and to increase risk while maintaining a certain ratio.

The use of uniform risk weights may even worsen the problem, because banks can invest in risky assets at a low capital charge. In contrast, the risk-weighted capital ratio requires banks to hold more equity if they hold risky assets. It is therefore unclear whether using a simple leverage ratio is an improvement—especially if it replaces a risk-based capital ratio. Even though the risk weights are not perfect in constraining bank risk, they are likely to be superior to a situation with uniform risk weights. Dodd-Frank and Basel III impose joint weights: leverage and risk-weighted ratios. This is a sensible approach in addressing the potential for gaming with respect to a single ratio.[28]

---

[27] The estimates are provided by the FDIC and can be accessed at https://www.fdic.gov/about/learn/board/hoenig/capitalizationratio2q16.pdf

[28] Acharya and Schnabl (2009) provide a discussion of this issue. They argue that a single ratio is unlikely to be optimal. They point out that a private investor would rarely make a decision based on a single ratio, and neither should a regulator.

Choosing the Off-Ramp Threshold

The Financial CHOICE Act proposes a minimum capital threshold of 10%, but provides little analysis to justify this threshold. Arguably, 10% equity may still be too low to provide a sufficient buffer during a systemic crisis. A brief review of the literature suggests that 10% is at the lower end of range of estimates for suggested minimum capital requirements.

Admati and Hellwig (2013) suggest that bank equity should be at least 20% of bank assets. They argue that any potential costs of equity are negligible at levels below 20%-30%. In their assessment, any reduction in bank value below a 20% capital requirement is likely to come from reduced implicit and explicit guarantees. It is therefore recommended to set bank capital requirements to 20% or higher.

Hoenig (2012) points out that that banks had significantly higher capital ratios before the founding of the Federal Reserve Board in 1913 and the introduction of the Federal Deposit Insurance Corporation (FDIC) in 1933. The likelihood of government bailouts was low, and capital levels were market driven. During this period, the U.S. banking industry's ratio of tangible equity to total assets was between 13% and 16%. Arguably, these levels might be a good starting point even for today's banking system.

A group at the Minneapolis Federal Reserve Bank (2016) has estimated required capital levels based on historical data on banking crises with the goal of limiting the likelihood of a systemic crisis. Their proposal calls for a risk-weighted ratio of 23.5%, which is estimated to be equivalent to a 15% leverage requirement. After five years, if an institution continues to be deemed systemic, the plan calls for ratcheting up the capital requirement by five percentage points annually until it reaches 38% (roughly 24% leverage requirement).

Other works suggest a threshold closer to 10%. Calomiris (2012) argues that 10% is a sensible capital requirement. A group of International Monetary Fund (IMF) researchers uses historical banking crisis data and argues for a Tier 1 requirement of 15%-23%, which translates to a leverage ratio of 9% (Dagher et al. (2016)).

To summarize, the required thresholds vary greatly across proposals with recommended capital ratios ranging from 9% to 30%. It is clear that all recommendations come with a number of assumptions on the economic magnitude of the costs and benefits of bank capital. Even though there is no unanimous consensus on the recommended level, none of the proposals recommends a number clearly below 10%, and most proposals recommend a number significantly above 10%. A prudent regulator may prefer a threshold that puts more weight on some of the higher estimates.

Summary and Conclusion

The Financial CHOICE Act proposes an off-ramp for financial institutions. The off-ramp allows banks to opt out of Dodd-Frank regulation if their capital level exceeds a certain threshold. The logic behind the proposal is that banks with sufficient capital pose no systemic risk and therefore do not require regulation.

We believe that any implementation of the off-ramp requires regulators to take into the account banks' responses to using a leverage ratio. The history of bank regulation has shown that a single target may not be sufficient in containing risk. Regulators therefore need to make sure that banks have sufficient capital not only during regular times but also during crises. In practice, this requires regulators to measure capital during a crisis using credible stress tests. It also requires that regulators monitor bank risk using proper measures of leverage, off-balance sheet exposure, and bank risk exposure.

References

Acharya, Viral V., Thomas F. Cooley, Matthew P. Richardson, Ingo Walter, eds., 2011, *Regulating Wall Street: The Dodd-Frank Act and the New Architecture of Global Finance* (John Wiley & Sons).

Acharya, Viral, Robert Engle, and Diane Pierret, 2014, Testing macroprudential stress tests: The risk of regulatory risk weights, *Journal of Monetary Economics* 65(C), pages 36-53.

Acharya, Viral, Lasse Pedersen, Thomas Philippon, Matthew Richardson, 2017, Measuring system risk, *Review of Financial Studies* 30 (1), 2-47.

Acharya, Viral, and Matthew Richardson, eds., 2009, *Restoring Financial Stability: How to Repair a Failed System* (John Wiley & Sons).

Acharya, Viral V. and Philipp Schnabl, 2009, How banks played the leverage game, in Viral Acharya and Matthew Richardson, eds.: *Restoring Financial Stability: How to Repair a Failed System* (John Wiley & Sons).

Acharya, Viral, Philipp Schnabl and Gustavo Suarez, 2013, Securitization without risk transfer, *Journal of Financial Economics* 107 (3), 515-536.

Admati, Anat, and Martin Hellwig. 2013, *The Bankers' New Clothes: What's Wrong with Banking and What to Do about It* (Princeton University Press).

Begley, Taylor A., Amiyatosh Purnanandam, and Kuncheng Zheng, 2016, Strategic under-reporting of bank risk, *Review of Financial Studies* (forthcoming).

Behn, Markus, Rainer Haselman and Vikrant Vig, 2014, The limits of model-based regulation, Working paper, London Business School.

Calomiris, Charles, 2012, How to regulate bank capital, *National Affairs* No. 10 (Winter), 41-57.

Calomiris, Charles and Charles M. Kahn, 1991, The role of demandable debt in structuring optimal banking arrangements, *American Economic Review* 81 (3), 497–513.

Cecchetti, Stephen G., and Kermit L. Schoenholtz, 2016, Leverage and risk, *Money, Banking, and Financial Markets* (Blog).

Cornett, Marcia M., Jamie J. McNutt, Philip E. Strahan, and Hassan Tehranian, 2011, Liquidity risk management and credit supply in the financial crisis, *Journal of Financial Economics* 101 (2), 297-312.

Dagher, Jihad, Giovanni Dell'Ariccia, Luc Laeven, Lev Ratnovski, and Hui Tong, 2016, Benefits and costs of bank capital, Staff discussion note, IMF.

Diamond, Douglas W., and Raghuram G. Rajan, 2000, A theory of bank capital, *Journal of Finance* 55 (6), 2431- 2465.

Dewatripont, Mathias and Jean Tirole, 1994, The prudential regulation of banks, Walras-Pareto Lectures (MIT Press).

Farhi, Emmanuel and Jean Tirole, 2012, Collective moral hazard, maturity mismatch, and systemic bailouts, *American Economic Review* 102 (1), 60-93.

Federal Reserve Bank of Minneapolis, 2016, The Minneapolis Plan to end too big to fail.

Frame, W. Scott, Kristopher Gerardi, and Paul S. Willen, 2015, The failure of supervisory stress testing: Fannie Mae, Freddie Mac, and OFHEO, Working paper, Federal Reserve Bank of Atlanta.

Hoenig, Thomas M., 2012, Back to basics: A better alternative to Basel capital rules, speech delivered to the American Banker Regulatory Symposium.

Ivashina, Victoria, and David Scharfstein, 2010, Bank lending during the financial crisis of 2008, *Journal of Financial Economics* 97, 319-338.

Peek, Joe, and Eric S. Rosengren, 2000, Collateral damage: Effects of the Japanese bank crisis on real activity in the United States, *American Economic Review* 90 (1), 30-45.

Paravisini, Daniel, Veronica Rappoport, Philipp Schnabl and Daniel Wolfenzon, 2015, Dissecting the Effect of Credit Supply on Trade: Evidence from Matched Credit-Export Data, *Review of Economic Studies*, 82 (1), 333-359

Philippon, Thomas, and Philipp Schnabl, 2013, Efficient Recapitalization, *Journal of Finance* 68 (1), 1-42.

Plosser, Matthew C., and João A. C. Santos, 2015, Banks' incentives and the quality of internal risk models, Working paper, New York Federal Reserve Bank.

Schnabl, Philipp, 2012, The international transmission of bank liquidity shocks: Evidence from an emerging market, *Journal of Finance* 67 (3), 897-932.

CHOICE Act vs. Dodd-Frank

Resolution Authority Redux

By Barry E. Adler and Thomas Philippon

The economic and financial crisis of 2007-2009 caused the collapse or near collapse of several Systemically Important Financial Institutions (SIFIs), such as Bear Stearns, Lehman Brothers, Merrill Lynch, Fannie Mae, Freddie Mac, American International Group (AIG), and Citigroup in the U.S. and many others in the rest of the world. Except for Lehman, these financial giants were not allowed to fail, and many were bailed out by the taxpayers. The debate regarding the desirability of these bailouts will never be settled because it is impossible to assess the systemic consequences that disorderly failures would have had on the financial system and the broad economy. What is clear, however, is that citizens around the world do not want to be presented with the too-big-to-fail dilemma again. The job of regulators is therefore to make the system safer, and to create a process whereby SIFIs can fail in an orderly manner.

In 2010, Congress enacted the Dodd-Frank Act, which, among other provisions, took a dual approach to the prevention of systemic collapse. In this discussion, we focus on Dodd-Frank Title I—Systemic Risk Regulation and Oversight—and Title II—Orderly Liquidation Authority (OLA) for Systemic Risk Companies.

Title I insists that SIFIs maintain a sound capital structure and plan for dissolution in the event of crisis, i.e., create a Living Will.[29] A Living Will should ensure that a failed bank holding company can be resolved under the US bankruptcy code, as are other corporate debtors.

---

[29] Title I establishes the Financial Stability Oversight Council (FSOC) and the Office of Financial Research (within the Treasury), and it expands the authority of the Board of Governors of the Federal Reserve System to allow for supervision of certain nonbank SIFIs.

There are, however, legitimate doubts about whether the bankruptcy code in its current form can handle the failure of a SIFI, especially amidst a global crisis. In that spirit, Dodd-Frank Title II provides for orderly restructuring or liquidation of a SIFI that is severely distressed.[30] Title II provides an alternative to bankruptcy, in which the Federal Deposit Insurance Corporation (FDIC) is appointed as a receiver to carry out the bank's resolution over three to five years. OLA is meant to protect financial stability in the US economy.

Ever since Dodd-Frank's enactment, a debate has raged about the pros and cons of Title II. Now, the Financial CHOICE Act before Congress seeks to alter both Title I and Title II of Dodd-Frank. There are elements of the CHOICE Act that we admire, but also some elements that we consider dangerously counterproductive. The CHOICE Act relaxes or removes Dodd-Frank safeguards that providence mandates—safeguards such as required stress tests and Living Wills—and it fails to fill the gap, left by Dodd-Frank, in the government's ability to address systemic crisis as opposed to the mere failure of isolated institutions. While our primary task here is to address the CHOICE Act's treatment—proposed replacement, in fact—of Dodd Frank's Orderly Liquidation Authority, a proper analysis of that treatment necessarily includes consideration of Regulation and Oversight as well, the topic to which we turn next (and offer analysis described more fully in the chapter entitled Should There Be an Off-Ramp for Banks?).

---

[30] Although the title of the OLA refers to "liquidation," the Act does not envision a necessary winding up of a SIFI's business operations, but rather permits a restructuring of those operations, including through a refinancing of a holding company's subsidiaries. For this reason, we refer to restructuring or resolution, not merely to liquidation, in our discussion of the OLA.

The CHOICE Act's Dodd-Frank Off-Ramp

Per the report of the House Committee on Financial Services, under the Financial CHOICE Act, "banking organizations that maintain a leverage ratio of at least 10 percent and have a composite [Capital adequacy, Assets, Management capability, Earnings, Liquidity, Sensitivity, i.e.] CAMELS rating of 1 or 2, at the time of the election, may elect to be exempted from a number of regulatory requirements, including the Basel III capital and liquidity standards and the 'heightened prudential standards' applicable to larger institutions under [Title I] of the Dodd-Frank Act." The stated goal is to free the financial sector from what the drafters of the CHOICE Act see as a crippling regulatory burden imposed, in part, through strict and invasive stress tests.

In principle, sufficient capitalization is a solution to any problem of insolvency risk, including the risk of systemic financial collapse. But there is an ongoing debate about the proper level of capital in practice. An important study by researchers at the International Monetary Fund (IMF) shows that "bank capital in the range of 15–23 percent of risk-weighted assets would have been sufficient to absorb bank losses in the vast majority (85 percent) of past banking crises in OECD countries."[31] The costs of such capital requirements are more difficult to assess. Although the long-run (steady state) costs of additional equity capital may be small, probably less than ten basis points per additional percentage point of bank capital, recent papers have shown that the transition costs can be

---

[31] Jihad Dagher, Giovanni Dell'Ariccia, Luc Laeven, Lev Ratnovski, and Hui Tong, *A New Look at Bank Capital*, Oxford Business Law Blog (April, 2016).

substantial.[32] In any case, because the CHOICE Act's off-ramp is optional, banks might well choose to endure the costs and thus reduce their regulatory burden.

We are sympathetic to the CHOICE Act's emphasis on capitalization, but it is misleading to present the threshold capitalization as a way to solve the too-big-to-fail problem. Specifically, the roughly 20% of risk-weighted assets described in the IMF study corresponds roughly to 11% of total assets, so the ratio proposed in the CHOICE Act *could* give significant protection to taxpayers. That ratio would *not*, however, guarantee that banks do not fail, and it would not, by itself, guarantee that a SIFI could be resolved.

To understand the limitations in the proposed capitalization requirements, compare the ratio proposed in the CHOICE act to the one proposed in the 2016 Minneapolis Plan to End Too Big to Fail. [33] The Minneapolis Plan would increase capital requirements for all bank holding companies larger than $250 billion to 23.5% of risk-weighted assets, counting as capital only common equity and not long-term debt. Under that plan, if the Treasury Secretary deems a bank systemic, the capital requirement increases further, up to 38%. These ratios translate roughly into pure leverage requirements of 15% and 24%, respectively.

It is also useful to compare the CHOICE Act capital requirements to the actual ratios of U.S. Global Systemically Important Banks.

---

[32] For a comprehensive discussion of the literature, see Jihad Dagher, Giovanni Dell'Ariccia, Luc Laeven, Lev Ratnovski, and Hui Tong, *Benefits and Costs of Bank Capital*, IMF Discussion Paper (2016). These authors observe that "the long run impact of a 1 percentage point increase in capital requirements on lending rates ranges from merely 2 basis points to 20 basis points." They conclude, however, that in the short run "a 1 percentage point negative shock to capital (or increased capital requirement) is associated with a 5–8 percentage point contraction in lending volumes."

[33] See Federal Reserve Bank of Minneapolis, *The Minneapolis Plan to End Too Big to Fail* (November 16, 2016), available at https://www.minneapolisfed.org/publications/special-studies/endingtbtf

---

(GSIBs). According to FDIC estimates based on Generally Accepted Accounting Principles (GAAP), U.S. GSIBs have $10.7 trillion of assets and a leverage ratio of 8.24%. In this case, an increase to 10% would not be significant.[34] Moreover, for global banks with large derivative positions, it is not clear that GAAP is the right benchmark. International Financial Reporting Standards (IFRS) accounting rules are more conservative in their treatment of derivative exposures. According to FDIC estimates based on IFRS, U.S. GSIBs have $15.2 trillion of assets and a leverage ratio of only 5.75%. By this measure, an increase of capitalization from above 8% to 10% would be an anemic response to the risk that GSIBs in fact present.

In our view, it is simply incorrect to assume that a 10% leverage ratio would be enough, by itself, to negate the need for other forms of regulations. More generally, we are skeptical that any capital requirement lenient enough to permit the proper functioning of a large financial institution can be strict enough to be a one-stop solution.

There is an additional problem with the off-ramp proposed by the CHOICE Act. The proposal is to treat minimum capitalization as a substitute for extensive oversight. In our view, this is misguided because it assumes that the proper ratio will be maintained at all times despite relaxed supervision. In fact, in the absence of extensive oversight, one wonders whether minimum capitalization will be maintained. Violations of regulatory requirements are not unheard of, and without scrutiny, there is the concern that the first sign of insufficient capitalization at a SIFI may appear too late.

For these reasons, we believe that there is continuing benefit in multiple approaches to the prevention of crisis. The off-ramp should, perhaps, allow the SIFI to escape some regulation, but the

---

[34] The capital ratios are estimated by the FDIC. The numbers refer to 2016 Q2, available at
https://www.fdic.gov/about/learn/board/hoenig/capitalizationratio2q16.pdf

requirement for stress tests should be retained. The Dodd-Frank requirement of Living Wills, made optional by the CHOICE Act's off-ramp, is another regulation that should be maintained for large banks—even those that make a qualifying capital election.

Living Wills (Bail-In and Single Point of Entry)

The Dodd-Frank Act requires that every designated company, typically a bank holding company with $50 billion or more in assets, prepare and file with the Federal Reserve Board and the FDIC a resolution plan commonly known as a Living Will.[35] While the legislation requires that a Living Will describe the firm's assets and obligations, and provides that the plan should facilitate bankruptcy resolution, it does not offer detail on what a financial distress plan must include to receive approval. There is, however, a developed academic literature on just such an arrangement. As we discussed in an earlier policy paper,[36] the sort of Living Will suggested in the literature can help to accomplish an orderly resolution of financial distress in an automated fashion.

The concept of a corporate Living Will was first described in the academic literature as Chameleon Equity.[37] The idea is to divide a firm's capital structure into a hierarchy of priority tranches. In the event of an uncured default on a firm's debt obligations, the equity of the firm would be eliminated and the lowest-priority debt tranche would be converted to equity, just as a chameleon changes its colors as circumstances require. There would be no need for

---

[35] The threshold for designation, vehemently criticized by the drafters of the CHOICE Act, is neither capricious nor complicated, though it does present close questions difficult to adjudicate. Metlife is a case in point. One of the authors wrote an amicus brief for the court arguing that Metlife is indeed systemic, but this is a topic on which reasonable people can disagree.

[36] Viral Acharya, Barry E. Adler, Matthew Richardson, and Nouriel Roubini, Resolution Authority, in Acharya et al., editors, *Regulating Wall Street* (Wiley 2010).

[37] See Barry E. Adler, Financial and Political Theories of American Corporate Bankruptcy, 45 *Stanford Law Review* 311 (1993).

---

further restructuring if elimination of the lowest priority debt tranche reduced the firm's fixed liabilities sufficiently so that the remaining debt obligations could be paid from its assets. If obligations to the higher debt tranches remained in uncured default, the process would repeat until either all defaults were cured or the highest-priority tranche was converted to equity. Only at the point where a firm defaulted on its most senior obligations, after the elimination of all junior debt, would holders of those senior obligations have reason to foreclose on collateral. Elimination of the junior debt classes would, until that point, provide liquidity that could stabilize the firm and perhaps stem any run on the firm's assets.

Significantly, within a Chameleon Equity structure, there is no need for a judicial valuation or determination of which obligations are or are not entitled to satisfaction.[38] The prospect of default-driven transformations of the tranches from debt to equity would theoretically provide the firm with solvency until a class of secured claims was impaired, and without the need for bankruptcy restructuring beyond simple adherence to the prescribed capital structure or, to use the terminology of the current debate, without the need for bankruptcy beyond simple adherence to the firm's Living Will. Therefore, although the Dodd-Frank Act envisions Living Wills as blueprints for the bankruptcy process, a Living Will with the automatic conversion features we favor could also alleviate the need for that process and provide the speed of resolution that financial markets require.

---

[38] There are academic proposals to allow for a bankruptcy reorganization distribution of an insolvent debtor's value contrary to the creditors' contractual priority hierarchy if no creditor is thereby deprived of what it would have received in a liquidation. And while a Chameleon Equity structure could be devised to mimic such distribution, in our view deviation from contractual priority is undesirable whether the debtor is an industrial firm or a bank. See generally, Barry E. Adler and George G. Triantis, Debt Priority and Options in Bankruptcy: A Policy Intervention, *American Bankruptcy Law Journal* (forthcoming 2017).

To be sure, there are potential drawbacks to the Living Will we envision. The transformation, or winding down, of the firm must be triggered by an easily verifiable signal, such as default on obligations, rather than a difficult one such as inherent asset value.[39] The key to the proposal, after all, is to provide swift rescue and payment of those obligations that are still in-the-money, despite the firm's inability to make good on all its obligations. Such a transformation, or winding down, runs the risk that a firm in financial crisis will eliminate an interest that might have later proven to be valuable in a traditional bankruptcy reorganization, where time and the debtor's continued search for liquidity might resolve the crisis.[40] This problem could be exacerbated in a systemic financial crisis where a firm's assets are likely to be illiquid particularly so if debtors are permitted to invest in one another's risk securities. If, in such an environment, the firm cannot raise cash to pay even what should be its surviving obligations, creditors could bear large losses, and short-term creditors, despite theoretical seniority, might run or refuse to roll over their claims.

The Chameleon Equity concept—though it offers no panacea—has some empirical support. The concept depends on regulation to impose proper minimum size of loss-absorbing tranches. Prompted in large part by European legislators' or regulators' reaction to last decade's worldwide financial crisis, large banks have issued what is referred to as Bail-In capital, senior to common equity, but

---

[39] A modification of the Chameleon Equity approach could be designed specifically for large banks. Under this modification, a government administrator could be granted constrained discretion to initiate the conversion of a debtor's capital structure even before default, when a bank's equity market value sunk below a prescribed threshold, for example. See generally Stephen G. Cecchetti and Kermit L. Schoenholtz, Living Wills or Phoenix Plans: Making Sure Banks can Rise from Their Ashes, *Money & Banking* (October 13, 2014). Such an approach could alleviate the problems, described here, of a transformation occurring too late, but would introduce regulatory complexity and uncertainty.

[40] There are costs, too, to a traditional reorganization, including uncertainty and the potential paralysis of the financial markets that led to the Dodd-Frank requirement of Living Wills.

---

designed to absorb losses in the event the bank encounters financial distress. Shielded by Bail-In capital (as opposed to a bailout), even a foundering bank may be able to meet its obligations on systemically important assets such has short-term securities and derivatives treated as cash in the capital market.

On the topic of loss-absorbing capital, the experience of the United States is more complicated. As noted above, Title II of Dodd-Frank contains the OLA for the restructuring or liquidation of SIFIs that, per regulators, cannot be safely resolved in bankruptcy court. (The process is described in greater detail below.) Pursuant to Dodd-Frank, the FDIC has issued OLA regulations called the Single Point of Entry (SPOE) Strategy. The premise of SPOE is simple, and reflects the policy underlying Chameleon Equity and Bail-In. Under SPOE, among the entities that make up a SIFI—typically a bank holding company and subsidiaries—only the bank holding company would be subject to the orderly liquidation process; the subsidiaries, as operating companies, would continue unaffected by their parent's resolution, even its demise.

For the SPOE strategy to work, two conditions must hold. First, any subsidiary with systemically significant obligations must itself be sufficiently capitalized to avoid failure. Second, the holding company must be financed only through the issuance of expendable obligations—that is, not with systemically significant obligations. If these conditions are satisfied, the SPOE strategy operates essentially in the same way as Chameleon Equity or Bail-In: Each bank issues a significant amount of low-priority capital, beyond common equity, as a supplemental cushion for high-priority, systemically significant obligations. Under Chameleon Equity or Bail-In, capital is raised through the issuance of expendable obligations that fill low-priority tranches as part of a single entity's capital structure. Under SPOE, a holding company issues expendable obligations to raise capital that is then contributed to subsidiaries, which are permitted to issue systemically significant obligations.

It follows that the SPOE depends on requirements that the banks structure and finance themselves appropriately. The Living Will provisions of Title I establish an ideal platform for the imposition of these requirements, customized as they must be for each individual bank. Because Living Wills are not public documents, it is uncertain whether the plans produced by the banks have been required to meet these criteria.[41] But there is evidence that the banks have been so required. Last year, for instance, PricewaterhouseCoopers reported that most domestic SIFIs now have SPOE strategies for resolution of financial distress (a shift from the bridge-bank approach).[42]

We view the enhancement of loss-absorbing capital of the SIFIs since Dodd-Frank as real progress. Moreover, we do not oppose the CHOICE Act's off-ramp as a path to some regulatory relief (the details of which are beyond the scope of the current discussion). However, the off-ramp should not undermine the Living Will requirement, which allows regulators to ensure that a SIFI's capital structure is sufficiently robust to earn such regulatory relief.

---

[41] The Living Will process has not been a smooth one, with regulators continuing to call for a reduction in organizational complexity and other evidence of viability. See Key Points from the US G-SIBs' Resolution Plan Progress Reports, *Harvard Law School Forum on Corporate Governance and Financial Regulation* (October 29, 2016). Because, as noted, the details of the plans are not public, it is not possible to evaluate them directly or say more than offered here.

[42] See *Regulatory Brief of PwC* (July, 2015). The bridge-bank approach encompasses a transfer of solvent operating subsidiaries from a failed holding company to a well-financed bridge entity that will hold the operating companies until they can be sold in due course, freed from the exigencies of their parent's crisis. Although the processes differ somewhat, and although, in principle, SPOE accomplishes a bank's transformation more simply than the bridge-bank approach, the intended result of the latter approach is the same as that of SPOE or, for that matter, of bankruptcy, OLA, or Bail-In, each of which is designed to salvage viable operations from the collapse of the affiliate's financial structure. The adoption of the SPOE approach by most companies is significant not so much in the structure chosen but in the signal that regulators have been able to impose their chosen discipline, presumably including the isolation of systemically important debt, away from the bank's insolvency risk.

Bankruptcy not Bailout

A successful Living Will could quickly resolve a failed firm's affairs, freeing all but its impaired obligations (which would be transformed or eliminated) to trade at solvency values. This result would limit the scope of a firm's failure and reduce the extent to which a firm's insolvency could spread through the financial system. The orderly transformation of lower-priority obligations can restore the higher-priority claims to in-the-money status, which can cabin the contagion.

Nevertheless, some impairment of a firm's obligations would remain unavoidable, so ultimately Living Wills are limited in their ability to stem contagion. Moreover, no plan is fool proof. A Living Will could fail to achieve its purposes if, for example, Bail-In capital proved insufficient or, for another, if not only a bank holding company—the intended single point of entry to the restructuring process—but also its operating subsidiaries, proved insolvent. However well designed, Living Wills must be backstopped.

As noted above, the backstop under Dodd-Frank had two parts: the bankruptcy process and Dodd-Frank's own Orderly Liquidation Authority. If a financial institution, such as a bank holding company or one of its subsidiaries, failed, the Act's presumption is that the institution would go through the ordinary bankruptcy process or other applicable insolvency law. However, upon the recommendation of the Federal Reserve Board (by a two-thirds vote) and a similar vote by the FDIC (or, in some cases, the Securities and Exchange Commission for broker-dealers or the director of the Federal Insurance Office for insurance companies), the secretary of the Treasury could determine that the financial institution should be subject to the OLA. Such financial institutions are designated Covered Financial Companies (CFCs). The secretary would have to establish a number of conditions, including that the CFC had defaulted on its obligations or was about to and that failure of the company under ordinary procedures, such as under the bankruptcy code, would seriously undermine the stability of the U.S. financial system.

Under Dodd-Frank, if the board of a CFC does not acquiesce to an orderly liquidation, the Treasury secretary may petition the U.S. District Court for the District of Columbia. If the District Court does not find that the secretary's petition is "arbitrary and capricious," the petition must be granted. All of this must take place within 24 hours of the petition being filed. Further appeals are possible. Once appointed as a receiver, the FDIC would have broad powers to manage the CFC's affairs, including the authority to transfer or sell assets and to satisfy claims. The FDIC is not able to use any funding, however, unless an orderly liquidation plan has been approved by the Treasury secretary.

The Dodd-Frank Act shapes the OLA on the receivership model of the FDIC (though specialized alternative provisions apply where the CFC is a broker-dealer or insurance company). Consistent with the FDIC's current and continuing role in resolving depository institutions, the FDIC would have the power to take over the assets of and operate the CFC. The FDIC's authority includes the power to transfer assets or liabilities to a third party or bridge financial company. It is worth noting here, as we did in our earlier paper,[43] that the essence of the Act's receivership model is also consistent with the bankruptcy process. In each case, a financially distressed firm becomes subject to the supervision of an administrator—the FDIC or a bankruptcy judge, respectively—and in each case, the administrator oversees the operation of the firm and the disposition of its assets.

There are differences, however, between bankruptcy and OLA in the way creditors are paid and in the procedures applied. Take, for instance, the order of payments to creditors, which generally

---

[43] See Acharya et al. Resolution Authority, cited in note 36.

follows state law priorities under the bankruptcy code. Under the Dodd-Frank Act, the FDIC would be able to cherry-pick among obligations (paying some out of priority order or treating obligations with similar priorities differently) under the proviso that no creditor gets less than what it would have received in a liquidation under the bankruptcy code, and subject to certain provisions for specified financial contracts.

Beyond priority, under the provisions of Title II of the Dodd-Frank Act, the OLA's rules do, in some cases, follow those prescribed by the bankruptcy code. For example, secured debt, contingent claims, preferential payments, and fraudulent conveyances are treated under the OLA largely as they would be treated under bankruptcy law. But not all provisions are the same under the FDIC receivership model and the bankruptcy code. For example, the settlement of qualified contracts is subject to a stay of up to one business day after the commencement of an FDIC receivership but not subject to the stay at all under the bankruptcy code. And setoffs, which are generally honored under the bankruptcy code, are subject to alteration under FDIC receivership.

There is the potential for a mismatch between the insolvency regimes, and even where the substantive rules are effectively identical, their implementation under the new law may be uncertain. In general, at least initially, there could be great uncertainty as to how the new statute would be interpreted, and uncertainty can be costly.

One wonders, moreover, whether the FDIC has the institutional capacity to deal with the dissolution of covered firms, which are, by definition, large and complex. The FDIC has been a receiver for banks and savings and loan associations, which are simpler by comparison, in that as the deposit insurer and holder of the depositors' claims by subrogation, the FDIC is the natural location for the firm's assets. This is not a reason to have the FDIC administer the insolvency of CFCs. By contrast to the OLA, the bankruptcy code, while imperfect and subject to some uncertainty, has well-established provisions tested by litigation. And the bankruptcy courts are experienced with the management of large cases—Enron, General Motors, and Lehman Brothers, among them.

For these reasons, as we observed in our earlier paper,[44] any inadequacy of the current bankruptcy code to deal with SIFIs does not imply that the code should be scrapped and replaced by FDIC-like powers of the OLA. The FDIC generally deals with specific and narrowly defined institutions. The bankruptcy code, and years of practice under it, is broader in its design and reach.

So we applaud the decision under the Financial CHOICE Act to replace the OLA with what the House Report describes as "a new subchapter of the bankruptcy code tailored to address the failure of a large, complex financial institution." The new bankruptcy chapter, based on noted bankruptcy scholar Tom Jackson's proposal for a new Chapter 14 for SIFIs,[45] would provide a specialized forum and an expedited process to resolve SIFI insolvency all otherwise under the auspices of the well-evolved rules of the bankruptcy code.

We further agree with the CHOICE Act's elimination of Dodd-Frank's industrywide fund assessment, essentially a tax, to pay any shortfall in repayment of federal funds advanced to a SIFI undergoing OLA resolution. In our earlier paper,[46] we observed (in language quoted by the CHOICE Act Report) that such an *ex post* fund assessment would essentially require prudent financial companies to pay for the sins of the others. This would be bad enough even from merely an *ex post* perspective once a crisis had begun, as the costs to the financial system could be substantial, and would weigh against the ability of the system to provide credit. Ironically, an illiquid financial system is the very evil the Dodd-Frank Act is intended to avoid. But

---

[44] See Acharya et al. Resolution Authority, cited in note 36.

[45] See Kenneth E. Scott and John B. Taylor, Editors, *Bankruptcy Not Bailout: A Special Chapter 14* (Hoover Institution Press, 2012).

[46] See Acharya et al. Resolution Authority, cited in note 36.

---

it gets worse, as we said. Dodd-Frank's plan for successful financial institutions to pay the creditors of failed institutions may not be a bailout at the expense of the general taxpayer but would lead to an identical free rider problem.[47]

Having proposed the elimination of assessment as a means for taxpayers to recover improvidently advanced capital, the CHOICE Act goes on strictly to limit the use of federal funds as loans for SIFIs undergoing bankruptcy. In a section of the House Report titled "Bankruptcy not Bailout," the Report describes what its drafters see as too-permissive rules for the use of federal funds under Dodd-Frank. The report then describes the CHOICE Act's restriction on the use under section 13(3) of the Federal Reserve Act "to those instances that meet the specific criteria of Bagehot's Dictum, named after the noted British financial journalist Walter Bagehot, which stipulates that a central bank should lend freely in a financial crisis, but only to solvent borrowers, against good collateral, and at penalty rates." It is here that we part company with the CHOICE Act's drafters.

In our earlier policy paper's assessment of Dodd-Frank,[48] we observed that the lending rules under Dodd-Frank were, in our opinion, *too* strict, or more precisely, insufficiently broad. We observed that, ideally, in the event of a systemic liquidity crisis, during which private funds have become scarce, federal funds could be made available as a source of capital to financial institutions in bankruptcy—that is, as a debtor-in-possession (DIP) lender much in the same way the Treasury served as a DIP lender in the Chrysler and General Motors cases. That is, we said, one could advantageously strip away the process portions of the Orderly

---

[47] Proposals for an *ex ante* tax on the banking industry to fund liquidity in times of crisis would alleviate the problem of specially burdening financial institutions at the time they are most vulnerable, and such a tax may be preferable to a general taxpayer provision of a liquidity fund, but such an *ex ante* tax would not address the moral hazard problem described here and further addressed below.
[48] See Acharya et al. Resolution Authority, cited in note 36.

Liquidation Authority and leave its only truly unique element, an Orderly Liquidation Fund.

Further, we said, there would be an additional benefit to segregating the federal government's capacity to lend in times of crisis from the OLA. As an entity devoted to the management of systemic financial crisis, rather than a mere liquidation facilitator, the Orderly Liquidation Fund, perhaps renamed the Systemic Risk Avoidance Fund, could, at prescribed times of pending systemic illiquidity, lend not only to failed firms but also to struggling ones, perhaps to prevent their failure.[49] Put another way, a federal fund focused on liquidity rather than liquidation might prevent a crisis rather than attempt to rescue the financial system after a crisis has occurred, when problems are more expensive to address.[50]

We were not, and are not, unmindful of the moral hazard created by the potential availability of federal funds. Thus, we continue to stress, the importance of regulation and oversight, including the oversight that the CHOICE Act seeks to diminish.

Against all this, the drafters of the CHOICE Act argue that eliminating even the possibility of a bailout will discipline SIFIs and render them responsible citizens. This basis for reform is misguided, in our view, for at least five reasons:

---

[49] As we observed in our earlier work, id., the Dodd-Frank Act does allow the FDIC, in consultation with the Treasury secretary and by two-thirds vote of the FDIC and Board of Governors, to create a systemwide program to guarantee obligations of solvent depository institutions and holding companies for a fee that offsets projected losses and expenses. However, as we noted, in addition to these procedural hurdles, the creation of such a program requires a determination that a liquidity crisis is underway, and so any relief may come too late. The details of how a federal liquidity fund could be optimally designed and implemented is beyond our current scope.

[50] See Viral V. Acharya and Matthew Richardson, Implications of the Dodd-Frank Act, 4 *Annual Review of Financial Economics* 1 (2012).

- Managers of corporations, including financial institutions, are not always faithful agents of their principals and, motivated by private gain, might take unjustified risks with corporate funds.
- Even if managers were entirely faithful agents to their investors, SIFIs would take on more than the socially optimal level of risk because, by their nature, the *systemic* costs of risk are *externalized*.
- Whatever their intent, humans commit errors and managers of SIFIs have the capacity to err spectacularly, as we've seen, with the world's economy at stake.
- No matter how strident the anti-bailout rhetoric of the House Report, the CHOICE Act cannot bind a future Congress confronted with a financial meltdown. So, given the opportunity to invest unwisely, one might expect SIFIs to do so in anticipation of the CHOICE Act's repeal and a bailout should things go wrong.
- Even if none of this were true, a worldwide liquidity crisis could occur even without SIFI misbehavior, and so a prohibition on federal rescue would be overly restrictive.

For these reasons, we disagree with the CHOICE Act's attempt to play chicken with SIFIs, which remain too-big-to-fail with or without a safety net. The Bagehot Dictum's limitation on funding to "good collateral" could be dangerously restrictive in a financial crisis. This implies that this provision of the CHOICE Act is either counterproductive or, because it is subject to later repeal, essentially meaningless. Neither of these possibilities is an endorsement.

Summary and Conclusion

There is much to like—but also much to worry about—in the CHOICE Act. With respect to financial stability and the too-big-to-fail issue, the CHOICE Act's stated intentions are encouraging, but the proposals suffer from two main conceptual flaws.

First, the drafters seem unable to recognize the fact that not only regulators, but market actors as well, can be mistaken about financial risks. It is true that in the lead-up to our most recent crisis, regulators misjudged the enormous increase in leveraged exposure to housing risk. But it is equally true that junk bonds reached their narrowest spread in recorded history in June 2007, and the market willingly lent to Greece at the same rate as it lent to Germany. In fact, in many cases, narrow market spreads were used to explain to regulators that they had nothing to worry about. It is therefore equally dangerous to put one's faith entirely in market discipline, as it is to put it entirely with regulators.

Second, in its zeal to address moral hazard, the CHOICE Act forgets the lessons from the 1930s. It is a dangerous idea that the only option in a systemic crisis is simply to let firms fail, regardless of the consequences. The CHOICE Act's elimination of a rescue option would likely be ineffective, in any case, inasmuch as a future Congress would have both the power, and good reason, to restore the option of federal relief.

The goal of financial regulation is to strike the right balance between market discipline and regulation, and to be realistic about the limits of each.

We think that the off-ramp is a potentially good idea, but it should not relieve firms from the obligation to undergo stress tests or to write credible Living Wills. If regulated entities perceive other forms of enhanced supervisions as overly burdensome, these could perhaps be reduced in exchange for more capital.

We approve the idea of replacing the OLA with a new subchapter of the bankruptcy code and of eliminating the industrywide fund assessment. The bankruptcy chapter should, however, allow for DIP financing by the federal government as part of a more general authority to address *systemic* liquidity concerns. The moral hazard of potential relief should be policed through regulatory requirements, including Living Wills. Continuation of such regulation would also make the new chapter more credible.

The Volcker Rule and Regulations of Scope

By Matthew P. Richardson and Bruce Tuckman

Regulations of Scope

A key objective of bank regulation since the financial crisis of 2007- 2009 has been to reduce risk. Banks have been required to hold more risk-weighted capital, to operate within new restrictions on leverage and liquidity, and to pass newly introduced stress tests.

The Volcker Rule, section 619 of the Dodd-Frank Act, is another of these new bank regulations, but is best understood as a *regulation of scope*. Rather than restrict risk directly, the Volcker Rule restricts banks from particular holdings and activities. Broadly speaking, the rule prohibits banks from proprietary trading in most securities and derivatives and severely limits banks' connections to hedge funds and private equity funds.

Regulations of scope have a long history. National banks, first chartered at the time of the Civil War, were prohibited from managing trusts, making mortgage loans, and underwriting corporate securities. Mortgage loans on farmland were permitted only from 1913, in a political compromise to pass the Federal Reserve Act.

At about the same time, national banks began to create affiliates—with the tacit approval of regulators—to conduct businesses that were otherwise prohibited to them. The National City Bank, for example, the ancestor of Citigroup, used such affiliates to become the preeminent universal bank of its time.

Through the stock market crash of 1929, the Great Depression, and the Banking Crisis of 1933, securities affiliates of national banks were—without compelling evidence[51]—blamed for the troubles of

---

[51] See, for example, Benston (1990).

the time. Furthermore, Carter Glass, an extremely influential U.S. senator on the Committee on Banking and Currency, had long believed that banks should have nothing to do with "speculative" markets for stocks and corporate bonds. The result was the most famous regulation of scope, the separation of commercial and investment banking, by the Glass-Steagall Act of 1933.[52]

Securities markets remained subdued through the 1940s, but as activity picked up in the 1950s, banks once again pushed to become universal banks. A cat and mouse game ensued, with banks working around the rules and with counteractive legislation like the Bank Holding Company Acts of 1956 and 1970.

Eventually, however, as banks lost business both to nonbanking financial institutions in the United States and to foreign universal banks, regulators gradually loosened the restrictions of Glass-Steagall. In 1999, when banks were for all practical purposes already back in the securities businesses, Congress and President Clinton, with overwhelming bipartisan support, repealed Glass-Steagall.

The Volcker Rule, passed in the wake of the financial crisis of 2007-2009, is thus the latest iteration of regulations of scope.

Dodd-Frank and Supporting Rulemaking[53]

Dodd-Frank lists a number of objectives of the Volcker Rule: promoting the safety and soundness of banks and the financial

---

[52] While deposit insurance was introduced at the same time, the separation of commercial and investment banking was not proposed to allay fears of moral hazard arising from deposit insurance. Deposit insurance was added as a political necessity late in the life of a bill that had been years in the making. In fact, until just before its passage, both Senator Glass and President Roosevelt opposed deposit insurance.

[53] This section is neither intended nor appropriate as a legal guide to compliance with the rule.

system; limiting the benefits of deposit insurance and Federal Reserve liquidity facilities to regulated entities; and reducing conflicts of interest between banks and their clients.

To achieve these objectives, the Volcker Rule generally prohibits banks from proprietary trading of securities and derivatives and from investing in or sponsoring hedge funds or private equity funds.

At the same time, the rule includes a number of broad exclusions to allow banks to fulfill some of their functions as financial intermediaries, including the following: trading of securities sold by the U.S. government, U.S. agencies, government-sponsored entities (GSEs, e.g., Fannie Mae and Freddie Mac), and municipal obligations; underwriting and market-making activities; hedging; and trading on behalf of customers.

Despite such exclusions, however, "backstop prohibitions" outlaw transactions that result in any of the following: a material conflict of interest between a bank and its customers, clients, or counterparties; material exposure to high-risk assets or trading strategies; a threat to the safety and soundness of the banking entity; or a threat to the financial stability of the United States.

Rulemaking to implement the Volcker Rule started with a public comment period followed by recommendations by the Financial Stability Oversight Council (FSOC) in January 2011.

Between late 2011 and early 2012, proposed rules for public comment were released by the five regulators with jurisdiction: the Federal Reserve Board (FRB), the Office of the Comptroller of the Currency (OCC), the Federal Deposit Insurance Corporation (FDIC), the Commodity and Futures Trading Commission (CFTC), and the Securities and Exchange Commission (SEC).

The proposed rules were long and complex, and attracted more than 18,000 comment letters. The regulatory agencies went back to work and, in December 2013, jointly released the final rules.

To understand why the rules are long and complex, consider the ban on proprietary trading.[54] A short list of explicitly exempted securities (e.g., U.S. Treasuries) and explicitly exempted transactions (e.g., securities lending) are recognized as outside the realm of the Volcker Rule.

All other trades are essentially assumed to be proprietary and forbidden, unless they can be justified as part of one of the broad permitted activities (e.g., market-making) and can be shown not to violate a backstop prohibition (e.g., conflicts of interest or exposure to high-risk assets and trading strategies).

Justifying that a trade belongs to a permitted category, however, is difficult and subjective. With respect to market-making, for example, some of the criteria are: "routinely stands ready to purchase and sell;" "willing and available to quote, purchase, and sell... in commercially reasonable amounts... throughout market cycles... appropriate for the liquidity, maturity, and depth of the market;" "not exceeding on an ongoing basis, the reasonably expected near-term demands of clients, customers, and counterparties."[55]

The backstop prohibitions are similarly hard to interpret. Trades may not "result in the bank's interest being materially adverse to the interests of its client, customer, or counterparty." Similarly, high-risk assets and trading strategies "significantly increase the likelihood... of a substantial loss... or pose a threat to the financial stability of the United States."[56]

---

[54] See Davis Polk (2013) for details.
[55] Davis Polk (2013), p. 6.
[56] Davis Polk (2013), p. 16.

A particular problem with the backstop prohibitions is that any losses incurred might be used as *ex post* evidence that undue risks had been taken. Along these lines, after a large loss at Credit Suisse in March 2016, a U.S. senator wrote the chairs of all the regulatory agencies:

> *"To put it very simply, how can the American public have confidence that banking organizations are complying with the Volcker Rule when this type of massive loss can occur?"*[57]

Precisely because it is so difficult to demonstrate that a trade is permitted, the rules require that banks establish compliance programs to justify all of their trades, at the level of a trading desk, in a consistent way. The rules are quite detailed about the attributes of these compliance programs, including the specification of seven quantitative metrics to be used in the process.[58]

The rules with respect to restricting connections with hedge funds and private equity funds are also complex, from defining exactly what it means to be a "covered fund" under the rules to exactly what it means to invest in or sponsor such a fund.[59] Furthermore, any investments and sponsorships allowed under these tests are still subject to the backup prohibitions.

The complexities of compliance are further multiplied by the fact that five regulatory agencies have jurisdiction over any aspect of the rules.

---

[57] Merkley (2016).
[58] Davis Polk (2013), pp. 17-23.
[59] Davis Polk (2014).

The CHOICE Act

The CHOICE Act proposes to repeal the Volcker Rule in its entirety. The arguments given by the proposal in favor of repeal are the following:[60]

- Banks' proprietary trading and investments or sponsorship of hedge funds and private equity funds played no significant role in the crisis.
- It is not clear how the Volcker Rule makes the financial system less risky.
- The Volcker Rule inhibits market-making by banks, which, in turn, reduces liquidity available in financial markets.
- The Volcker Rule imposes costs not only on the largest Wall Street banks, but also on smaller, community banks that need to demonstrate that they are not engaged in proprietary trading.

Policy Analysis

Why Regulate Risk-Taking at Banks?

There are two reasons to believe that banks, without constraints, will take on too much risk relative to what is optimal for their creditors, customers, and the broader financial system.

First, the government provides an underpriced safety net in the form of deposit insurance, access to Federal Reserve liquidity facilities and, for the biggest banks, an implicit too-big-to-fail guarantee. The long-standing policy of undercharging banks for this safety net may increase the availability of credit and support economic growth, but it also incentivizes banks to take on too much risk.

---

[60] House Committee on Financial Services (2016), pp. 81-86.

Second, even without an underpriced safety net, individual banks do not bear the costs to others of a general financial crisis that may be caused or exacerbated by their own failure. In other words, these banks do not internalize systemic risk costs arising from excessive risk-taking or leverage. This, too, implies that banks may take on too much risk.[61]

While the best solution might be to charge banks appropriately for their reliance on the safety net and for their contribution to systemic spillovers, this approach has never found general acceptance.[62]

Instead, heading into the 2007-2009 crisis, risk-taking was regulated directly through bank examinations and risk-weighted capital requirements.

Regulatory Failures and Post-Crisis Responses

For the most part, the 2007-2009 crisis erupted not from the commercial banking system but rather from mortgage companies, government-sponsored enterprises (i.e., Fannie Mae and Freddie Mac), investment banks, nonbank subsidiaries, and vehicles of bank holding companies.

Nevertheless, banking supervision and regulation did fail in the sense that the government felt obliged in the fall of 2008 to save too-big-to-fail banks. Wachovia was to have received government assistance and be sold to Citigroup, although, in the end, Wells Fargo purchased Wachovia with the stimulant of newly instituted tax breaks. Most spectacularly, however, Citigroup was bailed out

---

[61] See Acharya, Pedersen, Philippon and Richardson (2017).

[62] One exception is the Dodd-Frank Act's imposition on SIFIs of a capital surcharge, which may be interpreted as a charge for their systemic impact. See Acharya, Pedersen, Philippon and Richardson (2013) for a discussion of how to charge for systemic risk costs.

by the government with a combination of capital injections and guarantees.

In response to the crisis, risk-weighted capital requirements, which had proved too low, were increased. At the same time, however, there was a recognition that this sort of capital requirement could not stand on its own.[63]

First, a firm with adequate capital might fail in a general crisis because its funding was too susceptible to runs—that is, over-reliant on repo, wholesale funding, etc. The failure of Northern Rock, a British Bank, was probably the best example of this.[64] Despite the high quality of its mortgage portfolio, it could not roll over its short-term funding nor securitize its assets through the general crisis. In any case, the regulatory response here was to introduce liquidity ratios that limit the extent of such funding.

Second, regulators might easily set some risk weights too low, as had been the case during the crisis for mortgage-backed securities and, in Europe, for bonds of "peripheral" governments, like Greece. Even worse, the effect of such errors will always be magnified by banks' loading up on precisely those assets with mistakenly low risk weights.

Third, banks manage to circumvent the risk weights through regulatory arbitrage. In the crisis of 2007-2009, this took forms ranging from setting up and guaranteeing off-balance-sheet vehicles to reducing underwriting standards on mortgages with set risk weights.

One response to concerns about risk weights was a leverage ratio, a minimum level of capital relative to total, rather than risk-weighted

---

[63] See Acharya and Richardson (2012).
[64] See Tuckman (2016). While Bear Stearns and Lehman Brothers are often cited as examples, it is arguable that funders ran because these firms were insolvent.

assets. In this way, leverage cannot get too high, even for assets with erroneously assigned risk weights.

Another response was to subject banks to stress tests that would detect risks not captured by other regulatory and internal risk models.[65] Furthermore, by varying stress scenarios relatively frequently and without much advance notice, regulators can respond quickly to perceived changes in the riskiness of particular asset classes and bank positions.[66]

Is the Volcker Rule a Reasonable Way to Reduce Risk-Taking at Banks?

Supporters of the CHOICE Act correctly note that neither banks' proprietary trading nor their connections with hedge funds and private equity funds played a significant role in the crisis of 2007-2009.[67] The more important question, however, is whether the Volcker Rule is a useful tool for reducing the likelihood and minimizing the damage of future crises.

The difficulty of defending the Volcker Rule as a means of regulating risk-taking, however, is that Volcker Rule prohibitions are not

---

[65] A fundamental problem remains unresolved. Capital regulation is ill-suited to deal with certain kinds of activities, like carry trades and financial guaranty insurance. These activities generate small gains with high probability and large losses—likely systemic—with low probability. Regulators should, therefore, require banks to hold sufficient capital to cover losses against these low probability events. Unfortunately, however, this policy would require banks to hold too much capital relative to the set of overwhelmingly likely outcomes. See Kashyap, Rajan, and Stein (2008).

[66] Banks have objected to the flexibility of stress tests to the extent that it becomes difficult to make a forward-looking business plan that will be consistent with regulatory constraints.

[67] The crisis was very much related to large, complex financial institutions' manufacturing securitized products and retaining tail risk that was systemic in nature and inadequately capitalized. See Acharya, Cooley, Richardson and Walter (2009, 2011).

closely aligned with risk. Here are some illustrations of this proposition:

- Consider three similar bank business lines that are treated differently by the Volcker Rule: making and trading corporate loans (permitted), buying and trading corporate bonds for the account of the bank (forbidden), and investing in a private equity fund that makes corporate loans (forbidden except in very small size).

- A trading strategy that buys some stocks and shorts others is probably safer than making corporate loans, but the Volcker Rule prohibits the former and permits the latter. There is a robust debate around whether banking businesses are more volatile (and more illiquid) than trading activities.[68]

- A market-maker in corporate bonds, facing interest rate risk and credit risk, may hedge both risks, one but not the other, neither, or may even overhedge to take on additional risk. When does permitted customer business become forbidden proprietary trading?

- A junk-bond trader at Goldman Sachs earned the bank more than $100 million by buying junk bonds from customers from January 2016 and selling out of the position to other customers by the end of June.[69] Is that customer or proprietary trading?

---

[68] See Chung, Keppo, and Yuan (2016) and Demirguc-Kunt and Huizinga (2010) compared with Stiroh (2006), Fraser, Madura and Weigand (2002), and DeYoung and Roland (2001).
[69] Market Watch (2016).

- Citigroup's proprietary mortgage trading group—because it traded only U.S. and GSE-backed mortgages—was in compliance with the Volcker Rule.[70]

Given these considerations, it is difficult to make a general case that trading and fund investment businesses are riskier than traditional banking businesses. In fact, a bank's loan portfolio is likely to do poorly in a general crisis and contribute to the capital shortfall of the financial sector as a whole.

Supporters of the Volcker Rule might counter that nonbanking businesses—from investment banking to insurance—are more correlated with market fluctuations and, therefore, increase the systemic risk of banks. The empirical evidence on this point, however, is mixed.[71]

Can Regulations of Scope Be Justified for Other Reasons?

Supporters of the Volcker Rule might argue that banks are given a safety net because their core businesses—taking deposits and lending to households and businesses—are systemic, highly levered, and not easily replicable outside the banking sector.[72] Trading and fund investments, by contrast, which are easily accomplished outside banking, are best left to institutions that generally carry less systemic risk, like pension funds, mutual funds, hedge funds, and sovereign wealth funds.

---

[70] *The Wall Street Journal* (2014). The business was closed down in August 2016.

[71] For papers finding that nonbank activities increase systemic risk, see Baele, De Jonghe, and Vennet (2007), Brunnermeier, Dong and Palia (2012) and King, Massoud, and Song (2013). For papers finding that nonbank activities decrease or do not change systemic risk, see Akhigbe and White (2004), Boyd, Graham, and Hewitt (1993), Cornett, Ors, and Tehranian (2002), Geyfman and Yeager (2009), and Jorion (2005).

[72] See Fama (1985), Diamond (1984, 1991) and Petersen & Rajan (1994) for a discussion of the unique lending services provided by banks.

To analyze this argument, consider a related, though more extreme, proposal: restrict banks to making only short-term personal and corporate loans. This proposal, however, is questionable for several reasons.

First, banks are really in two businesses: creating liabilities that customers want and lending or investing funds. Discussions of banking often lose sight of the first business. Individuals and businesses want a relatively liquid and safe place to park their money, from super-liquid deposits to less-liquid but more remunerative certificates of deposit or commercial paper.[73] Any profitable activity with appropriate risk characteristics on the assets side—whether making loans or proprietary trading—allows a bank to provide customers with relatively safe and liquid assets that pay interest.

Second, to the extent that there are synergies across financial services, regulations of scope reduce the efficiency of the banking sector. A corporation, for example, might easily find it efficient—from an informational and operational perspective—for a single bank to handle its operational deposits, its bank borrowings, its private debt offerings, the management of its pension plan, its insurance policies, etc.

There are even synergies across relatively pure customer trades and relatively pure proprietary trades. In a "back book," for example, traders try to profit through proprietary positions in particular markets. From time to time, customers of a bank who want to do large trades—but are turned away by the market-making desks— could be accommodated by the capacity created by the back book.

---

[73] See Gorton and Pennacchi (1990).

The empirical evidence on the synergies across financial services is mixed.[74] But the universal bank has been the reality in Europe and a recurring dream of financial service companies in the United States from the early 1900s.

The third reason why tight restrictions of scope are a bad idea is that they may simply push systemic risk from the banking system elsewhere. Systemic risk would probably be reduced, for example, if a stand-alone commodities trading business moved from a bank into a hedge fund.

But what if that trading business, because of its synergies with trade financing and with commodity derivatives trading and hedging, moved from a bank into a large and important nonbank financial intermediary? Systemic risk might very well increase. The failure of either the bank or nonbank, as significant intermediaries, might cause systemic disruption, but the bank might be better diversified and better regulated.

The potential danger of forcing synergistic intermediation businesses outside banking can be put more dramatically. By setting up stand-alone investment banks, was Glass-Steagall partially responsible for the crisis of 2007-2009?

Costs-Benefit Analysis and the Volcker Rule

One of the reasons that the Volcker Rule was passed as an amendment to the Bank Holding Company Act, rather than to securities laws, was to avoid the need for cost-benefit analysis in

---

[74] For papers finding evidence of synergies, see Cornett, Ors, and Tehranian (2002), Elsas, Hackethal, and Holzhauser (2009), Lown, Osler, Strahan, and Sufi (2000), and Yu (2003). For papers finding that diversification of financial businesses reduces value, see Delong (2001), King, Massoud, and Song (2013), Laeven and Levine (2007), and Stiroh (2004). Schmid and Walter (2009) find that synergies are evident in some combinations of businesses but not in others.

---

rulemaking.[75] It is certainly difficult to compare even large costs of compliance plus the costs of forgone business opportunities and financial innovation with the massive costs of a financial crisis. But cost-benefit analysis would be extremely useful to compare the efficiency of the Volcker Rule with the other tools of the regulatory regime with respect to reducing individual bank and systemic risks.

In comparisons of this sort, the Volcker Rule will almost certainly rank very poorly. First, with the need to justify all trades as proprietary or not and as prohibited investments or not, compliance costs are particularly high.[76] Second, Volcker Rule prohibitions simply do not correlate well with risk reductions. Risk-weighted capital requirements, leverage ratios, liquidity ratios, and stress tests, on the other hand, are all aimed directly at controlling risk.

The Volcker Rule has been particularly criticized as contributing to a decline in market liquidity. The argument is that dedicated market-makers and proprietary traders all provide liquidity by taking positions and bearing risks that others choose to avoid. By limiting risk-taking of this sort, the Volcker Rule reduces market liquidity.[77]

The empirical support for this claim, however, is mixed. In the corporate bond market, for example, bid-ask spreads, volume, and issuance all indicate that liquidity is the same as it was before the

---

[75] See Gallagher (2013) and Stein (2013).

[76] Richardson (2012) argues for a Volcker Rule to be principle-based with safe harbors as opposed to a strictly rule-based approach. The reason relates to the difficulty (and frankly irrelevance for risk) of measuring principal trading versus market-making. Proprietary and hedge activities would be permitted within well-defined confines of the Volcker Rule. These boundaries could reasonably be related to the firm's aggregate gross and net inventories of assets. Any trading activity outside these inventory constraints would require permission by the bank's (or nonbank SIFI's) regulator.

[77] For a more detailed analysis, see Duffie (2012).

crisis or better.[78] On the other hand, execution of large corporate bond trades has become more expensive and riskier.[79] In any case, however, the Volcker Rule is only one of several relevant factors bearing on liquidity; others include regulatory changes at banks (i.e., increased capital requirements and the newly imposed leverage ratio); decreased risk appetites at banks; and the structural shift to high-frequency trading in U.S. Treasuries.

The entire debate about liquidity, however, may be off point. To the extent that banks took too much risk before the crisis, because of an underpriced safety net or systemic risk externalities, banks may very well have also provided too much liquidity. In that case, liquidity should be appropriately lower post-crisis.

Conclusion

The debate about regulations of scope is an old one. Carter Glass argued in the 1920s and 1930s that banks should have no connection with stock or corporate bond markets. Charles Mitchell, the chairman of National City Bank, argued that credit markets were an integrated whole that did not divide sensibly into loans versus securities.

Without an anchor to risk, the Volcker Rule makes artificial and superficial distinctions across credit markets. This has already led to confusion and regulatory arbitrage. Investments in local infrastructure projects under the Community Reinvestment Act may

---

[78] See the survey on market liquidity after the financial crisis by Adrian, Fleming, Shachar and Vogt (2016), and, more broadly, Mizrach (2015), Trebbi and Xiao (2015), Adrian, Fleming, Shachar and Vogt (2015), Adrian, Fleming, Vogt and Wojtowicz (2016) and Bessembinder, Jacobsen, Maxwell and Venkataraman (2016).

[79] See recent papers by Bao, O'Hara, and Zhou (2016) and Dick-Nielsen and Rossi (2016), and Blackrock (2015, 2016), BIS (2016) and Committee on Capital Markets Regulation (2015), and Deutsche Bank (2016), among others, for concerns about market liquidity in the corporate bond sector.

---

or may not be allowed. Regulators and market participants spar over collateralized loan obligations—which are generally permitted, unless they contain some bonds, in which case they are not.[80] And banks move to structure investments as merchant banking or business development companies to avoid the classification of "covered funds" under the Volcker Rule.[81]

Echoing Charles Mitchell in the 1930s, a spokesman from Goldman Sachs captured these ambiguities:

> *"Banks are in the business of providing businesses with the capital they need to grow. Sometimes that means offering a loan and other times making an equity investment... We ensure our investments comply with all regulations, including the Volcker Rule."*[82]

Taking into account the disconnect between the Volcker Rule and risk, along with its steep costs of compliance, this paper concludes that the Volcker Rule should be scrapped in favor of other prudential tools, such as risk-weighted capital requirements, leverage ratios, liquidity ratios, Living Wills, and stress tests.[83]

To the extent that the risks of particular positions are especially difficult to assess,[84] stricter applications of the tools might be appropriate. In these cases, it would be appropriate to conduct a cost-benefit analysis of the value-added of these positions to the bank and its customers, the synergies of such positions with other

---

[80] Bloomberg (2016).

[81] See Lykken (2013), Popper (2015), Trefis (2013a), and Trefis (2013b).

[82] Popper (2015).

[83] Dodd-Frank's stated goal of preventing conflicts of interest between banks and its customers and counterparties can be achieved at much less cost in other ways.

[84] White (2009), for example, differentiates between bank activities that are "examinable and supervisable" and those that are not.

---

bank activities, and the systemic risk implications of pushing positions out of the bank into other systemic entities that are less regulated.

Cost-benefit analysis often includes only the costs to the regulated, but should also include the costs to the regulators. There are estimates that, to comply with the Volcker Rule, banks spent more than 6 million hours initially and need to spend an additional 1.75 million hours annually.[85] On top of this, however, are the many hours spent by the staff at the relevant regulatory agencies, both initially and on an ongoing basis, to the exclusion of their other responsibilities and possible activities.

Would it not be better for the regulators to improve the quality of their bank examinations, monitor market conditions, and talk with banks about risk than to have semantic and legalistic discussions about whether a trade is "proprietary" and whether an investment is in a "covered fund"?

If repeal proves politically impossible, there are several useful compromises that could substantially reduce the regulatory burden of the rule:

First, the rule could prohibit "bright-line" proprietary trading, as defined in the initial FSOC study on the Volcker Rule.[86] The phrase denotes businesses within banks that are organized like internal hedge funds and have no formal market-making responsibilities. This relatively narrow definition would leave a lot of room for banks to take positions that are anathema to supporters of the Volcker Rule. But the prohibition would be enormously simpler to implement, would—almost by definition—not disturb synergies within banking organizations too much, and would abolish a significant share of pure proprietary trading.

---

[85] Piasio (2013).
[86] FSOC (2011), pp. 27-28.

Second, any compromise to go beyond this "bright-line" should scrap the current form of the Volcker Rule and its minutiae.[87] Rather than judge each and every trade, the rule should instead permit most transactions within some safe harbor, possibly based on gross and net inventory. Beyond that safe harbor, transactions could be subject to additional scrutiny.

Third, the Volcker Rule is really aimed at universal banks that have widespread trading operations and the means to exploit leverage requirements and government guarantees. By all reports, however, small- to medium-sized banks have been caught in the compliance net of the Volcker Rule. Any revision of the rule should effectively exempt these smaller banks.[88]

References

Acharya, V., and Richardson, M. (2012), "Implications of the Dodd-Frank Act," *Annual Review of Financial Economics* 4:1-38.

Acharya, V., Cooley, T., Richardson, M. and I. Walter (2010) "Manufacturing Tail Risk: A Perspective on the Financial Crisis of 2007-2009," (with Viral Acharya, Thomas Cooley and Ingo Walter, *Foundations and Trends in Finance*, Vol. 4: No. 4, 247-325).

Acharya, V., Cooley, T., Richardson, M. and I. Walter (2011) "Prologue: A Bird's Eye View — The Dodd-Frank Wall Street Reform and Consumer Protection Act," in *Regulating Wall Street: The Dodd-Frank Act and the New Architecture of Global Finance*, Viral V. Acharya, Thomas Cooley, Matthew Richardson and Ingo Walter, editors, New York University Stern School of Business, John Wiley & Sons, 2011.

---

[87] As an illustration, the final rule issued by the CFTC on January 31, 2014, is 269 pages long in small type.

[88] This exemption can be revisited over time should it lead to regulatory arbitrage with implications for systemic risk.

Acharya, V., Pedersen, L., Philippon, T. and M. Richardson (2013), "How to Calculate Systemic Risk Charges," Chapter 5, *Quantifying Systemic Risk, NBER*, edited by Joseph Haubrich and Andrew Lo.

Acharya, V., Pedersen, L., Philippon, T. and M. Richardson (2017), Measuring Systemic Risk, forthcoming *Review of Financial Studies*.

Adrian, T., Fleming, M., Shachar, O., and Vogt, E. (2015), "Has U.S. Corporate Bond Market Liquidity Deteriorated?" *Liberty Street Economics*, October 5.

Adrian, T., Fleming, M., Shachar, O., and Vogt, E. (2016), "Market Liquidity after the Financial Crisis," forthcoming *Annual Reviews of Financial Economics*.

Adrian, R., Fleming, M., Vogt, E., and Wojtowicz, Z. (2016), "Corporate Bond Market Liquidity Redux: More Price-Based Evidence," February 9.

Akhigbe, A., and Whyte, A. (2004), "The Gramm-Leach-Bliley Act of 1999: Risk Implications for the Financial Services Industry," *The Journal of Financial Research*, 27(3), Fall, pp. 435-446.

Baele, L., De Jonghe, O., and Vennet, R. (2007), "Does the Stock Market Value Bank Diversification?" *Journal of Banking and Finance*, 31, pp. 1999-2023.

Bao, J., O'Hara, M., and Zhou, X. (2016), "The Volcker Rule and Market-Making in Times of Stress," Working Paper, September.

BIS (2016), "Fixed-Income Market Liquidity," January.

Benston, G. (1990), The Separation of Commercial and Investment Banking, Oxford University Press.

Bessembinder, H., Jacobsen, S., Maxwell, W., and Venkataraman, K. (2016), "Capital Commitment and Illiquidity in Corporate Bonds," Working Paper, July.

Blackrock (2015), "Addressing Market Liquidity," July.

Blackrock (2016), "Addressing Market Liquidity: A Broader Perspective on Today's Bond Markets," February.

Boyd, J., Graham, S, and Hewitt, R. (1993), "Bank Holding Company Mergers with Nonbank Financial Firms: Effect on the Risk of Failure," 17(1), February, pp. 43-63.

Brunnermeier, Markus K., G. Nathan Dong, and Darius Palia. "Banks' Non-Interest Income and Systemic Risk." (2012).

Chung, S., Keppo, J., and Yuan, X. (2016), "The Impact of Volcker Rule on Bank Profits and Default Probabilities," Working Paper, June.

Committee on Capital Markets Regulation (2015), "Nothing but the Facts: U.S. Bond Market Liquidity," December 14.

Cornett, M., Ors, E., and Tehranian, H. (2002), "Bank Performance around the Introduction of a Section 20 Subsidiary," *The Journal of Finance*, 57(1), February, pp. 501-521.

Credit Suisse (2015), "Diminished Market Depth and the Illusion of Liquidity," May 13.

Davis Polk (2013), "Final Volcker Rule Flowcharts: Prop Trading," December 23.

Davis Polk (2014), "Final Volcker Rule Regulations Flowcharts: Funds Substantive Rules, January 6.

DeLong, G. (2001), "Stockholder Gains from Focusing versus Diversifying Bank Mergers," *Journal of Financial Economics,* 59, pp. 221-252.

Demirguc-Kunt, Asli and Harry Huizinga, 2010, "Bank Activity and Funding Strategies," *Journal of Financial Economics* 98, 626-650.

Deutsche Bank (2016), "Searching for Liquidity," March.

Diamond, Douglas, 1984, "Financial Intermediation and Delegated Monitoring," Review of Economic Studies 51, 393-414.

Duffie, D. (2012), "Market Making Under the Proposed Volcker Rule," Working Paper, January 16.

Elsas, R., Hackethal, A., and Holzhäuser, M. (2010), "The Anatomy of Bank Diversification," *Journal of Banking & Finance,* 34, pp. 1274-1287.

Fama, Eugene, 1985, "What's Different About Banks?" *Journal of Monetary Economics* 15, 29- 39.

Fraser, Donald, Jeff Madura, and Robert Weigand, 2002, "Sources of Bank Interest Rate Risk," *Financial Review* 37, 351-367.

FSCO (2011), "Study & Recommendations on Prohibitions on Proprietary Trading & Certain Relationships with Hedge Funds & Private Equity Funds," January.

Gallagher, D. (2013), "Dissenting Statement Regarding the Adoption of Rule Implementing the Volcker Rule," December 10.

Geyfman, V., and Yeager, T. (2009), "On the Riskiness of Universal Banking: Evidence from Banks in the Investment Banking Business

Pre- and Post-GLBA," *Journal of Money, Credit and Banking*, 41(8), December, pp. 1649-1669.

Gorton, G., and Pennacchi, G. (1990), "Financial Intermediaries and Liquidity Creation," *Journal of Finance* 45(1), 49-71.

House Committee on Financial Services (2016), "The Financial CHOICE Act," June 23.

Jorion, P. (2005), "Bank Trading Risk and Systemic Risk," NBER Working Paper, January.

King, R., Massoud, N., and Song, K. (2013), "How Does Bank Trading Activity Affect Performance? An Investigation Before and After the Crisis," Working Paper, September.

Laeven, L., and Levine, R. (2007), "Is There a Diversification Discount in Financial Conglomerates?" *Journal of Financial Economics*, 85, pp. 331-367.

Lown, C., Osler, C., Strahan, P., and Sufi, A. (2000), "The Changing Landscape of the Financial Services Industry: What Lies Ahead?" *FRB of New York Economic Policy Review*, 6(4), pp. 39-55.

Lykken, A. (2013), "Getting Around the Volcker Rule," PitchBook, November 27.

Market Watch (2016), "How a Goldman Sachs Trader Can Make $100 Million in the Volcker Rule Era," October 20.

Merkley, J. (2016), letter to Janet Yellen, Thomas Curry, Mary Jo White, Timothy Massad, and Martin Gruenberg, May 5.

Mizrach, B. (2015), "Analysis of Corporate Bond Liquidity," *Research Note*, FINRA Office of the Chief Economist.

Piasio, C. (2013), "It's Complicated: Why the Volcker Rule is Unworkable," *Seton Hall Law Review*, 43, pp. 737-771.

Popper, N. (2015), "Goldman Sachs Investments Test the Volcker Rule," *The New York Times*, January 21.

Richardson, M. (2012), "Why the Volcker Rule Is a Useful Tool for Managing Systemic Risk," White Paper. Summarized in *Perspectives on Dodd-Frank and Finance*, Paul Schultz editor, MIT Press, 2014.

Schmid, M., and Walter, I. (2009), "Do Financial Conglomerates Create or Destroy Economic Value?" *J. Finan. Intermediation*, 18, pp. 193-216.

Stein, K. (2013), "Statement Regarding Adoption of Rule Implementing the Volcker Rule," December 10.

Stiroh, K. (2004), "Diversification in Banking: Is Noninterest Income the Answer?" *Journal of Money, Credit, and Banking*, 36(5), October, pp. 853-82.

Stiroh, K. (2006), "A Portfolio View of Banking with Interest and Noninterest Activities," *Journal of Money, Credit and Banking*, 38(5), pp. 1351-1361.

The Wall Street Journal (2014), "Citigroup Team's Mortgage Bets Undeterred by Volcker Rule," June 25.

Trebbi, F., and Xiao, K. (2015), "Regulation and Market Liquidity," NBER Working Paper No. 21739, November.

Trefis (2013a), "Goldman Volcker Rule Policy: Creative and Profitable Compliance," February 13.

Trefis (2013b), "Here's Why Wells Fargo's PE Unit Will Flourish Despite the Volcker Rule," February 25.

White (2009), "Wal-Mart and Banks: Should the Twain Meet? A Principles-Based Approach to the Issues of the Separation of Banking and Commerce," *Contemporary Economic Policy* 27(4), October, pp. 440-449.

Yu (2003), "On the Wealth and Risk Effects of the Glass-Steagall Overhaul: Evidence from the Stock Market," Working Paper.

Regulating Insurance Companies and the FSOC Designation of SIFIs

By Ralph S. J. Koijen and Matthew P. Richardson

Introduction

The insurance sector is a crucial part of the real economy, directly and indirectly employing millions of people, with virtually every household and firm as a client. In addition, insurance companies are important financial intermediaries, as they are a primary source of capital, especially for corporations and commercial mortgages.

On the surface, traditional insurance companies pool and diversify idiosyncratic risks that have potentially catastrophic consequences for individuals and businesses. In competitive markets, insurers price diversifiable risks on an actuarial basis, yielding tremendous utility gains to the previously exposed individuals and businesses.

More recently, however, some insurers have deviated from this traditional business model by: (i) providing insurance or similar financial products protecting against macroeconomic events and other nondiversifiable risks; (ii) being more prone to runs due to changes in their liability structure; and (iii) having expanded their overall role in financial markets. These nontraditional insurance activities are more systemically risky than insurers' traditional activities and can lead to the insurance sector performing particularly poorly in systemic states—that is, when other parts of the financial sector are struggling.

In the United States, regulation of insurance companies—including prudential regulation—is carried out by the states, as has been the case since the 19th century. As the financial sector has become more interconnected, and financial activities and functions have become more blurred across institutional forms, the question arises whether insurance companies need Federal supervision and, in particular, enhanced supervision due to systemic risk creation.[89]

To this point, while the financial crisis of 2007-2009 was very much a banking (or "shadow banking") crisis, insurance companies played their role too. Monoline insurers of mortgage products (such as MGIC Investment Corporation, PMI Group and Radian Group) experienced severe financial distress that spilled over to other parts of the financial sector. Large life insurers (such as Hartford Financial Services Group) aggressively wrote investment-oriented life insurance and annuity products with minimum guarantees and other contract features that exposed them to equity and other investment markets. And the largest insurance companies (such as AXA, MetLife and Prudential) also came under stress with large spikes in their debt and credit default swap spreads. And, of course, AIG effectively failed through large losses in its securities lending business and writing insurance derivatives on a half-trillion dollars of nominal asset-backed securities. In hindsight, since AIG was vastly undercapitalized at the holding company level, and not subject to any serious regulation or oversight, it became the poster child for why enhanced prudential regulation may be needed for nonbank, large financial institutions.

While neither the Dodd-Frank Act nor the CHOICE Act addresses the insurance sector in any substantive way, there are a few key parts contained in these Acts that are especially relevant for insurance companies. We discuss these below.

The Dodd-Frank Act

---

[89] For two balanced books that analyze various points of view on insurance regulation, see Biggs and Richardson (2014) and Hufeld, Koijen and Thimann (2016).

As a result of the financial crisis, the Congress passed the Dodd-Frank Wall Street Reform and Consumer Protection Act and it was signed into law by President Barack Obama on July 21, 2010. The Dodd-Frank Act affected insurance companies in two ways.

First, while the Dodd-Frank Act did not create a new direct regulator of insurance, it did impose on nonbank holding companies, potentially including insurance entities, a major new form of regulation for those deemed systemically important financial institutions (SIFIs).[90] This regulation called for stricter prudential standards, including additional leverage and liquidity requirements, possible restrictions on the concentration and mix of activities of the company, and resolution plans, among other regulations. To date, the Financial Stability Oversight Council (FSOC) has designated four nonbank companies as SIFIs, three of which are insurance companies: AIG, Prudential and MetLife.[91] MetLife fought its designation in courts, and the FSOC order was rescinded. The case is under appeal.

Second, the Dodd-Frank Act created a Federal Insurance Office (FIO) inside the Department of Treasury. While the FIO has no direct

---

[90] The designation decision is made by the newly formed Financial Stability Oversight Council, which is chaired by the Secretary of the Treasury and consists of the top financial officers from various governmental and regulatory agencies—the Federal Reserve, the Office of the Comptroller of the Currency (OCC), the Bureau of Consumer Financial Protection, the Securities and Exchange Commission (SEC), the Federal Deposit Insurance Corporation (FDIC), the Commodity Futures Trading Commission (CFTC), the Federal Housing Finance Agency (FHFA), and the National Credit Union Administration (NCUA)—and an independent member with insurance expertise. The criteria for SIFI designation is to "identify risks to the financial stability of the United States that could arise from material financial distress or failure, or ongoing activities, of large, interconnected bank holding companies or nonbank financial companies or that could arise outside the financial services marketplace." (HR4173, Title I, "Financial Stability," Subtitle A, "Financial Stability Oversight Council," Sec. 112, "Council Authority."

[91] The designation of the fourth company (General Electric) was removed after GE restructured its business, in particular, spinning off a large part of its capital arm.

---

regulatory powers, its mandate is to investigate and represent the insurance industry, and refer any regulatory problems that it identifies to other regulators. For example, it would recommend to FSOC any insurance companies that it believes to be systemically important.[92] Also, the Dodd-Frank Act created an odd structure that the voting member of FSOC would be a "member appointed by the President, by and with the advice and consent of the Senate, having insurance expertise," but not from the Federal Insurance Office.

The CHOICE Act

The CHOICE Act proposes changes to the Dodd-Frank Act in two regards: (i) combining the roles of the FIO director and FSOC Independent Member with Insurance Expertise; and (ii) repealing FSOC's authority to designate nonbanks as SIFIs.

With respect to the former, it can be reasonably argued that the Dodd-Frank Act's creation of two insurance roles is counterproductive. To the extent that there is currently little oversight of insurance at the federal level, consolidating the federal insurance positions into one unified role makes ample sense. Regardless of one's views on FSOC's designation of SIFIs, it is important to keep the FIO and to clearly outline its authority and responsibilities.

First, the FIO should aggregate information and disseminate this information to state regulators. For example, large insurance companies should be required to prepare the same "statutory

---

[92] While the FIO director plays an important initial role if, and when, a systemically important insurance company becomes distressed, there is no follow-on function. Specifically, for a failing insurance company to go through the Dodd-Frank orderly liquidation authority, the director and at least two-thirds of the Federal Reserve Board of Governors must make the recommendation to the Treasury secretary. However, the liquidation and/or receivership would be carried out by the relevant state regulator, who most likely does not have either experience or expertise at managing systemic risk.

accounting principles" (SAP) filings for all their captive reinsurance activities, and to share them with the FIO. The FIO can consolidate this information and return it to the state regulators.[93]

Of particular interest are assumptions about reserves, hedging programs involving derivatives, investment risks including securities lending, and letters of credit including all (parental) guarantees. This information should be provided for all captives, including those domiciled offshore (for instance, in the Cayman Islands). Without this information, it is virtually impossible for state regulators to analyze the risks in captives. It is nevertheless the case that when a captive fails, all reinsured policies transfer back to the balance sheet of the original insurance company, and a failure of the operating company would result in losses of the guarantee fund in the state in which the policy has been sold. Hence, as a first step to ensure the stability of the state guarantee funds and the insurance sector as a whole, the FIO needs to provide transparency to all state regulators of the activities of insurance companies in other states. In response to this information, state regulators can use their judgment and expertise to choose to no longer provide, for instance, reserve credit to certain reinsurance transactions if they deem the captive to be too risky or insufficiently capitalized.

Second, the FIO should try to coordinate regulation with international regulators. At this point, there is little coordination across different regulators, while many of the largest companies are global. For instance, among the top ten variable annuity sellers are Jackson National (Prudential UK), Voya (ING, the Netherlands), Aegon (the Netherlands), and AXA (France). The Solvency II

---

[93] New York Department of Financial Services completed such an investigation for the companies doing business in New York in 2013, but this information should be readily available to all state regulators: http://www.dfs.ny.gov/reportpub/shadow_insurance_report_2013.pdf. Furthermore, the Iowa Insurance Division published the regulatory filings of captive reinsurers domiciled in Iowa for the years 2014 and 2015, https://iid.iowa.gov/financial-statements?category=22.

framework that was enacted in January 2016 is focused much more on mark-to-market valuation and one-year risk measures, which is very different from the SAP framework in the United States. Without proper coordination of regulatory frameworks across countries, loopholes undoubtedly open up, which can be exploited perhaps in particular by the largest and global insurance companies.

With respect to repealing FSOC's authority to designate nonbanks as SIFIs, we first outline the general arguments of the CHOICE Act and comment on its line of reasoning. Then, in the next section, we discuss the degree to which a large, modern insurance company may or may not fit into the SIFI designation.

The authors of the CHOICE Act basically make two arguments for repealing the FSOC's designation authority: First, the FSOC is made up of political appointees, i.e., the heads of the various regulatory agencies (see footnote 90), and these persons are not qualified to judge the systemic nature of financial firms. Second, the process for designating nonbanks as SIFIs is not well-defined. In other words, the specific criteria laid out in Dodd-Frank are too vague and therefore gives too much power to regulatory authorities.[94]

With respect to the first point, if it is truly about the qualifications of the FSOC members, then a reasonable suggestion might be to create a systemic risk board that is qualified to make such designations. That said, it is a sad state of affairs if the heads (or chairs) of the various financial regulatory agencies, with all their available staff (and commissioners) expertise, cannot be brought up to speed on the few nonbank firms or activities that fit into the SIFI category. The appropriate question is whether there exist nonbank SIFIs or systemic activities. If there is agreement on this point, then surely an inadequate governance structure of FSOC is not a good reason to repeal SIFI designation. Rather, the governance should be improved to make better decisions.

---

[94] The general criteria provided by Dodd-Frank is that the material financial distress, failure, or ongoing activities of large, interconnected financial institutions cause risk to the financial stability of the United States. Specific standards laid out are: "(A) the extent of the leverage of the company; (B) the extent and nature of the off-balance sheet exposures of the company; (C) the extent and nature of the transactions and relationships of the company with other significant nonbank financial companies and significant bank holding companies; (D) the importance of the company as a source of credit for households, businesses, and State and local governments and as a source of liquidity for the United States financial system; (E) the importance of the company as a source of credit for low-income, minority, or underserved communities, and the impact that the failure of such company would have on the availability of credit in such communities; (F) the extent to which assets are managed rather than owned by the company, and the extent to which ownership of assets under management is diffuse; (G) the nature, scope, size, scale, concentration, interconnectedness, and mix of the activities of the company; (H) the degree to which the company is already regulated by 1 or more primary financial regulatory agencies; (I) the amount and nature of the financial assets of the company; (J) the amount and types of the liabilities of the company, including the degree of reliance on short-term funding; and (K) any other risk-related factors that the Council deems appropriate." (HR 4173, Title I, Subtitle A, Sec. 113, "Authority to require supervision and regulation of certain nonbank financial companies.").

With respect to the second point, and the issue of what it means for nonbanks to be SIFIs and whether these SIFIs can be identified, the right solution is surely not to repeal the designation authority but instead to improve it. If there are possible problems with constitutional or practical implementation of the designation—or with too vague and poorly defined language—then this should be corrected. But the idea that banks can be SIFIs but nonbanks cannot is weak in light of the evidence, particularly based on the last financial crisis.

To this point, consider the last crisis as an example: Compare the Dodd-Frank Act to the CHOICE Act under a hypothetical scenario just prior to the emergence of the financial crisis in 2007. Without SIFI designation of nonbanks, the five large investment banks (Bear Stearns, Lehman Brothers, Goldman Sachs, Merrill Lynch, and Morgan Stanley) were for the most part under the regulation of the SEC. These investment banks engaged in capital market activities not unlike their large commercial bank counterparts, yet were extraordinarily levered and relied on wholesale liquid funding. During the crisis, at some point or another, all of them suffered bank-like runs on their liabilities; and, given their activities, some of the firms reached insolvency.[95] If large banks are considered SIFIs, then it is hard to comprehend why these large investment banks would also not be considered SIFIs. Under the CHOICE Act, these firms would not be SIFIs, and instead regulation would rest with the

---

[95] In March 2008, Bear Stearns was bought by JP Morgan Chase when it appeared insolvent and was suffering a run on its liabilities. The Fed provided a backstop to JP Morgan Chase for certain asset-backed securities of Bear Stearns. In September 2008, under similar circumstances, Lehman Brothers declared bankruptcy and Merrill Lynch was bought by Bank of America, which shortly after also received guarantees on particular Merrill Lynch holdings. While *ex post,* Goldman Sachs and Morgan Stanley were recognized as clearly solvent, both suffered bank-like runs and came under severe stress following Lehman's failure. Only after government intervention in markets as a whole and the transition of these firms to bank holding companies did the runs, especially on Morgan Stanley, curtail. The transition allowed access to the Federal Reserve's lending facilities, as well as other sources of funding, e.g., deposits.

SEC. Suppose, for example, large bank holding companies, like Goldman Sachs and Morgan Stanley, were to drop their bank status, or boutique investment banks were to accumulate large amounts of assets without future FSOC designation.[96] Would this not increase the likelihood of a financial crisis in magnitude similar to that of 2007-2009?

Of course, the relative systemic risk of large investment banks versus the universal commercial banks is plain to see. What about other nonbank financial institutions? During the recent financial crisis, there were runs on money market funds, collateralized repos, asset-backed commercial paper, and securities lending businesses. All these entities act very much like banks by borrowing in short-term markets, providing deposit-like liquid securities to investors, and investing in less liquid longer-term assets. Moreover, if, and when housing finance reform is enacted, possible counterparts to the Government-Sponsored Enterprises (GSEs)—Fannie Mae and Freddie Mac—might be created. Will these entities not be SIFIs? Finally, as the FSOC designation of SIFIs disappears, and higher capital requirements on banks are put in place, it seems likely that a number of activities will move outside the banking sector to a new (and yet unknown) *de facto* banking sector (sometimes called "shadow banking").[97] Without the possibility of enhanced prudential regulation of large firms that arise in this sector, regulatory capital arbitrage will result, putting the system in greater jeopardy.

---

[96] In theory, under Dodd-Frank, Goldman Sachs and Morgan Stanley cannot undo their bank holding company status. But with FSOC's SIFI designation, this change would be moot. Obviously, this point is not true with the elimination of the SIFI designation.

[97] "De facto or shadow" banking is a system of financial institutions that mostly function like banks. These financial institutions borrow short term in rollover debt markets, leverage significantly, and lend and invest in longer-term and illiquid assets.

The authors of the CHOICE Act describe a potential inconsistency or flaw with Dodd-Frank's FSOC designation of SIFIs. They argue that, while the Dodd-Frank Act attempts to constrain leverage and risk-taking of SIFIs through enhanced prudential regulation, it creates moral hazard through a "too-big-to-fail" mantra that in turn encourages leverage and risk-taking.

But the authors of the CHOICE Act have the causality the wrong way. It is precisely because these SIFIs will be treated differently in a financial crisis—either through liquidity support if solvent (i.e., Walter Bagehot's dictum) or special bankruptcy proceedings if insolvent (whether the Orderly Liquidation Authority of Dodd-Frank or a new bankruptcy code for large, complex financial institutions under the CHOICE Act)—that these firms must be subject to enhanced regulation. If market participants recognize that these firms are "special," then excess leverage and risk-taking may take place unless these firms are constrained in the broader financial system. There is no better example than Fannie Mae and Freddie Mac, which were poorly regulated on a prudential basis and yet were repeatedly described as not having access to a government backstop. The financial markets rightly did not believe these claims, and the actions and subsequent failures of these two firms greatly contributed to the debacle of mortgage finance.[98]

The Regulation of Insurance Companies

As described above, three of the four SIFI designations by FSOC have been insurance companies. These designations have been controversial, and MetLife's was rescinded by the courts and is now under appeal. It seems worthwhile therefore to comment generally on the potential systemic risk of insurance companies.[99] Indeed, the

---

[98] See the book by Acharya, Richardson, Van Nieuwerburgh, and White (2011) for a detailed analysis of this point for the GSEs.

[99] For a detailed discussion and varied views of systemic risk of insurance companies, see Acharya and Richardson (2014), Cummins and Weiss (2014) and Harrington (2014).

authors of the CHOICE Act question the logic of designating financial companies that by and large just "sell insurance."

In order to regulate and manage systemic risk, one needs to be able to define it. Dodd-Frank's criteria are that "the material financial distress, failure, or ongoing activities of large, interconnected financial institutions cause risk to the financial stability of the United States." These criteria highlight an important idea: The core problem is a firm's difficulty in performing financial services when it fails—i.e., when its capital falls short—and that systemic risk matters only to the extent there is an impact on the broader economy.

Specifically, systemic risk can only arise when there is a breakdown in aggregate financial intermediation that accompanies the firm's failure. When one financial firm's capital is low, that firm can no longer perform intermediation services (e.g., obtain funds from depositors or investors and provide financing to other firms or entities). This generally has minimal consequences because other financial firms can fill in for the failed firm. But when capital is low in the aggregate, it is not possible for other financial firms to step into the breach. When investors or depositors question the extent to which a class of financial institutions or the financial system as a whole can absorb losses, access to short-term funding and liquidity dries up, preventing even solvent institutions from taking over the financial intermediation activities of failed firms. Thus, it is this breakdown in aggregate financial intermediation that causes severe consequences for the broader economy.

Acharya, Pedersen, Philippon, and Richardson (2015, 2016) develop a framework to measure systemic risk of financial firms. They incorporate externalities arising from an aggregate capital shortfall, which leads to a reduction in intermediation activity, and from fire sales caused by the degree to which liabilities are liquid and under the threat of potential runs. The question is whether large insurance companies fall into this class of financial firms or are just simply selling insurance.

Historically, with respect to their liability structure, insurance liabilities have been mostly long-term and relatively illiquid. This is quite different from bank liabilities, which are predominantly short-term and withdrawable at will. That said, life insurance premiums are no longer as sticky for modern insurance companies. Paulson, Plestis, Rosen, McMenamin, and Mohey-Deen (2014) provide a detailed analysis of this issue. They provide evidence that approximately 50% of liabilities are in a moderately to highly liquid category, allowing for some type of withdrawal. Projected onto stress scenarios, they estimate that, respectively, 43% or 31% of the life insurance industry's liabilities are subject to withdrawals in an extreme or moderate stress environment. This is important because life insurance companies are prominent investors in commercial mortgage-backed securities and corporate bonds, both of which are susceptible to fire sales. Indeed, the evidence supports this being a potential problem in the life insurance sector.[100]

In terms of understanding the risk of insurance companies, it is important to distinguish idiosyncratic risks that are unique to the insurance sector, such as property, health, and life risks, and aggregate financial risks coming from modern insurance products (such as variable annuities) and investments in assets that create an aggregate risk mismatch between assets and liabilities. This latter risk can expose the insurance sector to common shocks, even if insurance companies are not directly connected to each other.

For example, some large life insurers aggressively wrote investment-oriented life insurance policies with minimum guarantees and other contract features that exposed them to equity and other asset markets. These policies expose the insurers

---

[100] See Becker and Opp (2014), Ellul, Jotikasthira, and Lundblad (2011, 2016), and Ellul, Jotikasthira, Lundblad, and Wang (2015).

to potentially large losses when markets decline. Other insurers have deviated from the traditional insurance business model by providing so-called insurance or similar financial products, protecting against loss due to macroeconomic events and other nondiversifiable risks. For example, in the years leading up to the financial crisis, the monoline insurers and AIG wrote financial guarantees on structured financial products tied to subprime mortgages. If these risks materialize (and the risks by nature are more likely to do so during a financial and economic crisis), then insurance companies collectively will suffer investment losses. For example, the credit default swap (CDS) premiums—the cost of buying protection against default of senior, subordinated bonds—of large life insurance companies, among others, rose well above 500 basis points in the fall of 2008 after Lehman's collapse.

More broadly, the line between insurance companies and other financial services companies has become blurred over time. New tools that insurance companies use to manage their capital— securities lending, new reinsurance schemes between affiliated companies ("shadow insurance"), and derivatives—have been developed. Koijen and Yogo (2016b) measure the trends in these activities from 2002 to 2014 in the U.S. and use the financial crisis as a case study to quantify the risks. One example is detailed in Koijen and Yogo (2016a) and is reminiscent of the special purpose vehicles of large complex banks during the financial crisis.[101]

As a final comment, because the insurance sector can perform poorly in systemic states—that is, when other parts of the financial

---

[101]Koijen and Yogo (2016a) show that some of the larger life insurance companies are now using reinsurance to move liabilities from operating companies that sell policies to less regulated (i.e., less capitalized) "shadow insurers" in regulation-friendly U.S. states (e.g., South Carolina and Vermont) and offshore locales (e.g., Bermuda and the Cayman Islands). Since the liabilities stay within the insurer's holding company, there is not the usual risk transfer between the insurer and reinsurer. The authors show that this type of regulatory arbitrage has grown from $10 billion to $363 billion over the past decade, and, when accounted for, expected losses are almost $16 billion higher in the industry.

sector are struggling—and because the insurance sector is an important part of the economy-wide financial intermediation process, it follows that significant capital shortfalls of the insurance sector contribute to systemic risk. The source for an aggregate capital shortfall can take many forms, including exposure to common aggregate shocks, interconnectedness, fire sales and bank-like "runs" on liabilities. As described earlier, the emergence of systemic risk means that financial firms will no longer be able to provide intermediation, causing knock-on effects to households and businesses. As an important source for financing (i.e., corporate bonds and commercial mortgages), disintermediation of the insurance sector can have important consequences.[102] Moreover, households may reduce their demand for insurance if they experience losses when an insurance company fails. This additional exposure to idiosyncratic risk can lead to significant welfare costs.

References

Acharya, V. V., Biggs, J., Le, H. Richardson, M. and S. Ryan, "Systemic Risk and the Regulation of Insurance Companies," Chapter 9 of *Regulating Wall Street: The Dodd-Frank Act and the New Architecture of Global Finance*, editors Viral V. Acharya, Thomas F. Cooley, Matthew Richardson and Ingo Walter, John Wiley and Sons, 2011.

Acharya, V. V., Pedersen, L. H., Philippon, T., & Richardson, M. (2017). Measuring Systemic Risk. *Review of Financial Studies, 30*(1), 2-47.

Acharya, Viral V., Thomas Philippon, and Matthew Richardson. "Measuring Systemic Risk for Insurance Companies" in *The Economics, Regulation, and Systemic Risk of Insurance*

---

[102] For example, see Becker (2016) and Paulson and Rosen (2016) for a discussion of the investment grade corporate bond market.

Markets (2016), editors Hufeld, Felix, Ralph Koijen, and Christian Thimann, Oxford University Press, 2017.

Acharya, Viral V., and Matthew Richardson, 2014. "Is the Insurance Industry Systemically Risky?" Chapter 9 of Modernizing Insurance Regulation, editors John Biggs and Matthew Richardson, John Wiley & Sons, 151-80.

Acharya, V. V., Richardson, M., Van Nieuwerburgh and L. J. White, 2011, Guaranteed to Fail: Fannie Mae, Freddie Mac and the Debacle of Mortgage Finance, Princeton University Press.

Becker, Bo. "How the Insurance Industry's Asset Portfolio Responds to Regulation" The Economics, Regulation, and Systemic Risk of Insurance Markets (2016), editors Hufeld, Felix, Ralph Koijen, and Christian Thimann, Oxford University Press, 2017.

Becker, Bo, and Marcus Opp. Regulatory Reform and Risk-Taking: Replacing Ratings. No. w19257. National Bureau of Economic Research, 2013.

Biggs, John and Matthew Richardson, eds., Modernizing Insurance Regulation, John Wiley and Sons, 2014.

J. David Cummins and Mary A. Weiss, 2014 "Systemic Risk and Regulation of the U.S. Insurance Industry," Chapter 7 of Modernizing Insurance Regulation, eds. John Biggs and Matthew Richardson and Ingo Walter, Hoboken, NJ: John Wiley & Sons

Ellul, Andrew, Chotibhak Jotikasthira, and Christian T. Lundblad. "Regulatory Pressure and Fire Sales in the Corporate Bond Market" Journal of Financial Economics 101.3 (2011): 596-620.

Ellul, Andrew, Chotibhak Jotikasthira, and Christian T. Lundblad. "Spillover Effects of Risk Regulation on the Asset Side to Asset

Markets" *The Economics, Regulation, and Systemic Risk of Insurance Markets* (2016): 165.

Ellul, A., Jotikasthira, C., Lundblad, C. T., & Wang, Y. (2015). DP10450 Is Historical Cost Accounting a Panacea? Market Stress, Incentive Distortions, and Gains Trading.

Scott E. Harrington, "Designation and Supervision of Insurance SIFIs," Chapter 8 of *Modernizing Insurance Regulation*, eds. John Biggs and Matthew Richardson and Ingo Walter, Hoboken, NJ: John Wiley & Sons.

Koijen, Ralph SJ, and Motohiro Yogo. "Shadow insurance" *Econometrica* 84.3 (2016a): 1265-1287.

Koijen, Ralph SJ, and Motohiro Yogo. "Risk of Life Insurers: Recent Trends and Transmission Mechanisms." (2016b), in *The Economics, Regulation, and Systemic Risk of Insurance Markets*, editors Hufeld, Felix, Ralph Koijen, and Christian Thimann, Oxford University Press, 2017.

Hufeld, Felix, Ralph Koijen, and Christian Thimann, *The Economics, Regulation and Systemic Risk of Insurance Markets*, Oxford University Press, 2017.

Paulson, Anna, and Richard Rosen. "The Life Insurance Industry and Systemic Risk: A Bond Market Perspective." *Annual Review of Financial Economics* 8 (2016): 155-174.

Paulson, Anna, Thanases Plestis, Richard Rosen, Robert McMenamin, and Zain Mohey-Deen, "Assessing the Vulnerability of the U.S. Life Insurance Industry," Chapter 6 *Modernizing Insurance Regulation*, eds. John Biggs and Matthew Richardson and Ingo Walter, Hoboken, NJ: John Wiley & Sons.

Don't Forget the Plumbing: Payment, Clearing, and Settlement Companies in the Dodd-Frank and Financial CHOICE Acts

By Bruce Tuckman

Introduction

On an average day, about $15 trillion in U.S. dollar-denominated payments settle around the world.[103] The operations behind this massive volume of transactions are known as the "plumbing" of the financial system, which is managed by central banks and by a relatively small number of large payment, clearing, and settlement (PCS) companies.[104]

PCS companies have always been systemically important. Should a large PCS company cease operations, it would become difficult, or even temporarily impossible, to conduct a wide range of transactions. The resulting disruption of retail or securities trading could easily have severe economic and financial consequences.

Title VIII of Dodd-Frank aims to protect systemically important PCS companies, or Financial Market Utilities (FMUs), by subjecting them to heightened regulation and by giving them access to emergency liquidity at the discretion of the Federal Reserve.

---

[103] Payments Risk Committee (2016), p. 9.

[104] Payment refers, obviously enough, to transfers of cash. Clearing refers to the preparation of trades for settlement. Settlement refers to the exchange of cash for securities and the discharge of derivatives obligations.

Title VIII might have been a response to some plumbing issues that arose during 2008,[105] and might, in the post-crisis spirit, be understood as filling holes in the regulatory landscape. Most directly, however, Title VIII was deemed necessary in the wake of Title VII.

Title VII mandated that most over-the-counter (OTC) derivatives be cleared. In other words, a derivative contract that had previously been settled between its two counterparties would now have to be settled through a PCS company known as a clearinghouse.

Proponents of Title VII argue that, overall, the clearing mandate reduces systemic risk. But it certainly increases the systemic risk of OTC derivatives clearinghouses. Were these to fail, it would become operationally difficult, if not impossible, and also illegal, to trade many OTC derivatives. From this perspective, Title VIII contends with the systemic risk created as a by-product of Title VII.

The CHOICE Act argues that Title VIII designations and access to emergency liquidity increase moral hazard and, thereby, increase the likelihood that PCS companies will fail. The CHOICE Act proposes, therefore, to repeal Title VIII.

This paper argues that both the implementation of Dodd-Frank to date and the CHOICE Act unwisely neglect the need for a resolution plan for PCS companies.

---

[105] On the whole, the PCS system worked well in 2008. See Bech, Martin, and McAndrews (2012). Intraday credit provision in tri-party repo was seriously flawed, however, and contributed to stresses around Bear Stearns and Lehman Brothers. See Tuckman (2010). But it is not clear that tri-party repo issues motivated Title VIII. First, tri-party repo clearing was at two banks, not a PCS company. Second, the issues were mostly corrected by regulators and the industry soon after the crisis, without Dodd-Frank. Third, tri-party repo and the clearing banks were never designated as Title VIII FMUs.

Given the systemic importance of the PCS system, government cannot credibly claim to let failing PCS companies cease operations. It is highly preferable, therefore, to develop a resolution plan in advance, rather than devise one, on the fly, during a crisis. Any such plan should certainly be sensitive to moral hazard by wiping out clearinghouse equity and other interests. But a workable resolution plan may very well require the use of public funds.

We find no harm in allowing PCS companies access to the Federal Reserve, but object to a designation process that restricts such access to incumbent PCS companies. At present, with rapid advances in financial technology, the regulatory apparatus should not entrench incumbents. A better approach would aim to level the playing field by permitting new entrants to accept regulation by the Federal Reserve in exchange for equal access to the system.

The Benefits and Risks of PCS Systems and Central Counterparties (CCPs)

To illustrate the benefits and risks of PCS systems, consider the following simple example: a broker-dealer (B/D) makes markets in a particular stock on a particular day; the stock trades at $1 per share; and the B/D executes ten trades with ten different counterparties, five purchases of 100 shares and five sales of 100 shares. Each trade is "bilateral," meaning that settlement obligations lie with the two counterparties to each trade.

If trades settle individually, the B/D executes ten different transactions, even though, at the end of the day, it has neither bought nor sold any stock on a net basis. These ten settlements, therefore, introduce needless operational expense and risk.

Settling trades individually also requires intraday financing. If the first trade to settle is a purchase, the B/D has to raise $100 to buy the stock. If the first trade to settle is a sale, the B/D has to borrow 100 shares to deliver. But intraday financing is both costly and risky:

If the B/D cannot raise the needed cash or securities, it will fail to settle. Furthermore, the B/D's failure to settle could cascade through the system by causing its counterparties to fail on their trades with others.

Many PCS systems use a CCP to reduce the costs and risks just described. When a CCP clears a trade, it steps in as the legal counterparty to both sides of the trade. In the example, with CCP clearing, the B/D's ten trades would all legally face the CCP rather than its ten trading counterparties. Similarly, all of these counterparties would legally face the CCP.

With CCP clearing, the B/D settles its five purchases and five sales of the stock with a single counterparty, namely, the CCP. The CCP can, therefore, net the ten trades and inform the B/D that it has no settlement requirements that day. Through netting, then, in this stylized example, the number of required settlements and the need for intraday financing has vanished.

Changing the example somewhat, say that the B/D makes five purchases but only four sales that day. Its netted requirement would be to pay $100 in exchange for 100 shares of stock. If the B/D cannot come up with $100 according to schedule, the chain of settlements might be delayed or disrupted. Worse, if the B/D defaults on its settlement obligation, the CCP is on the hook to purchase the stock for $100.

To protect itself against such an eventuality, the CCP requires that the B/D post margin in proportion to its obligations. To calculate an appropriate margin amount, the CCP might assume that the stock price could fall over the day by at most $0.10, to $0.90 per share. Under that assumption, the CCP would require $10 in margin.

If the B/D defaulted and the stock did fall to $0.90, the CCP would: substitute itself for the B/D and buy 100 shares for $100; sell these

100 shares at market for $90; and use the B/D's $10 of margin to make up for the loss.

If the CCP's assumption was too optimistic, however, and the stock falls to $0.85 per share, the CCP would suffer a loss of $15 from taking over the B/D's position. With only $10 of margin on hand, the CCP would be left with a loss of $5.

In practice, a CCP clears trades only for its members. These members must demonstrate financial wherewithal, post required margin, and contribute to a "guarantee fund" to help the CCP withstand losses over and above posted margin.

This structure reveals that CCPs mutualize the risks of their members. In bilateral trades, members bear the risks of their counterparties' defaulting directly. With CCP clearing, members bear these risks through their contributions to the CCP.

CCPs establish a "waterfall" that assigns any losses it incurs. Typically, losses are first absorbed by the margin of the defaulting member, as in the example, along with that member's guarantee fund contribution. Additional losses would be absorbed first by the CCPs own capital and then by the margin and guaranty funds of the non-defaulting members, plus, if the bylaws allow, by additional assessments on those surviving members.

If CCP losses exceed all of these resources, it reaches the "end of the waterfall" and fails. In this dire scenario, the CCP is unable to honor all of its commitments to settle the trades of its members.

At some threshold of losses before the end of the waterfall, however, members would stop trusting the CCP's ability to honor settlements. At this point the CCP would have to either replenish capital and guarantee funds—which may be hard to do in a crisis— or shut down. And if a CCP with a dominant market position does shut down, trading in the securities it clears would, at least for some time, shut down as well.

Over-the-Counter (OTC) Derivatives Clearing

Before the financial crisis of 2007-2009, derivatives were traded either on an exchange or OTC. Derivatives that traded on an exchange had standardized terms and were cleared through a CCP. By contrast, derivatives that traded OTC before the crisis had customized terms and were traded bilaterally.

There is disagreement on the extent to which OTC derivatives played a role in the financial crisis and the extent to which bilateral trading poses risks to the financial system.[106] Underlying the Dodd-Frank Act, however, is the strong belief that OTC derivatives markets should be much more highly regulated than they were before the crisis.

Title VII of Dodd-Frank mandates CCP clearing of OTC derivatives whenever possible.[107] As illustrated in the simple examples earlier, netting across cleared positions reduces risk by reducing total settlement obligations. More generally, a portfolio of trades against a CCP, by the principle of diversification, has less counterparty risk than isolated bilateral trades against individual member firms.

This does not necessarily imply that mandatory clearing reduces systemic risk. Taking into account how OTC derivatives are used, forcing all trades to be cleared sacrifices certain benefits of bilateral

---

[106] On the dangers of uncleared OTC derivatives, see, for example, Financial Crisis Inquiry Commission (2011) and Cecchetti, Gyntelberg, and Hollanders (2009). In their defense, see, for example, Duffie and Zhu (2011), Pirrong (2010), Pirrong (2012), and Tuckman (2015).

[107] Some exemptions are available for end-users—that is, commercial firms that use derivatives to hedge, as opposed to financial firms engaged in the derivatives businesses.

---

trading. An important example is risk reduction across cleared and noncleared products.

Consider a B/D that lends money to a client against a portfolio of corporate bonds and has sold the client, bilaterally, Credit Default Swap (CDS) protection on corporate bonds. If the value of the bonds increases, the B/D returns margin to the client against the loan but takes back margin from the client against the sale of protection. Similarly, if the value of the bonds decreases, the B/D takes additional margin against the loan but posts additional margin against the CDS. Hence, the B/D's counterparty risk exposure to the client is small, as is the client's exposure to the B/D.

Under mandatory clearing of CDS, however, the B/D's exposure to the CDS is against the CCP, while its loan exposure, which is not cleared, is against the client. The risks no longer offset, and the B/D's counterparty risk exposure is greater than under the bilateral arrangements. More generally, a clearing mandate sacrifices risk reduction across cleared and non-cleared products.

For this and a number of other reasons, it can be argued that, while clearing has great advantages, mandatory clearing does not minimize systemic risk.[108]

---

[108] See, for example, Duffie and Zhu (2011), Pirrong (2010), Pirrong (2012), and Tuckman (2015). Another drawback of mandatory clearing is that dealers are not free to set up alternative risk protocols. To take one example, a dealer might charge a "credit value adjustment" instead of requiring margin. Relative to clearing, this arrangement has more counterparty risk but less liquidity risk. To take another example, dealers may choose to fix initial margin requirements for some term, which reduces the procyclicality of margin calls. Clearinghouse margin, by contrast, can typically be changed at any time. Finally, while a CCP naturally nets payments and exposures, bilateral contracts can and have been netted—at some cost—through a multilateral process known as compression.

Dodd-Frank's Title VIII on PCS Companies

Title VIII of Dodd-Frank is designed to identify and protect systemically important PCS companies. This title empowers the Financial Stability Oversight Council (FSOC) to designate individual PCS companies as systemically important financial market utilities (FMUs). Once designated, an FMU is subject to supervision and regulation by the Federal Reserve in addition to the Securities and Exchange Commission (SEC) or the Commodity Futures Trading Commission (CFTC).

Title VIII also permits the Federal Reserve to grant FMUs privileges that have historically been available only to member banks. In particular, FMUs may hold interest-bearing accounts in the Federal Reserve system and, in "unusual or exigent circumstances," be given access to the "discount window," or liquidity facility, under Section 10B of the Federal Reserve Act.

To date, FSOC has designated eight FMUs as systemically significant. Three are payment and settlement systems that do not take any credit risk, though there are always, of course, operational risks: The Clearing House Interbank Payment System (CHIPS), for large dollar payments; Continuous Linked Settlement Bank (CLS), for settlement of foreign exchange transactions; and The Depository Trust Company (DTC), for settlement of various securities transactions.

Two other designated FMUs are CCPs for securities settlement: National Securities Clearing Corporation (NSCC), for settlement of equities, corporate bonds, municipal bonds, and money market instruments; and Fixed Income Clearing Corporation (FICC), for settlement of government bonds and government-sponsored mortgage-backed securities.

The remaining three designated FMUs are derivatives CCPs: Chicago Mercantile Exchange Clearing (CME), for a wide variety of derivatives; ICE Clear Credit (ICC), for credit default swaps; and The Options Clearing Corporation (OCC), for a variety of options.

Analysis

Dodd-Frank: No Resolution Protocol for PCS Companies

PCS companies pose systemic risk because there are no ready alternatives to their services. Were they to shut down, massive volumes of retail and security transactions would shut down as well.

Dodd-Frank's Title VII makes OTC derivatives clearinghouses systemic in the same way. The legal requirement to clear most derivatives will atrophy the operational ability to clear those derivatives bilaterally. Hence, after the failure of a CCP, it would be illegal, and also operationally difficult or impossible, to trade most derivatives.

Title VIII partially addresses the systemic risk of PCS companies. Once a company is designated as an FMU, it is subject to heightened supervision, may be allowed to keep an interest-bearing account at the Federal Reserve, and may be given access to Federal Reserve liquidity in a crisis.

The accounts at the Federal Reserve play a number of roles. First, receiving interest on these super-safe accounts is a perk in a world of low interest rates, both for an FMU and its customers.[109] Second, these accounts allow an FMU direct access to the payment systems run by the Federal Reserve, are convenient for holding reserves or liquidity buffers required by regulators, and simplify operations should the Federal Reserve ever decide to provide emergency liquidity to the FMU.

---

[109] In addition to depositing its own funds, a CCP can hold some of its customers' funds in segregated accounts at the Federal Reserve. See Burne (2016).

By itself, however, Title VIII is not an adequate solution to the systemic risk of FMUs. While the failure of an FMU is very unlikely, it is not impossible.[110] Nevertheless, more than six years after the passage of Dodd-Frank, there is still no plan for the resolution of a failing CCP.

With respect to the Federal Reserve, there are limits as to what it could do. Under Title VIII, it can lend money to an FMU against satisfactory collateral. But this might very well not be enough to keep an FMU up-and-running, even under optimistic collateral valuations.

The Federal Reserve also has emergency lending powers under Section 13(3) of the Federal Reserve Act. These were limited by Dodd-Frank, however, to programs of "broad eligibility," which do not seem to fit the case of a failing FMU. In addition, these powers are not meant to be used in the case of a clearly insolvent FMU.

Another possibility of FMU resolution under Dodd-Frank might be Title II's "Orderly Liquidation Authority." Not all scholars believe, however, that this would be legal, and, in any case, no plans are in place for resolving an FMU under Title II.[111]

Title VIII and Competition Among PCS Companies

Title VIII raises a concern with respect to market structure. PCS incumbents are already entrenched by large fixed costs, which include those of regulatory compliance. FMU designations, which grant special access to Federal Reserve accounts and emergency liquidity facilities, further entrench these incumbents.

---

[110] The CME nearly failed after the stock market crash of 1987. See Melamed (2009), pp. 149-151.

[111] On the legal question, see Lubben (2015). With respect to the absence of CCP resolution plans, see, for example, Duffie (2016) and Massad (2016).

The general problem with a policy of entrenching incumbents is that it stifles competition and, in the process, lessens market discipline and innovation. Stifling innovation in the PCS industry today is particularly troubling in light of the rapidly developing field of financial technology, which holds great promise for improving PCS systems.[112] Singing the praises of competition in this industry is not new, by the way. The Monetary Control Act of 1980 required the Federal Reserve to price its own PCS services so as to encourage competition and innovation.[113]

Competition across PCS companies does present some challenges. PCS systems have traditionally enjoyed significant economies of scale that might be lost in an industry with many smaller players. On the other hand, new developments in financial technology may very well achieve more than offsetting efficiencies.

Concerns have also been raised that competition in the PCS space might lead to a race-to-the-bottom, in which risk standards are lowered to gain market share. The incentives to engage in such a race, however, have historically been significantly blunted by the nature of the business. Clearing members have a lot of skin in the game through their posting of margin and guarantee funds. Furthermore, several PCS companies do not operate for profit but, instead, merely recover costs from their member firms. In any case, the industry should certainly be monitored to detect any such race-to-the-bottom.

The CHOICE Act, Resolution, and Competition

The CHOICE Act proposes to repeal Title VIII in the expectation that removing FMU designations and access to Federal Reserve facilities

---

[112] See, for example, Michel (2015), Philippon (2016), and Tapscott and Tapscott (2016), Chapter 3.
[113] See, for example, Schultz (1980).

will lower moral hazard and, therefore, reduce the likelihood that an FMU will take on too much risk and fail.

But even if moral hazard can be significantly reduced, there will always be some probability that a PCS company will fail. Furthermore, given the systemic importance of PCS systems, the government cannot credibly pre-commit to allow such a failure.[114] Hence, like Dodd-Frank, the CHOICE Act unwisely neglects to provide a resolution plan for a failing PCS company.

With respect to competition, of course, repealing Title VIII would remove the advantages conferred on incumbents by Dodd-Frank.

Repeal Mandatory Clearing?

Many provisions of Title VII aim to make OTC derivatives markets safer, namely, regulation of trades that are cleared, minimum margin requirements for non-cleared trades, and reporting requirements for all trades.

The mandatory clearing provision, however, has the drawback of making OTC derivatives CCPs too-big-to-fail. Proponents of the provision argue that mandatory clearing reduces systemic risk sufficiently to justify dealing with its undesirable consequences.

As discussed earlier, others disagree. From their perspective, repealing the mandate would not necessarily increase overall systemic risk, but would reduce the systemic importance of CCPs.

---

[114] Governments have historically changed, stretched, or outright violated existing law to bail out financial systems in crisis. Examples range from the suspension of specie payments in New York in the 19th century, despite repeated prohibitions of such suspensions (see Gorton (2012), pp. 103-107), to various actions taken by the government in 2008, e.g., the Treasury's creative use of its exchange stabilization fund to guarantee money market funds, the enactment of the Troubled Asset Relief Program (TARP), and the Treasury's diversion of TARP funds from troubled asset purchases to large bank recapitalizations.

Fewer derivative trades would pass through CCPs, and the plumbing of bilateral trades would be operational in the event of a CCP failure.

With or without mandatory clearing, however, the systemic risk of CCPs is significant enough to warrant well-developed resolution plans.

It might be noted, in passing, that repeal of mandatory clearing is very unlikely. The clearing mandate has many adherents, and the financial industry is not pressing for repeal.[115]

Other Ways to Reduce the Systemic Risk of OTC Derivatives CCPs

Two proposals, not included in either Dodd-Frank or the CHOICE Act, have been put forward to reduce the systemic risk of OTC derivatives CCPs.

First, provide higher quality transparency as to how firms' derivatives positions affect their holistic risks. Such transparency would allow investors, creditors, and regulators to better monitor both individual and systemic risks.[116]

---

[115] One reason is that the industry has largely adjusted to the current regulatory framework and wants to move on. Citigroup's CFO, for example, said after the 2016 election, "The first thing I would ask for is nothing new, no new rules." Rexrode and Glazer (2016). Another reason is that the extensive fixed costs of complying with Dodd-Frank, including the clearing mandate, have raised barriers to entry to the benefit of large derivatives dealers. Jamie Dimon, CEO of JPMorgan Chase, was quoted as saying that "higher capital rules, Volcker [Rule], and OTC derivative reforms... make it more expensive and tend to make it tougher for smaller players to enter the market, effectively widening JPM's 'moat.'" Weisenthal (2013). Lloyd Blankfein, CEO of Goldman Sachs, said that "More intense regulatory and technology requirements have raised the barriers to entry higher than at any other time in modern history." *The Wall Street Journal* (2015).

[116] See, for example, Acharya (2014) and Acharya, Sachar, and Subrahmanyam (2011).

Second, derivatives safe harbors should be narrowed. These exemptions from the bankruptcy code enable counterparties to manage through a crisis by allowing them to tear up derivatives trades with a defaulting entity and to liquidate collateral held against those trades. At the same time, however, these tear-ups and liquidations complicate the resolution or liquidation of the defaulting entity, which could be a CCP.[117]

Some academic and policy analysts argue that derivatives safe harbors should be completely eliminated, while others argue that they should be retained only for relatively liquid derivatives. Opinion is nearly unanimous, however, that the safe harbors should be narrowed in some way.[118]

Recommendations

If a PCS company were to fail, the government would almost certainly intervene to keep it operating. This reality suggests a resolution protocol in the form of nationalization.[119] The word "nationalization" implies that all margin, equity, and guarantee funds would be wiped out, which is consistent with the intention of the CHOICE Act to reduce moral hazard.

Contrary to the intention of the CHOICE Act, however, such a nationalization would allow for the temporary infusion of public funds to keep the PCS system running and to keep retail and securities transactions flowing. While the necessity of using public funds is regrettable, there is some comfort in the argument that authorities might be more likely to let individual financial firms fail when those failures would be prevented from shutting down the operations of PCS companies.

---

[117] Some progress has been made with respect to limiting the safe harbors in the case of a government resolution. See Duffie (2016).

[118] See, for example, Acharya et al. (2011), pp. 229-231, Duffie and Skeel (2012), Lubben (2010), and Tuckman (2010).

[119] See Lubben (2015) for a detailed proposal along these lines.

Title VIII's idea of formalizing the relationship between PCS companies and the Federal Reserve is sensible. The practice of a clearinghouse providing temporary liquidity to its members precedes the creation of the Federal Reserve, and in today's system, the Federal Reserve is the only sure supplier of liquidity in a crisis. Indeed, in the PCS services managed by the Federal Reserve (i.e., Fedwire and the National Settlement Service), the Federal Reserve regularly supplies intraday liquidity to participants.

A formal relationship between PCS companies and the Federal Reserve can also head off the need for a much more intrusive government intervention or resolution. In 1985, for example, the Federal Reserve made the largest discount window loan in its history to Bank of New York, which was temporarily unable, because of a computer system malfunction, to settle government bond trades for customers.[120]

With respect to market structure, however, Title VIII worryingly entrenches incumbents in the PCS industry. An alternative approach would be for the Federal Reserve to permit PCS companies to subject themselves to regulation and supervision in exchange for access to Federal Reserve accounts and liquidity facilities.

A framework of this sort would be analogous to small and large banks competing on the even playing field of membership in the Federal Reserve System. Furthermore, both the Reverse Repo Facility[121] and Title VIII have already set the precedent of the Federal Reserve's dealing directly with entities other than banks.

---

[120] See Zweig and Sullivan (1985).

[121] Through the Reverse Repo Facility, banks, broker/dealers, government-sponsored entities, and money market funds can all lend money directly to the Federal Reserve, taking its securities as collateral.

References

Acharya, V., (2014), "A Transparency Standard for Derivatives," in Risk Topography, M. Brunnermeier and A. Krishnamurthy, eds., Chapter 6.

Acharya, V., et al. (2009b), "Derivatives: The Ultimate Financial Innovation," in Restoring Financial Stability, Wiley, Chapter 10.

Acharya, V., et al. (2009a), "Centralized Clearing for Credit Derivatives," in Restoring Financial Stability, Wiley, Chapter 11.

Acharya, V., et al. (2011), "Resolution Authority," in Regulating Wall Street, Wiley, Chapter 8.

Acharya, V., and Bisin, A. (2013), "Counterparty Risk Externality: Centralized versus Over-the-Counter Markets," Working Paper.

Acharya, V., Iyer A., and Sundaram, R. (2016), "Risk Sharing and the Creation of Systemic Risk," Working Paper.

Acharya, V., Sachar, O., and Subrahmanyam, M. (2011), "Regulating OTC Derivatives," in Regulating Wall Street, Wiley, Chapter 13.

Bech, M., Martin, A., and McAndrews, J. (2012), "Settlement Liquidity and Monetary Policy Implementation—Lessons from the Financial Crisis," March.

Burne, K. (2016), "Clearinghouses Park Billions in New Fed Accounts," The Wall Street Journal, November 23.

Cecchetti, S., Gyntelberg, J., and Hollanders, M. (2009), "Central Counterparties for Over-the-Counter Derivatives," BIS Quarterly Review, September.

Duffie, D. (2016), "Financial Regulatory Reform After the Crisis: An Assessment," ECB Forum on Central Banking, June 27-29.

Duffie, D., and Skeel, D. (2012), "A Dialogue on the Costs and Benefits of Automatic Stays for Derivatives and Repurchase Agreements," *Faculty Scholarship*, University of Pennsylvania Law School.

Duffie, D., and Zhu, H. (2011), "Does a Central Clearing Counterparty Reduce Counterparty Risk?" *The Review of Asset Pricing Studies* 1(1), pp. 74-95.

Financial Crisis Inquiry Commission (2011), "Financial Crisis Inquiry Report," Government Printing Office, Washington.

Gorton, G. (2012), Misunderstanding Financial Crises, Oxford.

ISDA (2016), "Key Trends in Clearing for Small Derivatives Users," ISDA Research Note, October 2016.

Lubben (2010), "Repeal the Safe Harbors," *American Bankruptcy Institute Law Review* 18.

Lubben, S. (2016), "Failure of the Clearinghouse: Dodd-Frank's Fatal Flaw?" *Virginia Law & Business Review* 10(1), pp. 127-160.

Massad, T. (2016), "Taking Stock of Financial Resilience," OFR-FSOC 2016 Annual Conference, February 5.

Melamed, L. (2009), For Crying Out Loud, John Wiley & Sons.

Michel, N. (2015), "Financial Market Utilities: One More Dangerous Concept in Dodd-Frank," Backgrounder, Heritage Foundation.

Payments Risk Committee (2016), "Intraday Liquidity Flows," November 16.

Philippon, T. (2016), "The FinTech Opportunity," Working Paper, July.

Pirrong, C. (2010), "Derivatives Clearing Mandates: Cure or Curse?" *Journal of Applied Corporate Finance* 22(3), Summer.

Pirrong, C. (2012), "Clearing and Collateral Mandates: A New Liquidity Trap?" *Journal of Applied Corporate Finance* 24(1), Winter.

Rexrode, C., and Glazer, E. (2016), "Banks to Donald Trump: Don't Kill Dodd-Frank," *The Wall Street Journal*, December 8.

Schultz, F. (1980), "The Monetary Control Act of 1980 and the Payment System," remarks at the Banking and Payment Systems International Conference, April 4.

Tapscott, D., and Tapscott A., (2016), Blockchain Revolution, Portfolio/Penguin.

The Wall Street Journal (2015), "Regulation is Good for Goldman," Opinion: Review & Outlook, February 11.

Tuckman, B. (2010), "Systemic Risk and the Tri-Party Repo Clearing Banks," CFS Policy Paper, February 2.

Tuckman, B. (2010), "Amending Safe Harbors to Reduce Systemic Risk in OTC Derivatives Markets," *Policy Paper*, Center for Financial Stability, April 22.

Tuckman, B. (2015), "In Defense of Derivatives: from Beer to the Financial Crisis," *Policy Analysis* (781), Cato Institute, September 29.

Weisenthal, J. (2013), "The 4 Things That Worry Jamie Dimon," *Business Insider*, February 4.

Zweig, P, and Sullivan, A. (1985), "A Computer Snafu Snarls the Handling of Treasury Issues," *The Wall Street Journal*, November 25.

Limiting Government Discretion: Other Aspects of the CHOICE Act

Monetary Policy and the Financial CHOICE Act

By Paul A. Wachtel

The Financial CHOICE Act is a comprehensive piece of legislation that, if enacted, will eliminate many of the provisions of the 2010 Dodd-Frank Act, thus changing the financial regulatory structure profoundly. The CHOICE Act will also affect the operations of the Federal Reserve and alter its ability to fulfill its core functions to conduct monetary policy and act as the lender of last resort. The focus on the Fed is not surprising, given the view taken by the writers of the CHOICE Act:

> *"Dodd-Frank rewarded the governmental entity arguably most responsible for the financial crisis – the Federal Reserve – with expansive new regulatory powers, lending credence to the adage that at least in Washington, nothing succeeds like failure."*[122]

In this section, we discuss how the CHOICE Act affects the conduct of macroeconomic policy and the use of the lender of last resort facility. We conclude that the rules imposed and the oversight over the conduct of monetary policy will hamper the Fed's ability to conduct monetary policy independent of political interference. The limits placed on the lender of last resort are likely to constrain the Fed's ability to react quickly in a crisis situation to maintain financial stability. The CHOICE Act will make the Fed's monetary policymaking less effective and will hamper its ability to respond to financial crises.

---

[122]http://financialservices.house.gov/uploadedfiles/financial_choice_act_comp rehensive_outline.pdf   The House Committee on Financial Services, Comprehensive summary of the act, p.56.

Background

Central banks are venerable institutions with roots that date back almost 400 years. However, both the goals of central banks and the scope of their activity have changed dramatically over time. The Federal Reserve System is very different today from the institution that was created just over 100 years ago. The Federal Reserve emerged from one crisis, the Panic of 1907, and has been shaped by subsequent crises, the Great Depression and the recent financial crisis of 2007-2009. Today, the Fed is most closely associated with the conduct of monetary policy—a role that simply did not exist 100 years ago.

The main goal of the Fed, at the time of its founding, was to provide financial stability ("furnish an elastic currency" in the words of the legislation), and its principal tool was discounting or lending to the banking system. The Fed's role in making macroeconomic monetary policy developed after World War II, as policymakers and the economics profession began to understand the potency of changes in interest rate and credit aggregates. The Employment Act of 1946 added the goal of "maximum employment" to the traditional goal of price stability, thus creating the Fed's "dual mandate."[123] By the end of the 20th century, the Fed was primarily associated with its macroeconomic policy role, although it continued to have significant regulatory responsibilities.

Traditional thinking about central bank functions is usually associated with the 19th century British journalist, Walter Bagehot, who articulated the idea that a central bank should act as the lender of last resort to the financial system. By providing liquidity, the central bank can prevent crises and preserve stability. The lending functions of the Federal Reserve diminished in importance

---

[123] The dual mandate was implicit in the Employment Act and spelled out in 1977 legislation that gave the Fed the mandate to "promote effectively the goals of maximum employment, stable prices, and moderate long-term interest rates" (that makes three mandates but the last is usually subsumed into the first two).

through the latter half of the 20th century.[124] However, the financial crisis of 2007-2009 brought a renewed emphasis on the Federal Reserve as the lender of last resort and on its role in using its lending to ensure that financial institutions are safe and the financial system is stable. Financial stability became the Fed's implicit third mandate.

Central bank lending in a crisis is controversial because the central bank should not be engaged in the bailout of insolvent institutions. The lender of last resort facility exists to support solvent but illiquid institutions. The facility would be less useful if there were stigma attached to the borrower. Access to the lender of last resort by insolvent institutions introduces an element of moral hazard, as banks would count on a bailout facility being available. Further, lending to an insolvent borrower does not end its need for support, and it can subordinate private creditors in any bankruptcy. These concerns were clear to Bagehot years ago, but are hard to maintain in contemporary crisis situations where it can be difficult to determine whether an institution is insolvent or merely illiquid.

As a result, a 21st century central bank has three complex and closely related functions: (i) setting monetary policy to attain its goals of price stability and maximum sustainable growth; (ii) providing a lender of last resort facility to financial institutions, which leads to an involvement with regulation and supervision; and (iii) maintaining the stability of the financial system as a whole. This broad remit and the high expectations of success place the Fed under intense scrutiny.

---

[124] The eminent monetary historian, Anna J. Schwartz, concluded in 1992 that "A Federal Reserve System without the discount window would be a better functioning institution," p.68, "The Misuse of the Fed's Discount Window," Federal Reserve Bank of St. Louis, *Review,* September/October 1992. The Fed did not follow her advice but took several steps in the 1990s to strengthen the discount window and encourage bank borrowing.

The CHOICE Act is a reaction to the expanded role of the Fed over time. Monetary policy became the principle tool of macroeconomic management since the Volcker and Greenspan Feds tamed inflation. Fed lending and regulatory actions took center stage during the financial crisis. As a principal player with a degree of independence, the Fed attracts criticism from all quarters. Critics find it easy to blame this powerful institution for all that is wrong with the economy and the financial sector and are eager to place it under tight control. The CHOICE Act pretends to introduce greater clarity to the role of the Fed and its conduct of monetary policy, but in reality, it shifts control over the central bank to Congress.

The CHOICE Act goes much further than earlier legislation, which set out broad goals or objectives for the central bank—the dual mandate of monetary policy. The legislation specifies exactly how policy should be determined and conducted. As a result, it contradicts a tenet of modern central banking that is universally supported: the independence of the central bank to conduct monetary policy.[125] This independence is valued for three reasons, all linked to the problem of time consistency (the incentive for a policymaker to renege on a long-term commitment).

- It insulates policymaking from political cycles and the temptation to pump up economic activity in advance of an election.[126]

---

[125] For a central banker's explanation of the importance of the Fed's independence, see Timothy Geithner, "Perspectives on Monetary Policy and Central Banking," March 30, 2005, a speech given at Central Bank of Brazil, a country that has suffered the consequences of non-independence https://www.newyorkfed.org/newsevents/speeches/2005/gei050329 . See also, the empirical evidence in the *Annual Report, 2009* of the Federal Reserve Bank of St. Louis, https://www.stlouisfed.org/annual-report/2009/central-bank-independence-and-inflation

[126] Of course, even an independent central banker might be subverted by politics. Board Chairman Arthur Burns has been criticized for the role that the Fed played in the 1972 re-election of Richard Nixon.

- Central bank independence protects against the age-old temptation that governments have to finance their activities by printing money.
- Independence gives the central bank the ability to ignore criticism and maintain policies that are consistent with its long-run objectives of stable prices and sustainable growth. That is, central bank independence promotes policy credibility, which helps keep inflation expectations low without sacrificing long-run economic growth.

Indeed, central bank independence has relevance beyond the conduct of monetary policy. The lender of last resort function that is needed to maintain financial stability is essentially a banking function. The central bank is lending to a customer, and just like any bank, it needs to know its customers. Thus, the central bank has a role in bank supervision partly because it should be familiar with the condition of its potential loan customers. Further, the Fed should be able to maintain some secrecy regarding lending so that solvent banks that access the discount window are not stigmatized or subject to runs. To conduct its banking functions, particularly in a crisis, the Fed needs to operate independently and out of the public eye.

Central bank independence does not mean that it should be unaccountable or free from scrutiny. Accountability and transparency are also important objectives, but the mechanisms for achieving these goals should not *and need not* interfere with the ability to make policy. The CHOICE Act crosses the line between legislative oversight and the central bank's ability to independently pursue its mandate.

These issues are not new. Populist attacks on the Fed have been around for years, and there have been many legislative efforts to rein in the central bank. We will examine a few earlier efforts where Congress passed legislation that affected the Fed's operations and goals. Specifically, we look at the Federal Reserve Reform Act of

1977, the Full Employment and Balanced Growth Act of 1978 (the Humphrey-Hawkins Act) and the 2010 Dodd-Frank legislation. Although this legislation changed the way in which the Fed conducts and communicates policy, these laws did not interfere with the Fed's ability to make monetary policy. We will show that the Financial CHOICE Act is fundamentally different.

The 1970s Legislative Initiatives

Hubert Humphrey, the liberal Democratic Senator from Minnesota, sought to place monetary policy under closer, even direct, Congressional supervision, because he thought that the Fed paid too little attention to the full employment mandate set out in 1946.[127] At the same time, the Fed was criticized for being unable to rein in inflation, which accelerated through the 1970s. The 1970s also saw the intellectual ascendancy of monetarism and its emphasis on the rate of growth of the money supply. These different forces came together and led to legislative changes to clarify the goals of the Fed (the formal establishment of the dual mandate) and to increase the Fed's reporting to Congress regarding its policymaking. The earlier statements of goals were vague, and the Fed, along with other central banks, largely operated in secret. Secrecy about short-term intentions—and even about actual policy changes—was thought to preserve the Fed's discretion and influence over financial markets. Importantly, the legislative initiatives of the 1970s did not constrain the Fed's ability to make monetary policy or direct its policy actions. As we will see, the CHOICE Act proposals are very different.

The Reform Act of 1977 increased Congressional oversight by requiring the Fed to "consult with Congress at semiannual hearings about the Board of Governors' and the Federal Open Market

---

[127] It is ironic that in the 1970s, the most liberal wing of Congress was eager to control the Fed, while 40 years later, it is the rallying cry of the most conservative elements. In fact, populist elements on both sides the aisle—from Rand Paul to Bernie Sanders—are often critical of the Fed's independence.

Committee's objectives and plans with respect to the ranges of growth or diminution of monetary and credit aggregates for the upcoming twelve months, taking account of past and prospective developments in production, employment, and prices." Congress specified a policy approach, a monetarist emphasis on growth targets and formalized accountability for the first time. However, it went on to add "Nothing in this Act shall be interpreted to require that such ranges of growth or diminution be achieved if the Board of Governors and the Federal Open Market Committee determine that they cannot or should not be achieved because of changing conditions."[128] A year later, the Humphrey Hawkins Act called for a broader written report, the semiannual Monetary Policy Report to Congress on both monetary policy and macroeconomic performance. It also gave the committees an opportunity to respond and required the Fed to report on any revisions to or deviations from its objectives and plans. These reports continue today, long after monetary growth targets were abandoned.

Another element of Congressional oversight introduced in the 1977 Reform Act was that it made the designation of the Chairman and Vice Chairman of the Federal Reserve Board (from among the Governors) as Presidential designations that are subject to Senate confirmation, with a four-year term. This tied the appointment of the leading policymakers to the political structure. It did not alter the membership of the policymaking body, the Federal Open Market Committee, which includes all of the Governors (who are Presidential appointees, with 14-year terms) and the Presidents of the regional Federal Reserve Banks (who are not Presidential appointees).

The semiannual reporting to Congress had provided mixed benefits. In his history of the Fed, Allan Meltzer suggested that the semiannual reporting led the Fed to give more attention to

---

[128] Section 2A of the Act from https://www.govtrack.us/congress/bills/95/hr9710/text .

medium-term objectives.[129] However, a central feature of the Humphrey-Hawkins bill was the specific requirement for the presentation of "the objectives and plans of the Board of Governors and the Federal Open Market Committee with respect to the ranges of growth or diminution of the monetary and credit aggregates for the calendar year during which the report is transmitted..."[130] One result was a constant and excessive focus on target growth ranges for an array of aggregates (M1, M2, M3 and Total Credit). The target ranges were often very wide and of little value because of the problem of base drift, i.e., growth rate targets do not reflect prior growth that determines the base. Moreover, by the time the procedures were put in place, confidence in the efficacy of a strict monetarist approach was waning. The relationships between money aggregates and economic performance started to fall apart because of structural changes in the financial system at just the time that Congress enshrined the money growth targets in law. Even Meltzer, a monetarist, argued that by "the time President Carter signed the legislation, a common belief was that the act would not achieve its stated goals" (p. 991).

The Fed dutifully voted on and presented monetary growth targets until the Humphrey Hawkins legislation expired in 2000. There is a lesson to be learned from this experience: With a dynamic financial system, it is a mistake to define the way monetary policy should be conducted by legislating a particular approach. The experience with money growth targets was benign, because the legislation did not require the Fed to do anything more than provide an explanation when targets were not met. As we will see below, some 40 years later, the CHOICE Act includes a new attempt to legislate how policy should be conducted.

---

[129] Allan H. Meltzer, *A History of the Fed: Volume 2, Book 2, 1979-1986*, U. of Chicago Press, 2009, pp. 985-992.

[130] Sec. 108, https://www.gpo.gov/fdsys/pkg/STATUTE-92/pdf/STATUTE-92-Pg1887.pdf

In 1994, a Treasury proposal aimed to control the powers of the Fed by consolidating all financial regulation in a single new executive branch commission. The Greenspan Fed fought the proposal on the grounds that it would diminish the influence of the Fed, especially the regional Federal Reserve Banks that are deeply involved in bank supervision. Much financial sector regulation is conducted by other agencies, such as the Securities and Exchange Commission, the Office of the Comptroller of the Currency and the Federal Deposit Insurance Corporation; it does not have to be in the central bank. However, there is an important reason why the central bank needs to maintain some engagement with bank supervision: The Fed needs to know its loan customers if the lender of last resort function is to be used effectively in a crisis. The Clinton era proposal was made at a time when discount lending was inconsequential, and the importance of a customer relationship was overlooked.[131]

Dodd-Frank and Monetary Policy

The 2010 Dodd-Frank Act introduced extensive changes to financial regulation but did not address the way monetary policy is conducted. The goals of monetary policy—stable prices, maximum employment and moderate long-term interest rates—which had been codified earlier, were left unchanged. Early drafts of the Act included an additional goal—maintaining financial stability—but it is not part of the Act. However, the Act introduced new Fed functions and responsibilities that make such a goal implicit, and the Fed's own mission statement does include "maintaining the stability of the financial system and containing systemic risk that may arise in financial markets." [132]

---

[131] The United Kingdom did consolidate regulation in a single authority outside the central bank and regretted it during the crisis. The Bank of England had to make emergency lending decisions without having detailed knowledge of the condition of its customers. These were supervised by the Financial Supervisory Authority, which was abolished after the crisis.

[132] https://www.federalreserve.gov/aboutthefed/mission.htm

Dodd-Frank made no explicit changes to either the goals of monetary policy or the way in which monetary policies are determined or enacted, but it did place serious limitations on the lender of last resort function. Federal Reserve lending was the original tool of the central bank, but its importance diminished over time with the development of the Fed Funds market. However, the Fed started making vigorous use of its lending authority as the financial crisis began to emerge in 2007. Many new lending facilities were put in place to provide liquidity to the financial system, and lending once again became a tool of aggregate economic policy. As the crisis deepened, the Fed made use of emergency lending authority under Section 13(3) of the Federal Reserve Act, which then stated that "In unusual and exigent circumstances, the Board of Governors of the Federal Reserve System, by the affirmative vote of not less than five members, may …" lend to just about any institution.[133]

This unusual lending authority was added to the Federal Reserve Act in the Depression, subsequently repealed, and then reinstated in 1991. The lending authority was not used in the post-Depression era until the Fed invoked section 13(3) in connection with the purchase of Bear Stearns in March 2008. The Fed used 13(3) for some of its broad-based lending programs and for tailored assistance to four firms that the Fed considered too-big-to-fail. These four instances generated a great deal of controversy about the willingness of the Fed to bail out Wall Street, while it was accused of doing nothing for Main Street, where mortgage foreclosures created enormous dislocation. The proper scope of emergency lending by the central bank and whether it should extend to nonbank entities is a difficult question that has been the subject of much debate.[134] The negative public reaction to the Fed's

---

[133] Federal Reserve Bank of Minneapolis, "Lender of More than Last Resort," 2002. https://www.minneapolisfed.org/publications/the-region/lender-of-more-than-last-resort

[134] See Marc Labonte, *Federal Reserve: Emergency Lending*, Congressional Research Service, January 6, 2016. https://fas.org/sgp/crs/misc/R44185.pdf

actions resulted in provisions in Dodd-Frank designed to rein in emergency lending.

The Dodd-Frank Act sought to eliminate bailouts, in part by restricting the use of section 13(3). It restricts emergency lending to nonbanks to those participating in a broad-based program. The provision was specifically designed to prohibit the extension of credit to individual nonbanks. It also introduced some external oversight of Fed lending. The original provision only required the approval of not less than five members of the Board of Governors, while Dodd-Frank requires prior approval by the Secretary of the Treasury. In addition, the Act requires reporting to Congressional committees within seven days of the use of 13(3) and allows for Government Accountability Office (GAO) auditing. Dodd Frank also requires full public disclosure, with a time delay, of the terms and details of *all* Fed transactions. While transparency is valuable, the detailed disclosure policies (even with a lag) might inhibit the Fed's willingness to use its lending authority in a crisis.

The original section 13(3) lending provision was very open-ended. Dodd-Frank restricted the Fed and introduced some additional oversight; proponents argue that the restrictions on emergency lending were mitigated by other provisions of the Act. The orderly liquidation authority and the systemically important financial institution (SIFI) designation by the newly formed Financial Stability Oversight Council were designed to eliminate the dangers of too-big-to-fail. The ability of these provisions to do so in a crisis has not been tested. Moreover, the Financial CHOICE Act would eliminate these structures.

In summary, Dodd-Frank reflected anger with perceived bailouts by restricting 13(3) emergency lending. It introduced other mechanisms for responding to a crisis so the ability of the Fed to conduct monetary policy was not seriously affected. Importantly, Dodd-Frank mandates that financial crisis response is not the exclusive purview of the central bank. The Financial Stability

Oversight Council (FSOC) has an awkward structure that includes executive branch representatives, as well as the leadership of the Federal regulators and others. This structure runs the risk of delaying and politicizing decision making—just the opposite of what would be desirable in a crisis. Until such a test occurs, it remains hard to gauge whether these new structures, along with the Fed's limited emergency lending powers, will be an adequate substitute for 13(3) in a crisis.

The Financial CHOICE Act

The Financial CHOICE Act would dramatically change the way that macroeconomic monetary policy is conducted in the United States. Although it does not change the goals of monetary policy, it provides detailed instructions regarding the choice of policy targets and how the appropriate target value should be determined. In addition, the Fed will have to adhere to strict reporting and accountability standards should policy deviate from the rules in the law. The CHOICE Act provisions would restrict the Fed's independence and constrain its flexibility to respond to economic conditions.

From start to finish, the CHOICE Act provisions that relate to monetary policy reflect an anger at the Fed's history and practice. There is an underlying motif that the Fed consistently does the wrong thing and needs to be admonished and controlled; it is an institution that cannot be trusted. Short of replacing it with some other institution, the Act attempts to place monetary policy on a short leash and under a degree of scrutiny that will clearly compromise the independence of policymakers. Not only is the leash short, the direction that policy should take is made explicit. These changes, as we outline below, would move the United States away from the model of central bank independence and commitment to politically determined mandates. In its place, monetary policy would be subject to greater oversight and influence from the political sphere. The Act potentially takes governance of the world's most important central bank down to a political level that is found today only among failed or failing states.

To be clear, the independence of a central bank does not mean that it should be extra-legal or not subject to criticism or able to deliberate in secrecy. The public and its political representatives set the goals for monetary policy.[135] The central bank should clearly state how it intends to meet those goals and should be transparent in what actions it is taking to do so. Transparency is necessary to allow elected officials to hold the central bank accountable for its actions.

However, the central bank should have the independence to analyze economic and financial conditions and to determine what policy actions should be taken to reach its mandated goals and what operational instruments to use to get there. Put differently, it should have *instrument independence*, not *goal independence*. The goals are set legislatively in the form of the dual mandate, but the Fed should be free to choose which instruments to use (the Fed Funds rate or something else) and how they should be set.

All previous legislation has been consistent with these principles: It specified the dual mandate, required reporting and left the decision making and operational details to the Fed. Moreover, since the 1990s, the Fed has steadily enhanced its communications regarding policy and policymaking. It was only in 1994 that the Fed began to announce the numerical value of its Fed Funds rate target and only in 2011 that the Board Chair began to hold a press conference after the Federal Open Market Committee (FOMC) meeting. The FOMC now regularly publishes forecasts for key economic variables, along with projections for the policy interest rate. Like most central banks, its communications efforts remain a work in progress, with room for improvement.

---

[135] There is also some direction given to the Fed regarding the tools it can use to conduct policy. For example, legislation specifies a narrow range of assets that the Federal Reserve is authorized to acquire.

The CHOICE Act takes a drastically different approach. It specifies a fixed reference rule as a benchmark for assessing monetary policy and introduces complex procedures for GAO and Congressional oversight of the Fed's policymaking or adherence to that rule. While the Fed can set its own policy rule, its performance will be assessed against the CHOICE Act's reference rule in a way that can diminish the Fed's incentive to set policy optimally. The Act reflects the view that, as currently structured and staffed, the Fed is not making the right choices and therefore needs to be reined in and given explicit direction.

The Taylor Rule

The heart of the CHOICE Act's approach to monetary policy is the legislation's specification of the Taylor rule; it spells out the equation term by term in section 701. A strong argument can be made for the use of rules in guiding monetary policy and policy communication, but the CHOICE Act does more than guide policy by rule. It constrains policymakers and introduces a structure for second-guessing and criticizing the *instrument-setting* by Fed policymakers, rather than assessing the Fed's effectiveness in achieving its mandated objectives.[136] The GAO will be responsible for providing a "compliance report" to Congress within seven days of any material change in policy.

---

[136] The CHOICE Act does not comment on the goals set out earlier or on the Fed's ability to meet them, perhaps because the average inflation rate (using the Fed's preferred PCE deflator) for the past 20 years has been 1.74%.

There is a long history of economists who support the use of policy rules for monetary policy.[137] In broad terms, a rule provides the public with a context for understanding policy decisions and interpreting the intermediate-term objectives of policy. A publicly known rule makes the central bank's objectives clear and shows how it will use its policy targets to achieve those objectives. Importantly, a rule also helps the policymaker to maintain a stable policy designed to achieve long-term objectives. In an ideal world, the rule guides policy and provides the public with a full understanding of policy decisions, thus enhancing economic stability and confidence. Monetary policy should be systematic, predictable and focused on its long-run objectives; a rule can be useful as part of the communication strategy.

In a less than ideal world, the challenge is how to specify a rule and how to address economic conditions that might warrant deviations from the rule. The CHOICE Act is very specific about both of these issues and would introduce procedures that would unduly constrain the conduct of monetary policy.

In 1993, John Taylor offered a rule of thumb for determining the appropriate level for the Fed's target interest rate.[138] The Taylor Rule specifies that the target for the policy interest rate should be equal to the sum of:

---

[137] In 1977, Finn Kydland and Edward Prescott introduced the idea of time inconsistency, showing that the short-term and long-term objectives of the central bank might be at odds. This led to much discussion of policy rules as a way of solving the problem. They were awarded the Nobel Prize for this contribution in 2004. For a brief discussion see https://www.stlouisfed.org/publications/regional-economist/january-2003/rules-vs-discretion-the-wrong-choice-could-open-the-floodgates . Also pp. 64-67 of the House Committee on Financial Services, Comprehensive Outline for a summary of recent views http://financialservices.house.gov/uploadedfiles/financial_choice_act_compre hensive_outline.pdf

[138] Taylor, John B. (1993). "Discretion versus Policy Rules in Practice," *Carnegie-Rochester Conference Series on Public Policy. **39**: 195–214.*

- The real or natural rate of interest,
- The inflation rate,
- One-half of the percentage deviation of real Gross Domestic Product (GDP) from its potential level, and
- One-half the deviation of inflation from its target (2%).

Interestingly, over a long period of time, Taylor's specification tracks the Fed's actual policy rate rather closely—except for several periods when the Fed pursued a consistently tighter or looser policy than the rule would have dictated. Such deviations from the simple rule can arise frequently when policy decisions are influenced by considerations that are not reflected in the rule, such as financial conditions or international issues.

Policy observers and policymakers often find the Taylor Rule a useful construct for discussing the stance of policy or policy options; it provides a useful measuring stick that makes policy understandable. Although it is not used explicitly in Fed policy statements, many economists within the Federal Reserve System make reference to it, and estimates of the Fed Funds rate target based on the rule can be found on the websites of more than one Federal Reserve Bank.

However, to enshrine a particular equation into law overlooks all the uncertainties that surround such a simple rule. The CHOICE Act mandates that the Fed issue a 'policy directive rule' that specifies its plans to adjust the policy instrument (the Fed Funds rate), while it spells out the Taylor Rule in the legislation as the reference rule that is to be used to assess Fed policy setting. There are several problems with this rigid use of the Taylor Rule:

- The Taylor rule starts with the unobservable equilibrium real rate of interest; the legislation specifies it as 2%, which happens to be the number chosen by Taylor 20 years ago. The possibility that it has declined in recent decades has been suggested in recent academic work.[139] In any case, there is a wide range of uncertainty about the choice of 2%. It could be higher or it could be zero. The uncertainty from this source alone indicates that any Taylor Rule specification of policy necessarily would be of too wide a range to be useful in assessing the Fed's decisions regarding its policy instrument.

- The Taylor rule specifies that the policy interest rate target should adjust to one-half the percentage deviation of GDP from its potential and one-half the deviation of inflation from its target of 2%. These coefficients are not physical constants, but rather they are judgments regarding the appropriate response. These values were chosen because they appear consistent with the mandate to attain price stability and maximum sustainable output, and lead to a rule that tracks actual policy fairly well. Yet there might be situations when the Federal Reserve might want to respond to deviations more quickly or less quickly, and the appropriate responses might not be symmetric.[140]

- Finally, there are many measurement issues that need to be addressed before the rule can be applied. There is more than one measure of the GDP gap, and inflation measures can

---

[139] K. Holston, T. Laubach and J. Williams, "Measuring the Natural Rate of Interest: International Trends and Determinants," December 2016 http://www.frbsf.org/economic-research/files/wp2016-11.pdf . Also, "The fall in Interest Rates: Low Pressure," The Economist, September 24, 2016, http://www.economist.com/news/briefing/21707553-interest-rates-are-persistently-low-our-first-article-we-ask-who-or-what-blame
[140] Ben Bernanke suggested that the slack response coefficient should be one, which brings the rule's specification for the Fed Funds rate since the crisis much closer to the actual policy rate; see "The Taylor Rule: A Benchmark for Monetary Policy?" The Brookings Institution, April 28, 2015. https://www.brookings.edu/blog/ben-bernanke/2015/04/28/the-taylor-rule-a-benchmark-for-monetary-policy/ .

differ. For example, which price index and what time horizon should be used to calculate inflation?

The Taylor Rule policy rate target at the end of 2016 was 3.04%, considerably higher than the actual rate of 0.45%.[141] If the response coefficient is increased to one, the rule-driven Fed Funds rate falls to 2.51%. And, if the real rate estimates suggested by Laubach and Williams in their research at the Federal Reserve Bank of San Francisco is used, the target Fed Funds rate is just about where the rate is now. A reasonable range of uncertainty about the rule parameters spans the difference between the Fed's critics and its policy.[142]

The CHOICE Act would force policy communications to focus on the relationship between the rule and policy decisions. Given the uncertainty arising from various specifications of the Taylor Rule, it might do more to reduce the clarity of policy communication than it does to increase transparency. The rule and the procedures in the CHOICE Act to monitor adherence to the rule might make the FOMC reluctant to implement policy changes that they perceive as desirable. In this case, the rule could lead to less effective policy.

From 1977-2000, the Fed was required by law to set growth targets for monetary aggregates. It was soon apparent that the relationship between any definition of money and economic performance was unstable. The ranges for money growth became so wide that the targets soon played little if any role in policymaking, although they continued to appear in FOMC communications. Once the legislation expired, the Fed abandoned any mention or use of money growth targets. A more prominent role for the Taylor Rule in policymaking

---

[141] Using the Federal Reserve Bank of Atlanta, Taylor Rule utility with the parameter values specified in the CHOICE Act.

[142] Janet Yellen discusses the value of a Taylor Rule in an uncertain world in "The New Normal Monetary Policy," March 27, 2015, https://www.federalreserve.gov/newsevents/speech/yellen20150327a.htm

could have a similar fate, with limited usefulness in providing a uniform framework and, ultimately, with little influence.

The CHOICE Act procedures that would be put in place to force adherence to the rule are particularly troubling. The legislation has a complex structure: The reference policy rule (the Taylor Rule equation in the law) is used to prepare a directive policy rule (which appears to be a replacement for the Policy Statement released after each FOMC meeting, though it is not clear whether it would also be a pubic document).[143] Within two days of an FOMC meeting, the directive policy rule is submitted to the appropriate committees of Congress and to the GAO. It includes a statement of whether the directive policy rule conforms with the reference policy rule, and if not, it provides an explanation and justification. It also includes a certification by the Fed Chair that the directive policy rule is expected to support the Fed's goals of stable prices and maximum employment over the long term. Whenever there is a material change in policy, the GAO submits a "compliance report" to the Congressional Committees. In the event of noncompliance, the Chairman of the Board testifies before Congress within a week, and the GAO can be asked to audit the conduct of monetary policy.[144]

The legislation specifies that "Nothing in this Act shall be construed to require that the plans with respect to the systematic quantitative adjustment of the Policy Instrument Target ... be implemented if the Federal Open Market Committee determines that such plans cannot or should not be achieved due to changing market conditions." However, in the event of such a determination by the

---

[143] There are some additional specifications of what must be in the directive policy rule; for example, it must "include a calculation that describes with *mathematical* precision the expected annual inflation rate over a 5-year period" (my emphasis).

[144] These policy audits by the GAO are distinct from the annual audits of all the activities of the Board of Governors and the regional Federal Reserve Bank that are introduced elsewhere in the CHOICE Act.

FOMC, it has to submit, with an explanation, an updated directive policy rule, which is subject to further review by the GAO.

These complex procedures are designed to constrain the discretion of the FOMC. Embedding the Taylor Rule in legislation elevates it to more than its current role as a useful policy guide, giving it enhanced status as a policy benchmark. It reflects a particular school of thought that believes that the zero interest rate policy followed by the Fed (and all other major central banks) after the crisis was a serious mistake. It attempts to put into law a rule that Congressional overseers could have exploited to influence Fed instrument setting.

Oversight and Transparency

Congressional oversight of Fed policymaking is not particularly new: the Chairman of the Board of Governors testifies regularly before Congress and is unlikely to refuse to do so if asked more often. The CHOICE Act requires appearances when the GAO determines that there has been noncompliance. The Act also mandates that the Chairman appear before Congress four times a year, up from twice a year currently.

What is new is the introduction of the GAO as an auditor. It will be asked to judge compliance and audit monetary policy and make formal reports. In a very real sense, the GAO becomes a shadow FOMC. The public may wonder whether it should look to FOMC statements or GAO compliance reports to determine the direction of monetary policy.

Most important is the difference in the type of oversight. It does not focus on holding the Fed accountable for achieving its long-run objectives mandated by law. Instead, it introduces oversight and influence over instrument-setting itself, encouraging second-guessing of every policy decision. How should the Fed respond to a critical GAO compliance report? To what extent will Congress pressure the Fed to alter instrument setting? There is a clear risk that the Fed's hard-earned credibility as an independent policymaking institution would be surrendered to Congressional committees.

Transparency—the prompt publication of additional information about monetary policy—is generally viewed as a positive thing. Today, the FOMC provides an enormous amount of information about its policy setting. It has steadily increased the amount of information shared since it began announcing the Fed Funds target more than 20 years ago. Its regular communications now include useful, forward-looking information about the distribution of economic forecasts made by FOMC members, as well as their individual assessments for the interest rate instrument over a three-year horizon. As a result, the public now has considerable access to the policymaking process. The FOMC's economic forecasts and judgments regarding the appropriate policy responses indicate how it would respond to economic and financial developments. This information about the policy path and, implicitly, the Fed's 'reaction function' makes monetary policy more transparent than ever before and probably more effective. The Fed is already providing far *more* information than what is included in a simple policy rule.

The CHOICE Act does not mandate any improvement in the amount of information that the Fed already shares. It does set up a mechanism for public Congressional criticism of monetary policy decisions. A report to Congress within 24 hours of an FOMC meeting, a GAO determination of compliance, and the possibility of a policy audit will reduce Fed independence and potentially shift policymaking to Congressional committees. These complex procedures also could add to uncertainty about monetary policy, by raising doubts about the finality of FOMC decisions.

Summary and Conclusions

Our concern about the CHOICE Act's procedures for the direction and oversight of monetary policy is threefold: First, it creates an apparatus for monitoring and second-guessing the policy instrument setting in a way that diminishes central bank independence. Second, the existence of this apparatus would diminish the incentive of monetary policymakers to choose what they believe to be the optimal policy setting if it deviates from the simple benchmark rule. Third, the CHOICE Act procedures could increase, rather than reduce, uncertainty about policymaking.

With regard to discount lending, the CHOICE Act goes beyond Dodd-Frank, which seriously restricted the Fed's emergency lending authority. By eliminating the Systemically Important Financial Institution (SIFI) designation, the CHOICE Act will hamper the Fed's ability to address crisis situations. Specifically, the Act eliminates the Financial Market Utilities (FMUs) designation, which would deny access to the Fed discount window for solvent, but illiquid clearinghouses. Because that is unlikely to make these institutions less systemic, it may contribute to an unnecessary panic in a period of financial distress.

Finally, toward the end of Title VII (Fed Oversight Reform and Modernization), there is a section that calls for the establishment of a Centennial Monetary Commission (a little late since the Federal Reserve System started operations in 1914). There is nothing wrong with a commission examining the complex structure for financial system oversight that includes supervision of the financial industry, monetary policy and systemic risk regulation. The Fed is already very different from its 1914 incarnation, and some fresh thinking about the structure of the central bank might be beneficial. The proposed Commission would have just one year to examine some fundamental issues: the efficacy of different monetary policy operating regimes (including a gold standard); the value of macroprudential policy; the use of the lender of last resort; and the dual mandate. Furthermore, the appointment process would encourage partisanship, as all the voting Commission members will be appointed by the Congressional leadership, with two-thirds of the seats appointed by the majority party.

In conclusion, the CHOICE Act will impinge on the ability of the Fed to use its authorized tools to conduct monetary policy independently and without interference. The proposed oversight of instrument setting is more likely to boost, than to reduce, uncertainty. The Act would further limit the ability of the Fed to act as the lender of last resort for solvent, but illiquid, intermediaries in a crisis. With the elimination of SIFI and FMU designations, and the removal of the Orderly Liquidation Authority, it is not clear that the United States will have the institutions needed to prevent or contain a future financial crisis.

Rebalancing Consumer Protection in the Trump Era

By Ingo Walter

Before and after enactment of the Dodd-Frank legislation in 2010, concerns were raised that consumers often lacked the knowledge to evaluate and make informed decisions about important financial services. In the past, the government and employers often made some of the most important financial decisions on behalf of households—for example by providing Social Security or defined-benefit employee retirement plans. Today, households are mostly on their own when it comes to home mortgages, car loans, asset management, retirement planning, household credit for major durable purchases and credit lines for ongoing household expenses, life and nonlife insurance to keep a family secure, and many more such services.

On the plus side, there are plenty of financial products and competitors from all kinds financial firms to choose from. But over time, financial products have become more complex and less transparent, and there is a bewildering range of options to wade through. Often, financial salespeople are under heavy pressure to cross-sell, leading to unneeded new accounts or up-sold services, sometimes attached to an array of imbedded and sometimes-undisclosed fees. Certain products, such as some kinds of variable annuities, can be almost impossible for consumers and even salespeople to value and identify the associated risks.

Back in the glory days of the mortgage boom a decade ago, eager households were offered mortgage "affordability" resets, imbedded options and prepayment penalties. The financial crisis soon placed many of these issues in sharp relief in the U.S. housing market's mortgage-origination "fee machine" and, through financial contagion, its contribution to global systemic risk.

In a recent paper,[145] Harvard University's John Campbell addressed how consumers can make more rational financial choices in home purchases, retirement savings, paying for higher education and other major decisions when navigating the fog of modern finance compounded by financial ignorance. He summarized the key issues as lack of financial education, naiveté, overconfidence and inattention to detail, to which can be added lethargy and sloth. The results take the form of both real costs imposed on household by mistakes and opportunity costs that could have been avoided—and which in a broader context may be associated with the much-discussed pattern of income and wealth distribution in the United States.

The question is whether greater financial disclosure and transparency—together with financial education and vigorous enforcement of laws to ensure fair dealing and block financial bad actors—will help level the playing field. Examples include easy-to-understand choice options and target-date mutual funds in retirement plans—features that focus on transparency, costs and risk profiles. But Campbell also points out that uniform regulations that effectively raise costs do so on all households, whether or not there are benefits in overcoming financial disadvantages.

As in any market, there are buyers and sellers, and it's in the interest of both to come to market fully informed about the price and the exact terms of what is being bought and sold. There are always mistakes being made, but the playing field should be as level as possible for the market to do its work: wealth creation, rather than wealth redistribution.

The argument for regulatory intervention is that consumers frequently suffer from market attributes that are stacked against them, so that *caveat emptor* is an inappropriate model

---

[145] "Restoring Rational Choice: The Challenge of Consumer Finance," American Economic Association, 2016 Richard Ely Lecture, 3 January 2016.

for conduct in the retail financial marketplace. Many factors can account for consumers finding themselves at a disadvantage, including lack of education and financial skills, lack of transparency in financial products and services, lack of fiduciary responsibility on the part of financial services vendors, and exploitation of vendor conflicts of interest.

Few would argue that consumers should escape the need for proper due diligence, or not bear some accountability for their own errors. Moral hazard alone makes an excessively robust consumer safety net untenable. There should be plenty of holes in the safety net. But a systematically biased playing field that aggressively steers consumer choice, provides incomplete and biased information, and creates conditions of financial exploitation is no less toxic. It drains *trust* from the system. Without trust, neither financial efficiency nor stability can be assured; it ultimately encourages excessive regulation when the political costs get too high. So there is a legitimate argument that both remedial and preemptive improvements in some key dimensions of consumer finance are a good idea.

First, consumers need to be financially literate in order to make well-informed choices in complex financial decisions. There have been some severe gaps. Consumers often do not understand fundamental financial concepts such as compound interest, risk diversification, real versus nominal values, and e v e n the difference between stocks and bonds. Indeed, the evidence suggests that consumers with higher levels of financial literacy plan better for retirement, while those with lower levels of literacy borrow more, save less, and have more trouble repaying their debts, making ends meet, planning ahead, and making important financial choices.

Realistically, who's going to cut down on time devoted to their jobs and recreational priorities to take Adult School classes in basic finance? And sometimes *too much* information is provided and leads to information overload, which can cause consumers to focus on only a few pieces of easily understood information, not necessarily the key aspects for complex financial decisions.

There are, of course, counter-examples. One is lapsed life insurance that can be surrendered with total loss of capital, sold back to the insurance carrier at a substantial discount, or sold to third parties for securitization and marketed to investors—sometimes called "death bonds" or "mortality bonds." Another example is long-term care insurance, which can be an expensive but rational choice for consumers, or a combination of life insurance and long-term care insurance to lower the cost. Consumers sometimes seem to display remarkable clarity in thinking about the options, even though pricing and disclosure specifics may remain obscure.[146]

Still, consumers can be overly optimistic in interpreting information in a way that helps lead them to a desired, if irrational, conclusion. And there's concern that some financial firms purposely design and proactively advertise products to mislead consumers about benefits, leaving "financial health warnings" to the fine print. Some classes of consumers—such as older people preoccupied with life's other challenges, minorities and women—may be particularly vulnerable to aggressive marketing practices for financial products and thus exploitation. It has been argued that complex financial products survive in the marketplace because they enable cross-subsidizing sophisticated consumers at the expense of the unsuspecting. Regulatory intervention in that context will tend to redistribute income away from sophisticated customers, who prefer less consumer protection.

The underlying argument is that fairness embodies more than moral or ethical content in the financial architecture. Failure to provide equitable treatment undermines confidence in the system

---

[146] Paul Sullivan, "Life Insurance Plus Long-Term Care? Run the Numbers First," *The New York Times*, December 10, 2016.

and impacts liquidity, efficiency and growth. It distorts financial flows on the part of ultimate sources and uses of funds, and undermines the political legitimacy of financial intermediaries and those who regulate them. So sensible government intervention is needed as a matter of the public interest.

Dodd-Frank and the Consumer Financial Protection Bureau

This is the logic behind the 2010 Dodd-Frank Wall Street Reform and Consumer Protection Act, which created the Consumer Financial Protection Bureau (CFPB) as an independent unit within the Federal Reserve System. Dodd-Frank was mainly about financial stability and systemic risk. But "consumer protection" in the title signaled its political centrality in setting out the future rules of engagement.

Dodd-Frank's consumer protection legislation covers depository institutions with assets exceeding $10 billion, mortgage lenders, mortgage servicers, payday lenders, and private education lenders. It does not cover automobile financing.

The legislation created the CFPB with a mandate to aid consumers in understanding and using relevant information. Its intent was to shield them from abuse, deception, and fraud by ensuring that disclosures for financial products were easy to understand. It is also mandated consumer finance research and financial literacy education. It has the authority to set rules under existing consumer financial law and take appropriate enforcement action to address violations. It is charged with collecting, investigating, and responding to consumer complaints. And it has a mandate to ensure that suitable financial products and services are made available to consumer segments and communities that have traditionally been underserved.

The CFPB is an entity of the Federal Reserve System, and its budget is self-determined and funded out of Fed resources, not by Congressional appropriation, thereby offering some protection against inevitable lobbying pressure. It is managed by a Director (currently Richard Corday) who is appointed by the President with the advice and consent of the Senate, serving a five-year term and who (like that Chair of the Federal Reserve Board) can be dismissed only "for cause."

The Financial CHOICE Act

The consumer protection provisions of Dodd-Frank and the CFPB were controversial from the start, with criticism spanning a range of issues from the constitutionality of its mandate and the heavy hand of overregulation to the "blank check" funding through the Fed and the early cases demonstrating its allegedly excessive use of enforcement powers. Much of the criticism was concentrated in the draft Financial Choice Act tabled by Republicans on the House Committee on Financial Services in June 2016. There are two major themes in this proposed CFPB revision:

The first is governance and accountability. As a unit of the Federal Reserve System, CFPB governance was considered both indirect and lacking a clear public mandate and political accountability. Moreover, its budget (close to $1 billion in fiscal 2016) thought to escape the kinds of checks and balances that apply to other Federal agencies. The CHOICE Act would broadly extend to the CFPB the kinds of governance, accountability and budgetary appropriations that apply to other Federal agencies.

The second key issue is consumer choice and cost. The CFPB is thought to preempt free consumer choice, transferring key decisions—such as which financial products will be available and to whom, what product information needs to be disclosed, and how they are marketed and priced—to CFPB bureaucrats. The argument is that the CFPB has reflected a retrograde shift from the market economy toward increased paternalism of the state. It highlights presumptive cuts in access to financial services to the 'un-banked' and 'under-banked,' increases in the cost of financial services, violates consumer privacy, and harms small businesses that rely on consumer financial products.

That said, convincing empirical evidence suggests that tough consumer protection measures can, in fact, work. Take for example the 2009 Credit Card Accountability and Responsibility and Disclosure (CARD) Act, which capped credit card penalty fees that card issuers were using to make up for lost revenues during the recession.[147] A careful study of the CARD Act's impact finds that the reduction in fee revenue from cancelled "over-limit" and late fees did not lead to banks' increasing credit card interest rates or significantly raising other fees in the period through 2015—nor did it reduce access to credit for U.S. households. In combination, the Act cut the cost of financial services to consumers by about $11.6 billion annually.[148]

The Financial CHOICE Act proposes a range of specific reforms that would fundamentally change the operations, governance, accountability, and funding of the CFPB, although it does not propose to scrap it. Nor does it seem to be true that the CFPB has been out of control in pursuing its mandate, since it was created by the Dodd-Frank Act. In reviewing the record so far, John Campbell concludes, "The CFPB has produced a relatively small number of major new rules through a deliberate process. In 2013 a rule took effect requiring fee disclosures in remittance transfers to foreign

---

[147] The credit card industry levied $11.4 billion in penalty fees in 2015, about half the amount levied prior to the CARD Act and imposition of CFPB fee limits. In the United States, about 170 million credit card accounts (20% of the total active accounts) incurred late fees in 2015. Robin Sidel, "AmEx Raises Fee for Late Payers," *Wall Street Journal*, November 26, 2016.
[148] Agarwal, Sumit, Souphala Chomsisengphet, Neal Mahoney and Johannes Stroebel, "Regulating Consumer Financial Products: Evidence from Credit Cards." *Quarterly Journal of Economics* (2014) 130 (1): 111-164.

countries; in 2014 a rule defined the standards that lenders must use in assessing borrowers' ability to repay mortgages, and the standards for qualified mortgages that, under the Dodd-Frank Act, provide greater protection against litigation to lenders who issue them; in 2015 a rule took effect integrating and simplifying the disclosure forms that mortgage borrowers receive; and in 2016 the CFPB issued a rule scheduled to take effect in 2017 regulating the terms of prepaid cards. The CFPB has sought comments on proposed rules concerning arbitration in consumer financial disputes and the terms of payday lending. None of the rules currently in effect are plausibly responsible for major changes in the availability of household credit."[149] In his view, the CFPB's complaints registry and data collection are, themselves, a valuable contribution to a more level consumer finance playing field.

Where Should the Trump Administration Be Heading?

Where the Trump administration will come down on consumer financial protection and the fate of the CFPB and the Financial CHOICE Act is uncertain at this point. But at least the FCA offers a considered roadmap for change, one that deserves to be debated. It seeks to pare away some of the Dodd-Frank provisions considered superfluous or counterproductive, and increase the accountability and budgeting process of the CFPB to align it with governance of other important Federal agencies—all while increasing accountability to elected officials.

It is hard to argue against political accountability and financial discipline. Still, in a system driven by heavy lobbying and financial contributions by those who stand to gain or lose from consumer protection measures, the survival and impact of Financial CHOICE Act proposals, if enacted, are difficult to gauge. It is a major, highly complex exercise in cost-benefit analysis—one in which both costs

---

[149] John Campbell. "Consumer Protection in Need of Protection," at http://econofact.org/consumer-financial-protection-in-need-of-protection. February 2017.

and benefits are often obscure, and second-best solutions are welcome. Inserted into the coming overheated, lobbyist-driven political debate, it is not hard to imagine that consumer interests will once again come at the end of the line.

Of course, there is always the threat of overregulation, but there is also value in helping consumers gain financial literacy, in improving our understanding of how consumer financial markets work, in helping people access and use relevant information, and in protecting them from abuse, deception and fraud.

Fintech—shorthand for financial technology—is the wild card in the game. Several dozen competitors are now in the game and range from start-ups and proof-of-concept players to established survivors seeking "unicorn" status by disrupting a retail financial services industry that is considered overdue for disruption. Services range from marketplace lending to robo-advising, from financial aggregation to retail remittances, from e-brokerage to e-retirement planning. As these "direct-connect" linkages take root, some of the key household disadvantages in finance could melt away— especially as new generations of consumers enter the market—so that the case for consumer finance regulation may weaken.

On the other hand, the legacy players are sophisticated, and many fintech initiatives have already been internalized by the established financial intermediaries. Even the independent "disruptors" themselves have found it opportune to link up with fintech upstarts in joint ventures and as attractive acquisition targets. The fintech dynamic has its own ways of tilting the playing field and generating new forms of conflicts of interest. Good news or bad news? Some of both, no doubt, and time will tell. What is certain is that consumer financial protection will be a moving target and take on new forms.

What's also certain is that there will continue to be many "sticky fingers" in finance, amply reflected in the waves of wholesale and retail banking scandals since the financial crisis. If nobody's watching the store, bad things happen. The recent Wells Fargo case involving consumer cross-selling—a core strategy deeply ingrained in Wells Fargo's history, culture and incentive systems—shows how easily a good institution and good people can overstep even the most basic trust and fiduciary constraints in dealing with "soft target" consumers.

Indeed, in a highly competitive financial services market, profit often lurks in the shadows. Retail finance is particularly vulnerable to questionable financial practices, given its gaps in information and understanding. So it is surely in the public interest to focus on remedies for market imperfections and professional malfeasance as they appear, and if possible to preempt them. It may not be the "best" and most efficient approach, but "second best" can also leave the world better off. As always, the devil is in the details.

Whether the Trump administration and Congress ultimately choose the "high road" to consumer financial protection remains to be seen.

Credit Rating Agencies and the Financial CHOICE Act

By Matthew P. Richardson, Marti G. Subrahmanyam,
Laura L. Veldkamp, and Lawrence J. White

Introduction

Credit rating agencies (CRAs) provide judgments—typically in the form of a letter grade—about the creditworthiness of bonds that are issued by corporations, governments, and packagers of asset-backed securities. The lenders in credit markets, including investors in bonds, always try to ascertain the creditworthiness of borrowers, in making their decisions.[150] Credit rating agencies are, hence, one potential source of such information for bond investors.

Starting in the 1930s, and until the passage of the Dodd-Frank Act in 2010, financial regulators generally required that financial institutions rely on the judgments of the rating agencies in making their bond investments; these regulations, motivated by the desire for safety in bond portfolios, have played a major role in thrusting the agencies into the center of the bond markets.

It may not be surprising, therefore, that the major rating agencies in the U.S. played a central role in the housing bubble and then in the subsequent subprime mortgage debacle of 2007-2008.[151] The successful sale of the mortgage-related debt securities that had

---

[150] Equally important, more creditworthy borrowers want to distinguish themselves from less creditworthy borrowers, so that the former can receive better borrowing terms.

[151]The three major CRAs are Moody's, Standard & Poor's, and Fitch. By creating a category ("nationally recognized statistical rating organization," or NRSRO) of rating agency that had to be heeded and then subsequently maintaining a barrier to entry into the category in 1975, the Securities and Exchange Commission (SEC) further enhanced the importance of the three major rating agencies. See, for example, Altman, Oncu, Richardson, Schmeits and White (2011), and White (2013).

subprime residential mortgages and other debt obligations as their underlying collateral depended crucially on these CRAs' initial ratings of these securities. When house prices ceased rising and began to decline, these initial ratings proved to be excessively optimistic— especially for the mortgages that were originated in 2005 and 2006— and the mortgage bonds collapsed, bringing large parts of the U.S. financial sector crashing down as well.[152]

In order to better understand how credit ratings played such an important role in the financial crisis, consider the following illustrative examples: On page 122 of AIG's 2007 annual report, AIG reported that $379 billion of its $527 billion in credit defaults swap notional amount exposure to AAA-rated asset-backed securities sold by its now infamous financial products group was written not for hedging purposes but to facilitate regulatory capital relief for financial institutions. Meanwhile, Citigroup and ABN AMRO performed their own form of alchemy by financing, respectively, $93 billion and $69 billion worth of AAA-rated securities off-balance sheet through so-called "special purpose vehicles" (SPVs). Similarly, in an 18-month period, UBS increased its holdings of AAA nonprime mortgage-backed securities from $5 billion to over $50 billion which, as it turned out, was small relative to the $308 billion of such securities accumulated by Fannie Mae, Freddie Mac and other government-sponsored enterprises (GSEs). In fact, according to a Lehman Brothers report from April 2008, of the $1.64 trillion of these securities outstanding, an astonishing 48% was held by banks, broker-dealers and the GSEs.

---

[152] Today most market participants agree that the quality of collateralized debt obligation ratings was poor, even on an *ex ante* basis. A large theoretical and empirical literature in academia has developed over the last several years, commenting on the quality, and especially the inflation, of ratings. (See, for example, Ashcraft, Goldsmith-Pinkham, and Vickery (2010, 2011), Becker and Milbourn (2011), Griffin and Tang (2011, 2012), and He, Qian, and Strahan (2011, 2012), among others.)

What was going on? These securities offered attractive yields but, because of their AAA status, required little or no regulatory capital. And, of course, all of the firms mentioned here effectively failed, or would have, in the absence of a government bailout, during the financial crisis.

In the typical view of the role of ratings in the financial crisis, investors were asleep at the wheel because of the government's "seal of approval" of rating agencies. But the above description shows that it was not only investors who were tricked here but also taxpayers. How did this happen? Because the issuer pays the agency that rates the issuer, there is a huge conflict of interest to shop the security around until the issuer gets the desired rating, leading to inflated ratings.[153] There are numerous academic studies, as well as controversial testimony by former rating agency officials, that ratings were indeed inflated. And because the government had set its regulatory structure around these ratings, investors like AIG, Citigroup, ABN AMRO, UBS, Fannie Mae, Freddie Mac and, for that matter, Merrill Lynch and Lehman, among others, engaged in risky activities while having insufficient capital buffers due to the inflated ratings. Rating agencies effectively acquiesced with, and in some ways contributed to, this alliance between investors and issuers. It is arguable that the crisis could not have transpired the way it did without the rating agencies planted at the center of the financial system.[154]

---

[153] Of course, the rating agencies care about their long-run reputations, which would be a force to offset the conflict of interest. See, for example, Klein and Leffler (1981). But the short-run profit temptations to accede to an issuer's desire for a higher rating can overwhelm the long-run concerns, as apparently happened with respect to mortgage-related debt securities.

[154] Some of the papers that describe and analyze the conflicts of interests between CRAs, issuers and investors include Bolton, Freixas, and Shapiro (2012), Efing, Matthias, and Hau (2015), Griffin, Nickersen and Tang (2013), Richardson and White (2009), Mathis, McAndrews, and Rochet (2009), Skreta and Veldkamp (2009), and Stanton and Wallace (2012).

The Dodd-Frank Act: Six Years On

As a response to the impact that credit ratings had during the financial crisis, the Dodd-Frank Act instituted major changes to the manner in which CRAs were to be regulated. Most important, Dodd-Frank tried to address two major issues: the conflict of interest that is inherent in the "issuer-pays" model and the regulatory reliance on ratings.[155]

Aside from these major issues, Dodd-Frank prescribed new rules for internal control and governance, independence, transparency, and liability standards. It established an Office of Credit Ratings at the SEC to "administer the rules of the Commission (i) with respect to the practices of NRSROs in determining ratings, for the protection of users of credit ratings, and in the public interest; (ii) to promote accuracy in credit ratings issued by NRSROs; and (iii) to ensure that such ratings are not unduly influenced by conflicts of interest." (Title IX, Subtitle C, Sec. 932, "Enhanced Regulation, Accountability and Transparency of Nationally Recognized Statistical Rating Organizations.")

While oversight of NRSROs was needed, some of the Dodd-Frank provisions were quite onerous in terms of compliance, while appearing to yield only modest benefits. Since many of the costs of complying with the regulation are fixed or lumpy, it is more burdensome and costly for smaller firms. In turn, this makes it difficult for smaller firms to survive, and for new firms to enter the business, and innovation, which often is embodied in new firms, may be discouraged. This imposes a relatively heavier burden on innovative start-up rating firms, thereby strengthening the dominance of, and entrenching, the larger rating agencies. For example, Dodd-Frank focuses on "inputs" such as transparency as to their methodology rather than on "outputs" that would be

---

[155] For a detailed analysis of the reform of credit ratings agencies in the Dodd-Frank Act, see Altman, Oncu, Richardson, Schmeits and White (2011).

directly related to the accuracy of the ratings. Too much emphasis on transparency of the methodologies may endanger the intellectual property of the CRAs and, again, discourage innovation. Indeed, since Dodd-Frank was passed in 2010 the market share of the three large NRSROs – Fitch, Moody's, and S&P – has not decreased substantially, which *ex ante* may be surprising, given the past financial crisis.[156]

With respect to regulatory reliance, Dodd-Frank changed the way that regulators would use credit ratings to assess the risk of financial institutions. Sec. 939A of Dodd-Frank called for the regulatory agencies to review their reliance on ratings and, where possible, to eliminate such references and find alternative ways of achieving their regulatory goals. Note that while it did not mandate these eliminations, Dodd-Frank called for a more flexible creditworthiness standard. In particular, regulators ought to be looking at market risk, liquidity risk, model risk and even measures of default risk, in addition to credit ratings (e.g., those embedded in market prices).

Since Dodd-Frank, changes to the U.S. financial regulatory environment for ratings agencies have occurred—slowly but steadily. For example, by 2012-2013, bank regulators had removed both references and reliance on credit ratings. Instead, regulators placed the burden on each bank to provide a reasoned basis for its choice of information about its bond portfolio and the suitability of these bonds for that bank. In an important sense, this approach parallels the bank regulators' approach for commercial loans and other types of unrated loans that banks hold. Note that a bank is not prevented from using one or more CRA's ratings; but the bank has to have a reasoned basis for doing so. On the positive side, regulatory reliance was a feature of regulatory capital arbitrage, which, in turn, was a key factor underlying the financial crisis. On the negative side, this burden adds yet another level of compliance

---

[156] See USSEC (2016), especially Chart 5 on p. 15.

for banks, further adding to their costs. Moreover, allowing the banks to, in effect, model the risk of their bond portfolios may not solve the regulatory capital arbitrage issue.

Along with bank regulators, the SEC moved at a similar speed with respect to its capital requirements for broker-dealers and most other references to ratings.[157] The SEC took longer with respect to withdrawing references to ratings vis-à-vis its regulation of money market mutual funds. Those references were eliminated only in September 2015 (five years after Dodd-Frank). In other areas of the financial system, the Department of Labor (DOL) has not (to our knowledge) removed its references to ratings in its regulation of defined benefit pension funds (under ERISA). And, similarly, the state regulators of insurance companies (which were not covered by Dodd-Frank) have not eliminated their reliance on ratings.

There is some evidence regarding the informativeness of credit rating events, defined as changes in ratings, as a result of Dodd-Frank.[158] Informativeness is measured through the impact of credit rating changes on the pricing and liquidity of corporate bonds, controlling for bond characteristics. Following the passage of Dodd-Frank, Jankowitsch, Ottonello and Subrahmanyam (2016) find that the informativeness of rating changes is low when regulation favors better-rated securities, especially when their cost of information acquisition is high. However, following the increase in litigation risk and the dismantling of rating-contingent regulation enacted by Dodd-Frank, rating changes led to significantly stronger market reactions, but not for all securities. These results may be linked to differences in information-related costs and underlying credit risk across securities.

If all regulators cease relying on ratings, then the argument for regulating CRAs becomes much weaker. Since the bond markets are

---

[157]Note that it was a revision to its capital requirements for broker-dealers in 1975 that originally led the SEC to establish the aforementioned NRSRO system.
[158] See Jankowitsch, Ottonello and Subrahmanyam (2016) for details.

largely institutional, the "investors" in these markets are largely bond portfolio managers who should be expected to have a reasoned basis for where they seek their information about bonds. The portfolio managers ought to be able to understand the dangers of the issuer-pays model and also to learn from their mistakes.

Because credit ratings, however, do include independent information above and beyond what is in the market, it seems unlikely, and inefficient, for regulators to drop all forms of reliance (even if indirect).[159] Indeed, by providing financial institutions and regulators flexibility in terms of measuring creditworthiness, some form of regulatory reliance remains. To the extent that this is the case, the aforementioned conflict of interest issue still exists, and this "market failure" calls for some type of additional regulation.[160]

With respect to the conflict of interest issue, Section 939D of Dodd-Frank calls for a study of new regulatory structures for how ratings for asset-backed securities (such as residential mortgage-backed securities) might be assigned and, if no better alternative is found, to implement one based on a ratings board (which would be housed in the Office of Credit Ratings at the SEC) to assign CRAs to issuers (the Franken Amendment).[161]

The main idea underlying the Amendment is that these issuers would no longer choose the rating agency for their initial rating, but instead must go through a centralized clearing process. Specifically,

---

[159] See, for example, Ederington, Yawitz, and Roberts (1987), Goh and. Ederington (1993), Hilscher and Wilson (2016), and Kliger and Sarig (2000).

[160] Bolton, Freixas, and Shapiro (2008), Mathis, McAndrews, and Rochet (2009), and Skreta and Veldkamp (2009), as examples, provide a theoretical justification for regulation based on the conflict of interest argument. The conflicts of interest that are addressed in these papers include ratings inflation that reflects the fact that the rating agencies are paid by the issuers, as well as the practice of so-called ratings shopping, whereby the issuer can troll the NRSROs for the best rating.

[161] See Mathis, McAndrews, and Rochet (2009), Raboy (2009) and Richardson and White (2009) for an economic discussion of possible resolution of the conflict of interest problem along the lines of the Franken Amendment.

a company that wants its structured debt to be rated would go to the ratings board. Depending on the attributes of the security, a flat fee would be assessed. From a sample of approved rating agencies, the ratings board would choose, most likely via lottery, the rating agency that rates the security.

While this choice could be random, a more palatable lottery design could be based on some degree of excellence, such as the quality of the ratings methodology, the rating agency's experience at rating this type of debt, some historical perspective on how well the rating agency has rated this type of debt relative to other rating agencies, past audits of the rating agency's quality, and so forth. The issuer would be allowed to gather additional ratings, but the initial rating would have to go through this process, which no longer allows the issuer to choose the rater.

In theory, such a scheme could simultaneously solve several issues: (1) the information free-rider problem,[162] because the issuer still pays; (2) the conflict of interest problem, because the rating agency is chosen by the regulating body; and (3) the competition problem, because the regulator's choice can be based on some degree of excellence, thereby providing the rating agency with incentives to invest resources, to innovate, and to perform high-quality work.[163]

As required by the Dodd-Frank Act, the Office of Credit Ratings Agency at the SEC had to prepare a report on assigned credit ratings, specifically addressing the Franken Amendment and other possible structures. This report was produced in December 2012.[164] The report does not take a position per se on the feasibility of the

---

[162] This problem would arise under an investor-pays or "subscriber" model, since it may be difficult (especially in a digital environment) to prevent nonsubscribers from quickly (and without cost) obtaining the information, which would then discourage potential subscribers from signing up (and paying) for the information in the first place.

[163] See Altman, Oncu, Richardson, Schmeits and White (2011).

[164] See the SEC's "Report to Congress on Assigned Credit Ratings."

ratings board, but, along with the aforementioned benefits, does highlight several concerns, including the difficulty, complexity and cost of implementing and administering such a scheme (e.g., the expertise of the rating board members, the huge number of ratings that need to be assigned, the determination of the fee of the initial credit rater, the assumption that there would be a sufficient number of expert NRSROs participating, etc.) The mere fact that the SEC has made no progress toward implementing any such a scheme is telling. Moreover, there are potential constitutional issues related to imposing such a structure on private firms.[165]

The CHOICE Act and Analysis

As it pertains to credit ratings and ratings agencies, the Financial CHOICE Act changes the Dodd-Frank Act in two ways: (i) the SEC has exemptive authority for the Dodd-Frank Act's provisions if a provision creates a barrier to entry into the market for a potential NRSRO; and (ii) the CHOICE Act repeals the Franken Amendment.

As argued above, the Dodd-Frank Act imposed a multitude of regulations that are likely barriers to entry for new, and potentially innovative, NRSROs. While in theory the exemptive authority potentially corrects this issue, in practice, it requires that the SEC exerts this authority. A more efficient approach would be to provide immediate exemption to the Dodd-Frank rules for internal control and governance, independence, transparency, and liability standards for all NRSROs except the big three, and then to give the

---

[165] In its report, the SEC discusses several other options, but concentrates on one competing structure, the "Rule 17g-5 Program," which has been implemented. In this structure, the SEC calls for a mechanism by which non-hired NRSROs get access to the same information as the hired NRSRO to allow for a competing analysis of the ratings that were not solicited by the issuer. One problem with this program to date is that, while there has been some commentary provided by non-hired NRSROs, no competing ratings have been produced, presumably because NRSROs are not in the position of providing free ratings. Other issues relate to confidentiality of information.

SEC the right to impose such rules on other NRSROs, presumably at a time when these NRSROs reach a certain scale.

Of course, increasing competition for NRSROs is a potential problem if the conflict of interest for the issuer-pays model remains in place and is not addressed.[166] As we argued above, even without official regulatory reliance, credit ratings still play an important role in the regulatory framework. Increasing competition can lead to a race to the bottom. Therefore, it is crucial that the regulation of ratings agencies addresses the conflict of interest within the issuer-pays model.

The CHOICE Act repeals the Franken Amendment, which was one attempt at such a solution, but offers no alternative in its place. Because the Franken Amendment was never implemented, the CHOICE Act's repeal is somewhat moot. Nevertheless, the Act does provide some rationale for its repeal.

The CHOICE Act advances three arguments for why the Franken Amendment is harmful: (1) It conflicts with the mandate to reduce the regulators' reliance on ratings; (2) It conveys the impression that the government has approved the rating and, thus, encourages reliance on the rating; and (3) The requirement that rating agencies participate in the Franken mechanism for assigning agencies to rate asset-backed securities deters entry and reduces competition.

First, as argued above, reducing ratings bias and discouraging the use of ratings are not incompatible. The Franken Amendment deals with how ratings are produced, while other Dodd-Frank provisions focus on how the ratings would be employed in practice by regulators. The idea that if ratings are not used for risk regulations, they will disappear is not realistic. Many investors will still want a

---

[166] For various thoughts on competition in the ratings industry, see, Baghai, Servaes, and Tamayo (2014), Becker and Milbourn (2011), Griffin, Lowery, and Saretto (2014), Griffin and Maturana (2016), Kashyap and Kovrijnykh (2016), Mathis, McAndrews, and Rochet (2009), White (2013) and Xia (2014).

simple statistic to describe the risk characteristics of an asset. Even regulations that reduce reliance on ratings have mostly employed ratings as at least one of the inputs into the risk assessment. Hence, there are good reasons for even flawed ratings not to disappear. For every investor to collect and process this information individually is extremely costly. If every investor must bear this information cost to invest in debt, few will invest, and the cost of debt could skyrocket. That would inhibit the entry and expansion of all kinds of firms. Asking firms to provide risk information themselves is fraught with even more conflict of interest problems than are present for ratings. Therefore, CRAs enjoy the benefits of economies of scale and thus generate more information, even if some of it is flawed.

Second, it is not hard to make clear that ratings chosen by the NRSRO lottery are not "officially sanctioned" ratings. In fact, the lottery should serve as a visible reminder of the problems and risks that are associated with ratings reliance. If regulators do not trust ratings enough to rely on them, why would an investor, upon seeing that there is a lottery designed to ameliorate the bias in ratings, conclude that the government guarantees it? It's like saying that there should be no national weather service because that might convey the idea that the government guarantees the accuracy of the chance of rain. In addition, of course, most of the investors in question here are professional, institutional traders, not gullible innocents.

Third, there is no reason that a lottery assignment of rating agencies should necessarily discriminate against new entrants. In fact, the chance of being assigned to a new entrant could be bolstered to support new rating agencies and encourage diverse viewpoints. In fact, it would be much harder to encourage entry and support new entrants without such a mechanism that can direct business their way.[167]

We endorse the idea that regulators should find wider sources of reliable information on the creditworthiness of borrowers. We believe that this investigation is compatible with improving the incentives to rate structured credit products accurately. Ultimately, someone needs to incur a sizable fixed cost to collect and process information in order to assess credit risk. The question is: Who will bear this cost and what will their incentives be? Bond issuers could provide this information, but they will want to minimize reported risk to reduce their credit costs.[168] Investors could collect this information on their own, but that is extremely duplicative and costly. Investors who incur high information costs will only do so if they expect a large return, which would only happen if the assets were cheap, and debt issuance therefore expensive for firms that wish to grow. The government could assess all credit risk. But that is costly for government and risks politicization. Finally, some third party can assess risk. But that third party will need to be compensated, by either buyers or sellers. Either alternative creates a conflict of interest. The Franken Amendment offers a solution by setting out a third-party compensation mechanism that rewards providers of accurate, unbiased information. If it is not be implemented, then some similar alternative should be put in place.

---

[167] But it is, of course, possible that the actual practices of the selection board might tend to favor incumbents.

[168] One possibility for asset-backed bond issuances is that the issuer would have to release to the general public–and not just to the other NRSROs (as is currently true under Rule 17g-5, which we discussed in footnote 165—all of the information that the issuer provides to the rating agency that the issuer chooses. This would increase the likelihood that outside analysts might spot (and announce to the public) instances where the rating agency–either accidentally or as an effort to expand its market share—might unduly favor the issuer. And, in turn, this would make the rating agency more careful and diminish the conflict of interest. Such expanded information revelation should be quite consistent with the SEC general culture of encouraging securities issuers to release more information to the general public. See White (2013).

As an even more radical proposal: We urge the CHOICE Act drafters to carry through on their logic with respect to barriers to entry and to abolish the NRSRO category. Since almost all of the Federal financial regulators (except the DOL) have ceased their specific references to ratings in their regulations, the need for a category of approved (by the SEC) rating agencies to which those references would pertain—which was the origin of the NRSRO concept—has largely disappeared. Again, the financial regulators now require that their regulated entities directly justify their sources of information with respect to bonds, so, in principle, the SEC "blessing" for a specific set of rating agencies is contrary to the spirit of asking the regulated entities to justify their sources of information. And the regulation that surrounds the NRSRO category does raise barriers to entry.

Conclusion

The issuer-pays business model that is the standard for almost all credit rating agencies today embodies an obvious conflict of interest: The rating agency may be tempted to shade its rating of an issuer's bonds in favor of the issuer, so as to gain the issuer's business. Although this business model (which has been in place since the late 1960s) has not "blown up" in the areas of rating "plain vanilla" bonds, such as corporate and government bonds, the hundreds of billions of dollars of residential mortgage-backed and related securities were too tempting for the major credit rating agencies. The excessively optimistic ratings that these rating agencies assigned to these securities clearly played a significant role in triggering the financial crisis of 2007-2009.

It was no surprise, then, that the Dodd-Frank Act embodied provisions that entailed heavier regulation of the rating agencies by the SEC.[169] But this heavier regulation has also meant higher

---

[169] But, as we discussed above, Dodd-Frank concomitantly also encouraged financial regulators to reduce their reliance on ratings in their prudential regulation of their financial institutions.

barriers to entry for smaller creditworthiness advisory firms that might want to attain the status of a NRSRO that can be conveyed by the SEC. Dodd-Frank also specifically encouraged the SEC to explore an alternative mechanism—the Franken Amendment—for assigning raters to the issuers of asset-backed securities.

The Financial CHOICE Act largely leaves in place the added regulatory apparatus of Dodd-Frank. But it does provide the SEC with a greater ability to exempt rating agencies from otherwise mandated regulatory provisions, if those provisions would have the effect of raising barriers to entry. And it repeals the Franken Amendment.

We believe that the CHOICE Act could be more specific in its direction to the SEC to reduce the burden of regulation on smaller (and entrant) rating firms. And the repeal of the Franken Amendment is largely a moot point, since the SEC has never gone beyond the issuance of a report (which was mandated by Dodd-Frank) on the possible mechanisms (including the Franken Amendment) for assigning raters to issuers. However, the CHOICE Act drafters should be more forthright in acknowledging the dangers of the issuer-pays model and in encouraging the SEC to be more creative in considering alternatives. Further, we urge the CHOICE Act drafters to consider abolishing the NRSRO category itself, so as to lower the barriers to entry into the rating agency business generally.

References

Ashcraft, Adam B., Paul Goldsmith-Pinkham, and James I. Vickery. "MBS ratings and the mortgage credit boom." (2010).

Ashcraft, A., Goldsmith-Pinkham, P., Hull, P., & Vickery, J. (2011). Credit ratings and security prices in the subprime MBS market. *The American Economic Review*, *101*(3), 115-119.

Altman, E., Oncu, S., Richardson, M., Schmeits, A. and L. J. White, 2011, "Regulating Rating Agencies," in chapter 15 of *Regulating Wall Street: The Dodd-Frank Act and the New Architecture of Global Finance*, editors Viral V. Acharya, Tom Cooley, Matthew Richardson and Ingo Walter, John Wiley & Sons.

Baghai, Ramin P., Henri Servaes, and Ane Tamayo. "Have rating agencies become more conservative? Implications for capital structure and debt pricing." *The Journal of Finance* 69.5 (2014): 1961-2005.

Bar-Isaac, Heski, and Joel Shapiro. "Ratings quality over the business cycle." *Journal of Financial Economics* 108.1 (2013): 62-78.

Becker, Bo, and Todd Milbourn. "How did increased competition affect credit ratings?" *Journal of Financial Economics* 101.3 (2011): 493-514.

Begley, Taylor A., and Amiyatosh Purnanandam. "Design of financial securities: Empirical evidence from private-label RMBS deals." *Review of Financial Studies* 30.1 (2017): 120-161.

Bolton, Patrick, Xavier Freixas, and Joel Shapiro. "The credit ratings game." *The Journal of Finance* 67.1 (2012): 85-111.

Cornaggia, J. and Cornaggia, K. J.: 2011, Does the bond market want informative credit ratings? Working Paper.

Cornaggia, Jess, and Kimberly J. Cornaggia. "Estimating the costs of issuer-paid credit ratings." *Review of Financial Studies* 26.9 (2013): 2229-2269.

Ederington, Louis H., Jess B. Yawitz, and Brian E. Roberts. "The informational content of bond ratings." *Journal of Financial Research* 10.3 (1987): 211-226.

Efing, Matthias, and Harald Hau. "Structured debt ratings: Evidence on conflicts of interest." *Journal of Financial Economics* 116.1 (2015): 46-60.

Esaki, Howard and Lawrence J. White. "Rating mortgage-backed securities: How to end the race to the bottom." *Milken Institute Review* (2017, forthcoming).

Goh, Jeremy C., and Louis H. Ederington. "Is a bond rating downgrade bad news, good news, or no news for stockholders?" *The Journal of Finance* 48.5 (1993): 2001-2008.

Griffin, John M., and Dragon Yongjun Tang. "Did subjectivity play a role in CDO credit ratings?" *The Journal of Finance* 67.4 (2012): 1293-1328.

Griffin, John M., and Dragon Yongjun Tang. "Did credit rating agencies make unbiased assumptions on CDOs?" *The American Economic Review* 101.3 (2011): 125-130.

Griffin, John M., Jordan Nickerson, and Dragon Yongjun Tang. "Rating shopping or catering? An examination of the response to competitive pressure for CDO credit ratings." *Review of Financial Studies* 26.9 (2013): 2270-2310.

Griffin, John, Richard Lowery, and Alessio Saretto. "Complex Securities and Underwriter Reputation: Do Reputable Underwriters Produce Better Securities?" *Review of Financial Studies* 27.10 (2014): 2872-2925.

Griffin, John M., and Gonzalo Maturana. "Who facilitated misreporting in securitized loans?" *Review of Financial Studies* 29.2 (2016): 384-419.

He, Jie, Jun Qian, and Philip E. Strahan. "Credit ratings and the evolution of the mortgage-backed securities market." *The American Economic Review* 101.3 (2011): 131-135.

He, Jie Jack, Jun Qj Qian, and Philip E. Strahan. "Are All Ratings Created Equal? The Impact of Issuer Size on the Pricing of Mortgage-Backed Securities." *The Journal of Finance* 67.6 (2012): 2097-2137.

Hilscher, Jens, and Mungo Wilson. "Credit ratings and credit risk: Is one measure enough?" *Management Science* (2016).

Jankowitsch, R., Ottonello, G., and M. G. Subrahmanyam, 2016, "The Rules of the Rating Game: Market Perception of Corporate Ratings," working paper.

Kashyap, Anil K., and Natalia Kovrijnykh. "Who should pay for credit ratings and how?" *Review of Financial Studies* 29.2 (2016): 420-456.

Klein, Benjamin and Keith B. Leffler. "The role of market forces in assuring contractual performance." *Journal of Political Economy* 89 (1981): 615-641.

Kliger, Doron, and Oded Sarig. "The information value of bond ratings." *The Journal of Finance* 55.6 (2000): 2879-2902.

Manconi, Alberto, Massimo Massa, and Ayako Yasuda. "The role of institutional investors in propagating the crisis of 2007–2008." *Journal of Financial Economics* 104.3 (2012): 491-518.

Mathis, J., McAndrews, J. and Rochet, J.-C. 2009, Rating the raters: are reputation concerns powerful enough to discipline rating agencies? Journal of Monetary Economics 56, 657-674.

Opp, Christian C., Marcus M. Opp, and Milton Harris. "Rating agencies in the face of regulation." *Journal of Financial Economics* 108.1 (2013): 46-61.

Raboy, David. 2009. Concept paper on credit rating agency incentives. Congressional Oversight Panel, January 9.

Richardson, Matthew, and Lawrence J. White. 2009. The rating agencies: Is regulation the answer? In *Restoring financial stability: How to repair a failed system*, eds. Viral V. Acharya and Matthew Richardson. Hoboken, NJ: John Wiley & Sons.

SEC Staff, 2012, "Report to Congress on Assigned Credit Ratings."

Skreta, Vasiliki and Laura L. Veldkamp. 2009. Ratings shopping and asset complexity: A theory of ratings inflation, Journal of Monetary Economics 56(5), 678-695.

Stanton, Richard, and Nancy Wallace. "CMBS subordination, ratings inflation, and regulatory-capital arbitrage." (2012).

U.S. Securities and Exchange Commission. 2016. *Annual Report on Nationally Recognized Statistical Rating Organizations*, December 2016.

White, Lawrence J. "Credit rating agencies: An overview." *Annu. Rev. Financ. Econ.* 5.1 (2013): 93-122.

Wojtowicz, Marcin. "CDOs and the financial crisis: Credit ratings and fair premia." *Journal of Banking & Finance* 39 (2014): 1-13.

Xia, Han. "Can investor-paid credit rating agencies improve the information quality of issuer-paid rating agencies?" *Journal of Financial Economics* 111.2 (2014): 450-468.

Evaluation of Accounting-Related Proposals in the Financial CHOICE Act

By Yiwei Dou and Stephen G. Ryan

Introduction

Passed in the wake of the financial crisis of 2007-2009, the Dodd-Frank Wall Street Reform and Consumer Protection Act (Dodd-Frank) imposed many new regulations on insured depository institutions, bank holding companies, and certain nonbank financial institutions (hereafter referred to as banks, except where necessary to distinguish the different types of institutions). Republicans believe that Dodd-Frank, along with extensive preexisting regulations, saddles banks with an onerous and inefficient regulatory burden, and that this burden contributed to the relatively slow recovery of the economy from the recent financial crisis. They proposed the Financial CHOICE Act, which if adopted would eliminate much of this burden.

In this section, we explain how various proposals in the CHOICE Act depend on, provide incentives regarding, or influence the usefulness of banks' accounting numbers. Many of the effects of these proposals on banks' accounting numbers would flow through to banks' leverage and risk-based regulatory capital ratios, an important issue that the Act does not acknowledge or address. We evaluate the Act's proposals in the context of these accounting-related effects. The specific proposals we consider pertain to: (1) the use of a leverage ratio threshold to determine whether banks qualify for the Dodd-Frank "off-ramp;" (2) the interaction of securitization risk-retention requirements with on- versus off-balance sheet accounting treatment for securitizations and thus with the leverage ratio; (3) short-form regulatory call reports; and

(4) Congressional oversight of and restrictions on the Public Company Accounting Oversight Board (PCAOB).

The Leverage Ratio Threshold for the Dodd-Frank Off-Ramp

Background

A number of Dodd-Frank's regulations target very large bank holding companies (those with assets exceeding $50 billion or $10 billion, depending on the regulation) and similarly systematically risky nonbank financial institutions. These regulations aim to reduce the systemic risks that large banks impose on the financial system. These risks arise in part from the incentives of bank regulators to deem these institutions "too-big-to-fail," particularly during periods of high economic uncertainty. Title I of Dodd-Frank subjects (or allows the Board of Governors of the Federal Reserve to subject) these large banks to more stringent prudential standards, including risk-based capital and liquidity requirements, leverage and short-term debt limits, contingent capital requirements, credit exposure concentration limits and reporting requirements, periodic stress tests, requirements to plan for rapid and orderly resolution of the institution in the event of financial distress or failure, requirements to establish risk committees, and enhanced public disclosure requirements.[170]

Dodd-Frank also creates many new regulations for all banks. Compliance with these new regulations requires banks to incur sizable and partly fixed costs, which are particularly onerous for small and medium-sized community banks. A recent survey of over 200 community banks (defined as banks with assets less than $10 billion) reports that Dodd-Frank's creation of the Consumer Financial Protection Bureau (Title X) and mortgage regulations (Title XIV) are of greatest concern to these banks.

---

[170] Dodd-Frank, Title I, Section 165(b)-(e), (g), (h), (i), and (j).

The CHOICE Act Proposal

Any bank that qualifies based on criteria specified in Title I, Section 101 of the Act could elect the off-ramp, exempting the bank from certain of Dodd-Frank's and other regulations. Section 101 indicates that, to qualify for the off-ramp, banks must maintain average leverage ratios—defined as tangible equity divided by total assets (excluding any assets deducted from tier 1 capital) calculated in accordance with Generally Accepted Accounting Principles (GAAP)—of at least 10%.[171] This percentage is approximately double the current leverage ratio at which a bank is deemed well capitalized. Banks must also receive composite CAMELS ratings of 1 or 2.[172]

The CHOICE Act specifies that qualifying banks that elect the off-ramp would be exempt from the stringent prudential regulation in Dodd-Frank Title I described above. These banks would also be immune to regulatory objections to capital distributions and proposed mergers and acquisitions on grounds that these actions might compromise the stability of the U.S. financial system.[173]

Evaluation of the CHOICE Act Proposal

The Act would make the off-ramp available to all qualifying banks. As suggested in the comprehensive summary of the Act, however,

---

[171] The CHOICE Act, Title I, Section 105(5) and (6).
[172] CAMELS ratings are supervisory ratings of banks' overall condition. CAMELS stands for capital adequacy, assets, management capability, earnings, liquidity, and sensitivity to market risk. A CAMELS rating of 1 (2) indicates strong (satisfactory) performance and risk management and thus minimal supervisory concern.
[173] The CHOICE Act, Title I, Section 102(a)-(d).

such regulatory relief is most necessary for community banks.[174] Inconsistent with this fact, the most onerous regulations from which qualifying banks would be exempted apply mostly or entirely to very large banks. For example, community banks are not subject to the more stringent prudential regulation in Dodd-Frank Title I, Section 165 described above, and they infrequently acquire other banks. In contrast, the off-ramp does not eliminate Dodd-Frank's creation of the Consumer Financial Protection Bureau (Title X) and mortgage regulations (Title XIV) that community banks find most onerous.

A large body of empirical research demonstrates that banks exercise discretion over accounting numbers, usually within the bounds of GAAP, to manage their regulatory capital ratios.[175] The reliance on accounting numbers to measure the leverage ratio would yield incentives for banks to exercise discretion over these numbers to increase the leverage ratio to qualify for the off-ramp. Most of these avenues for accounting discretion have similar effects of risk-based capital ratios. For example, banks could increase regulatory capital by delaying loan loss provisions or realizing gains on available-for-sale securities, or they could smooth regulatory capital by accelerating loan loss provisions in boom periods.[176]

---

[174] For example, the second bullet on page 2 of the comprehensive summary of the Act states "Dodd-Frank's particular brand of regulatory complexity and government micromanagement has made basic financial services less accessible to small businesses and lower-income Americans, by saddling America's small and medium-sized community financial institutions with a crushing regulatory burden."

[175] For summaries of this research, see Stephen Ryan, 2011, Financial Reporting for Financial Instruments, *Foundations and Trends in Accounting*; Anne Beatty and Scott Liao, 2014, Financial Accounting in the Banking Industry: A Review of the Empirical Literature, *Journal of Accounting and Economics*; Viral Acharya and Stephen Ryan, 2016, Banks' Financial Reporting and Financial System Stability, *Journal of Accounting Research*.

[176] Chi-Chun Liu and Stephen Ryan, 2016, Income Smoothing over the Business Cycle: Changes in Banks' Coordinated Management of Provisions for Loan Losses and Loan Charge-Offs from the Pre-1990 Bust to the 1990 Boom, *The Accounting Review*.

Other avenues have considerably stronger effects on the leverage ratio than on risk-based capital ratios. Most importantly, securitization and other transactions that keep economic leverage off-balance sheet typically reduce the leverage ratio far more than risk-based capital ratios, because risk-based capital rules require banks to hold capital against most types of off-balance sheet positions.

Post-financial crisis changes in accounting rules (discussed below) made off-balance sheet treatment somewhat more difficult to attain. Even so, empirical research finds that securitizations of most types of financial assets—including subprime and other types of residential mortgages, perceived culprits in the genesis of the financial crisis—continue to remain almost entirely off-balance-sheet.[177] Hence, were the CHOICE Act adopted, it could be expected that banks would engage in off-balance sheet securitizations and other transactions to qualify for off-ramp status. Very large banks are more likely than community banks to have the capability to engage in such transactions.

Summary and Recommendations

The CHOICE Act provides community banks with relatively little regulatory relief compared with that provided to very large banks. Granting banks with off-ramp status based on their leverage ratios is likely to encourage more off-balance sheet securitization and other transactions, particularly by very large banks.

To avoid providing accounting-related incentives, we recommend that the financial leverage embedded in banks' off-balance sheet positions (excepting those where risk has been completely transferred to unrelated third parties) be incorporated into the

---

[177] Board of Governors of the Federal Reserve System, 2010, Report to the Congress on Risk Retention; Yiwei Dou, Stephen Ryan, and Biqin Xie, 2016, The Real Effects of FAS 166 and FAS 167, Working Paper, New York University.

leverage ratio used to assess whether banks qualify for the off-ramp. This recommendation would retain most of the simplicity of the Act's approach, while increasing its robustness with regard to accounting-motivated transaction structuring.

Interaction of Risk-Retention Requirements with On- versus Off-Balance Sheet Treatment for Securitizations

Background

During the financial crisis, originators of securitized nontraditional (e.g., subprime) residential mortgages and some other types of financial assets (originators) and securitization sponsors and issuers (securitizers) bore sizable securitization-related losses through the provision of contractual or noncontractual credit enhancement and liquidity support, as well as through the repurchases of securitized assets due to actual or credibly alleged violations of representations and warranties. These losses suggest that originators and securitizers did not have adequate incentives to originate assets with sufficiently high credit quality and to make accurate representations and warranties about the credit-risk characteristics of those assets in securitization prospectuses. To provide such incentives, Dodd-Frank, Title IX, Subtitle D, Section 941 requires securitizers to retain at least 5% of the credit risk of securitized assets, exempting qualified (i.e., relatively low risk) residential mortgages,[178] without subsequently transferring or hedging that risk. The final rules became effective in December 2015, for securitizations involving residential mortgages, and in December

---

[178] The definition of "qualified residential mortgages" corresponds to the Consumer Financial Products Bureau's definition of "qualified mortgages," which involves any lien or property type, no negative amortization features, 30-year term or less, 43% total debt-to-income ratio or less, documented borrower income and assets, and with the underwriting decision based on a fully adjusted (non-teaser) interest rate.

2016, for securitizations involving other types of securitized assets.[179]

For securitizations of non-exempted types of financial assets, securitizers can satisfy the risk-retention requirements by holding: (1) vertical interests (i.e., a constant proportion of each tranche issued) in securitizations of at least 5%; (2) horizontal residual (i.e., first-loss-bearing) interests constituting at least 5% of the fair value of all the securitized assets; or (3) any combination of (1) and (2) totaling at least 5%. Option (2) involves far more risk retention than option (1) and thus at least somewhat more risk retention than option (3). Thus, securitizers that prefer to retain the minimum allowed level of risk will choose to hold vertical interests.[180]

The CHOICE Act Proposal

Republicans consider Dodd-Frank's risk-retention requirements, which apply to all but one type of securitized financial assets, to be an overreaction to a problem that only affected securitization of certain nontraditional residential mortgage-related assets, and thus that it constitutes excessive governmental intrusion into capital markets. The Act's Title IV, Subtitle B, Section 442 exempts securitizations of pools of financial assets that are not wholly residential mortgages from these requirements.

Evaluation of the CHOICE Act Proposal

In principle, the Act could completely sterilize Dodd-Frank's risk-retention requirements, even for residential mortgage

---

[179] Credit Risk Retention, Final Rule, Federal Register, December 24, 2014, pp. 77601-77766.
[180] For further discussion of the economic implications of and likely responses to Dodd-Frank's risk retention rules, see Matthew Richardson, Joshua Ronen, and Marti Subrahmanyam, 2010, Chapter 16: Securitization Reform, in Regulating Wall Street: Dodd-Frank and the New Architecture of Global Finance, edited by Viral Acharya, Thomas Cooley, Matthew Richardson, and Ingo Walter.

securitizations, as a securitization with 99% residential mortgages would be exempt from those requirements. If this turned out to be the case, banks would retain risk only to the extent that market forces made it optimal from the banks' perspective.

A subtle accounting-related implication of Dodd-Frank's risk-retention requirements, and thus of the Act's proposal to eliminate these requirements, is that sufficient risk retention typically will cause securitizers to recognize securitizations on-balance sheet. On-balance sheet treatment reduces securitizing banks' leverage and other regulatory capital ratios, among other generally conservative accounting effects, compared with the transactions being off-balance sheet.

Specifically, under current GAAP, securitizers may account for securitizations on-balance sheet for two distinct reasons: First, securitizers may account for securitizations as secured borrowings rather than as sales under Accounting Standards Codification Topic 860, Transfers and Servicing (ASC 860). This rule requires secured borrowing accounting when securitizers retain control over the securitized assets. Retention of control is defined both legally (the assets are not isolated from securitizers) and effectively (securitizers retain effective control over the assets through contractual or noncontractual means). Second, securitizers may consolidate the securitization entities under Accounting Standards Codification Topic 810, Consolidation (ASC 810). This rule requires consolidation when securitizers retain control over the economically most significant activities of securitization entities, as well as the obligation to absorb a reasonable possibility of significant loss in the entities.

The more risk securitizers retain in securitization entities, the more they will desire to be able to manage this risk by retaining control over the entities. Sufficient risk retention thus will tend to be associated with retention of control. The retention of sufficient control and risk will lead to securitizers recognizing securitizations on-balance sheet. This treatment would be especially likely if securitizers retained 5% horizontal residual interests in securitizations. For many types of securitized financial assets, securitizers that bear the first 5% risk of loss on the assets likely bear most or even all of the risk of the assets, and so they will want to retain control over the assets.[181]

Summary and Recommendations

As written, the CHOICE Act proposal could sterilize Dodd-Frank's risk-retention requirements even for securitizations of residential mortgages. This aspect could easily be fixed, however, by exempting securitizations if they contained less than a threshold amount lower than 100% of residential mortgages.

The proposal might also contribute to more off-balance sheet accounting for securitizations. If so, it would increase securitizers' leverage and other regulatory capital ratios. In this respect, this proposal overlaps with the reliance on the leverage ratio in the Act's Dodd-Frank off-ramp proposal discussed earlier in this article.

---

[181] In the final rule of credit risk retention (https://www.gpo.gov/fdsys/pkg/FR-2014-12-24/pdf/2014-29256.pdf), regulators acknowledged: "One commenter expressed opposition to any requirement for a minimum vertical or horizontal component, claiming that such a requirement would increase compliance costs and increase the risk that sponsors would, as a result of accounting standards, have to consolidate securitization entities into their financial statements... Two commenters asserted that, because of the flexibility of the proposed standard risk retention option, in and of itself, the option would not cause a sponsor to have to consolidate its securitization vehicles. One of these commenters observed that case-by-case analyses would be required and that the likelihood of consolidation would increase as a sponsor retains a greater portion of its required interest as a horizontal interest. Another commenter asserted that, if potential investors require the sponsor to hold a horizontal rather than a vertical interest, or a combination, the consolidation risk will increase."

We recommend that any proposal to reduce or eliminate Dodd-Frank's risk-retention requirements be considered in part based on its implications for off-balance sheet treatment for securitizations.

Short-Form Call Reports

Background

Every national bank, state member bank, insured state nonmember bank, and savings association must file quarterly Reports of Condition and Income (Call Reports) with the relevant bank regulatory agencies. Call Reports contain much more detailed and standardized quantitative balance sheet, income statement, and other data than exists in public banks' financial reports. The specific requirements depend on the size of the institution, the nature of its activities, and whether it has foreign offices. Unlike financial reports, Call Reports do not contain qualitative data or management discussion and analysis.

The Federal Deposit Insurance Corporation (FDIC) website describes the nature and uses of Call Report data as follows:

> *"Call Report data serve a regulatory and public policy purpose by assisting the agencies in fulfilling their missions of ensuring the safety and soundness of financial institutions and the financial system and the protection of consumer financial rights, as well as agency-specific missions affecting national and state-chartered institutions, e.g., monetary policy, financial stability, and deposit insurance...Call Report data are also used by the public, state banking authorities, researchers, bank rating agencies, and the academic community."*[182]

---

[182] https://www.fdic.gov/regulations/resources/call/index.html

The CHOICE Act Proposal

The CHOICE Act, Title XI, Subtitle N, Section 1166 would permit highly rated and well-capitalized (covered) insured depository institutions to file short-form Call Reports in the first and third quarters of each year.

Evaluation of the CHOICE Act Proposal

The ability to file short-form Call Reports in the first and third quarters likely would yield cost savings for community banks relative to preparing full reports in those quarters. The extent of these cost savings are unlikely to be large, however, as the reported data are standardized and entirely quantitative. Banks must record almost all of these data in their accounting systems at least quarterly. Hence, the primary costs are those involved in compiling these accounting records into standardized Call Reports.

Consistent with the FDIC description above, bank regulators indicate they use these reports to monitor banks between supervisory examinations, which occur only once every year or 18 months.[183] Moreover, empirical research shows that the highly standardized, and thus comparable, quarterly Call Reports provide more information to market participants than do far less easily analyzed quarterly financial reports.[184] Hence, even for small community banks, quarterly Call Reports likely provide significant benefits in terms of regulatory and market discipline, and these benefits very well may outweigh the likely modest cost savings.

---

[183] Jessica Keeley, 2017, The Impact of Regulatory Enforcement Actions on Bank Risk, Working Paper, New York University.
[184] Brad Badertscher, Jeffrey Burks, and Peter Easton, 2016, Day 30: The Tacit Quarterly Information Event in the Banking Industry, Working Paper, University of Notre Dame.

Summary and Recommendation

Quarterly Call Reports yield benefits in regulatory and market discipline. We recommend that these benefits be weighed against the cost savings before passing the proposal to allow covered insured depository institutions to file short-form Call Reports.

Congressional Oversight of and Restrictions on the Public Company Accounting Oversight Board (PCAOB)

Background

In the wake of the revelation of numerous severe financial reporting failures by large publicly traded companies in 2001 and 2002 (e.g., Enron, WorldCom, Tyco, and Adelphia), as well as the demise of Enron's auditor, Arthur Andersen, the Sarbanes-Oxley Act (SOX) passed with almost unanimous bipartisan support. Among many other things, SOX created the PCAOB to supervise, investigate, and potentially sanction auditors of public companies. The PCAOB's activities effectively replaced auditors' prior self-regulatory practice of peer review of audits of these companies. SOX also vested auditing standard setting for these companies with the PCAOB, removing this responsibility from the Auditing Standards Board, a committee of the American Institute of Certified Public Accountants. Arguably, these changes diminished the professional status of auditors, possibly making auditing a less attractive career option.

SOX created the PCAOB as an independent nonprofit private corporation within the Securities and Exchange Commission, itself an independent federal agency. This, along with various other features of SOX, had the effect of providing the PCAOB with double insulation from both the executive and legislative branches of government. This insulation exists despite the PCAOB's *de facto* ability to act as an independent, and in some respects unusually powerful, federal agency. SOX also created the PCAOB to be independent of the auditing profession, most notably by limiting the number of certified public accountants on the five-member board to exactly two, and by not allowing the chairperson of the board to have been a practicing accountant for at least five years. The political insulation of the PCAOB and the limited auditing experience of its members involved various well-understood trade-offs (e.g., more independence from government and auditors, but less oversight and expertise) that Republican Senator Phil Gramm discusses in remarks supporting SOX reported in the Congressional Record.[185]

The CHOICE Act Proposals

The Act proposes two primary changes to SOX's provisions regarding the PCAOB. First, the CHOICE Act Title IV, Subtitle A, Section 425 requires the PCAOB to make information requested by specified Congressional committees available to them on a confidential basis. The comprehensive summary of the CHOICE Act indicates that this resolves "statutory ambiguity" regarding whether these committees can obtain this information. This ambiguity apparently results from SOX expressly allowing the SEC to receive such information, but not specifying whether the SEC can pass the information along to the committees on a confidential basis, despite Congressional oversight of the SEC.

Second, the CHOICE Act Title VI, Subtitle A, Section 620 requires the SEC to conduct a study within one year of the Act's enactment to set forth a plan to make the PCAOB subject to various provisions of this title. These provisions include requirements to: (1) conduct and explain, in notices of proposed rulemaking, quantitative and qualitative cost-benefit analyses for proposed new rules, both in isolation and relative to alternative approaches; (2) assess and explain who will bear the burden of the new rules; (3) consider comments on notices of proposed rulemaking; (4) predict changes

---

[185] Congressional Record, Vol. 148, No. 90, S6330-6340, July 8, 2002.

in market structure and behavior; (5) conduct retrospective regulatory impact analyses; and (6) enable adversely affected parties to bring actions in U.S. Appeals Court for judicial review of agency compliance with these requirements.

Evaluation of the Act's Proposals

We do not object to the Act's requirement that the PCAOB make information available on a confidential basis to specified Congressional committees. We raise a caution, however, about proceeding further down the slippery slope to political intrusion into the delicate and intertwined processes of setting, applying, and enforcing accounting and auditing standards. The history of such intrusions is deeply unfortunate, having consistently been driven by the political expediency of the moment to the detriment of the development of well-functioning and coherent processes.[186] Such development requires professional expertise and judgment, as well as a long-term perspective.

Relatedly, experience shows that auditors' reputations are easily lost but hard to regain (as noted above, Arthur Andersen's rapid demise after its Enron-related audit failures were factors contributing to the creation of the PCAOB). Moreover, auditors are subject to frequent and costly litigation, regardless of their culpability. These concerns are particularly salient given the highly concentrated audit market, in which very few firms (primarily the Big 4 auditors) are capable of auditing the largest and most far-flung companies. The loss of another auditor would raise significant competitive and practical problems.

---

[186] See discussion related to this point in Joshua Ronen and Stephen Ryan, Bank Regulators Should not Meddle in GAAP, Section 4 of Chapter 18, Accounting and Financial Reform, in Regulating Wall Street: Dodd-Frank and the New Architecture of Global Finance, edited by Viral Acharya, Thomas Cooley, Matthew Richardson, and Ingo Walter.

We believe these concerns require ongoing investigations of auditors to remain entirely confidential, whether or not information about the investigations is shared with Congressional committees. Many of the PCAOB's processes, and the ongoing improvement of auditing, require the cooperation of auditors. Such cooperation is less likely to be forthcoming if auditors cannot be sure that information provided is confidential prior to an evidence-based, reasoned, and fair determination of culpability.

We agree with the desire of the drafters of the CHOICE Act to deter the promulgation of rules for which the costs exceed the benefits. As a general rule, however, we do not believe that the costs and benefits of the PCAOB's oversight of auditors and setting of auditing standards are amenable to either quantification or judicial review. In most cases, these cost-benefit trade-offs are matters of professional judgment that must primarily be assessed qualitatively, and for which a certain amount of trial and error is inevitable.[187]

Summary and Recommendations

Sufficient time has passed since the creation of the PCAOB for the appropriate Congressional committees to evaluate whether and what extent this unusually powerful and politically insulated hybrid of nonprofit corporation and federal agency is serving its intended purposes, and whether and how these purposes can be better served. We believe it is critical to keep ongoing investigations of auditors confidential in order to avoid unnecessary loss of reputation and litigation costs.

More generally, we believe any Congressional oversight of the PCAOB's activities needs to be as nonpolitical as possible and to treat auditors as professionals and auditing as a profession. The best way for the profession to improve over time is to make it

---

[187] Mark Nelson, 2009, A Model and Literature Review of Professional Skepticism, *Auditing: A Journal of Practice & Theory.*

attractive to young people as they choose their careers. As Senator Gramm states in his remarks mentioned above, "if we don't attract smart young people into accounting, people who understand it is not talent, it is not personality, it is not cool, it is character that ultimately counts, then none of these systems is going to work very well."

Reining in the Regulators: Title VI of the Financial CHOICE Act

By Barry E. Adler, Thomas F. Cooley, and Lawrence J. White

Introduction

The drafters of the Financial CHOICE Act believe that the Dodd-Frank Act of 2010 mandated excessive regulation of the financial sector—especially banks—and also that U.S. financial regulators have not regulated wisely: both before and since Dodd-Frank. Although other parts of the CHOICE Act target specific provisions of Dodd-Frank (e.g., Title I provides an "off-ramp" from detailed Dodd-Frank regulation for well capitalized banks), Title VI addresses broader regulatory issues. In this chapter, we will address the following:

- Requiring cost-benefit analyses of all financial regulatory proposals;

- Requiring that Congress approve all major financial regulations;

- Eliminating the "Chevron deference" to regulatory agencies; and

- Requiring multi-person governing boards instead of single-heads of agencies.[188]

Background

There is little question that Dodd-Frank—enacted in the wake of the financial crisis of 2007-2009—constituted a major expansion of financial regulation. Its supporters believed that the expansion was needed to remedy the regulatory shortcomings that allowed the crisis to occur; its critics warned that (among other things) the expansion did not address all of the causes of the crisis, could increase the likelihood of a new crisis (because it enshrined large financial institutions as "too-big-to-fail"), would increase the costs of financial services firms, and would thus raise the prices of financial services to users.

In any event, Dodd-Frank instructed financial regulators to propose and finalize about 400 regulations ("rulemakings")[189] and created a major new financial agency—the Consumer Finance Protection Bureau (CFPB)—as well as a new multi-agency monitoring entity—the Financial Stability Oversight Council (FSOC)—and a new

---

[188] Recent news stories indicate that there may be a "2.0" version of the Financial CHOICE Act that would not replace single-headed agencies with multi-person boards. See, for example, Ian McKendry, Kate Berry, and John Heltman, "Cheat Sheet: Hensarling's Plans to Gut CFPB, Revamp Stress Tests," Credit Union Journal, February 9, 2017; available at: https://www.cujournal.com/news/cheat-sheet-hensarlings-plans-to-gut-cfpb-revamp-stress-tests. Because of the current uncertainty as to what the introduced Act will contain and because we believe that the issue of single-heads versus multi-person governing boards for financial regulatory agencies deserves some general discussion, we have retained this item in our discussion.

[189] The Davis Polk law firm puts the number at 390. See Davis Polk & Wardwell, "Dodd-Frank Progress Report," July 19, 2016.

---

financial research organization—the Office of Financial Research (OFR).[190] It is this expansion to which the CHOICE Act is a response.

Four Components of Title VI

We will address four components of the CHOICE Act's Title VI: cost-benefit analysis; Congressional approval; reduced deference; and agency boards. These are now discussed in turn.[191]

Requiring cost-benefit analyses of all financial regulatory proposals

Title VI specifies that a financial regulatory agency may not adopt a regulation if the agency determines that the "quantified" costs outweigh the "quantified" benefits. Further, the agency must identify all available alternatives and explain why the regulation meets the objectives of the regulation more effectively than do the alternatives. If an agency is challenged by an interested party and has not complied with these requirements, the regulation can be vacated by the courts.

Requiring that Congress approve all major financial regulations

Major regulations would take effect only if Congress passed a joint resolution of approval that is enacted into law within 70 days after the agency sends a report on the regulation to Congress. Major regulations are defined primarily as those that would have annual effects of $100 million or more, or significantly raise costs or prices, or have other adverse effects on the U.S. economy (as determined

---

[190] Dodd-Frank is also notable for what it did not do: It did little to simplify or streamline an already complex regulatory architecture, but overlaid these new regulations and organizations on top of the existing system.

[191] This summary draws heavily on Davis Polk & Wardwell, "Comparison of Legislation in the 115th Congress Affecting the Rulemaking Process," January 26, 2017; this document can be found at https://www.davispolk.com/publications/comparison-legislation-115th-congress-affecting-rulemaking-process/

by the Office of Information and Regulatory Affairs). In somewhat the same spirit, Congress could similarly render ineffective non-major rules by a joint resolution of disapproval.

Eliminating the "Chevron deference" to regulatory agencies

Under <u>Chevron v. NRDC</u>, 467 U.S. 837 (1984), the Supreme Court established the precedent that the courts should generally defer to the regulatory agency's interpretation of the statute under which the agency has promulgated a regulation. Title VI would override this judicial interpretation and require the courts to decide *de novo* the appropriate interpretation of the relevant statute.

Requiring multi-person governing boards instead of single-heads of agencies

Some financial regulatory agencies are headed by multi-person boards: specifically, the Federal Deposit Insurance Corporation (FDIC), the Securities and Exchange Commission (SEC), the Commodities and Futures Trading Corporation (CFTC), the National Credit Union Administration (NCUA), and the Federal Reserve. Other financial regulatory agencies are headed by a single individual: specifically, the CFPB, the Office of the Comptroller of the Currency (OCC), and the Federal Housing Finance Agency (FHFA).[192] For the latter three agencies, their single-headed structure would be replaced by a five-person board,[193] with a

---

[192] In addition, the Pension Benefit Guaranty Corporation (PBGC) is somewhat of a hybrid: It has a single Director but also a Board of Directors that is composed of the Secretaries of Labor, Treasury, and Commerce. Further, the U.S. Department of Labor (DOL)—an Executive Branch agency—has financial regulatory powers with respect to pension funds and retirement account arrangements.

[193] Also, the NCUA's three-person board would be replaced by a five-person board.

requirement that no more than three of the five could be from one of the two major political parties.[194]

An Assessment

Requiring cost-benefit analyses of all financial regulatory proposals

In principle, we endorse a cost-benefit test for any kind of regulation, including, of course, financial regulation. We should expect—or at least hope—that the benefits of a given regulation exceed its costs.[195] Indeed, there are already some specific areas of regulation, including some SEC regulations,[196] as well as some regulations by the FCC and the Environmental Protection Agency (EPA), for which cost-benefit analyses have been required and conducted.[197] Even for areas, such as environmental or safety regulations that involve saving lives (i.e., reductions in premature deaths), in which it would appear to be difficult to place a value on

---

[194] This specification of a majority/minority political structure for the board membership is typical for most multi-person regulatory agencies: not only for financial regulatory agencies, such as the FDIC, the SEC, the CFTC, and the NCUA, but also for other federal regulatory agencies, such as the Federal Trade Commission (FTC), the Federal Communications Commission (FCC), the Federal Energy Regulatory Commission (FERC), and the National Labor Relations Board (NLRB).

[195] As a technical matter, where a regulation involves quantitative gradations— for example, a minimum capital requirement for banks that is expressed as the percentage ratio of net worth divided by total assets—the appropriate criterion for maximizing social welfare is (other things being equal) that the marginal benefit be equal to the marginal cost.

[196] See, for example, Bruce Kraus and Connor Raso, "Rational Boundaries for SEC Cost-Benefit Analysis," Yale Journal on Regulation, 30 (#2, 2013), pp. 289-342; and John C. Coates, IV, "Cost-Benefit Analysis of Financial Regulation: Case Studies and Implications," Yale Law Journal, 124 (January-February 2015), pp. 882-1011.

[197] See, for example, the discussion in Coates, op. cit., as well as in Eric A. Posner and E. Glen Weyl, "Benefit-Cost Paradigms in Financial Regulation," Journal of Legal Studies, 43 (June 2013), pp. S1-S34; and Ryan Bubb, "Comment: The OIRA Model for Institutionalizing CBA of Financial Regulation, Law and Contemporary Problems, 78 (No. 3, 2015), pp. 47-53.

the benefits, the economics profession has developed methods—conceptually and empirically—for obtaining estimates (or at least bounds on estimates) that can help guide policy.

However, there are significant difficulties of measurement and valuation—of benefits and costs—in financial regulation. For example, higher capital requirements for large banks may well have the benefit of reducing the likelihood of a repeat of the crisis of 2007-2009. But can the reduced likelihood of another crisis be quantitatively linked to the size of the capital requirements? And what were the costs of that crisis—and thus the benefits of reducing the probability of a repeat of the crisis?

Although economists could surely develop estimates for both questions, the tradition of having economists provide quantitative estimates of costs and benefits in the context of proposed regulations is relatively recent.[198] And, indeed, there are diverse views among economists and lawyers as to the practicality and wisdom of requiring formal cost-benefit analyses for financial

---

[198] White—who was a regulator of the savings & loan industry in the late 1980s—can personally attest to the general absence of formal cost-benefit analyses among bank regulators through the late 1980s; and this absence appears to have persisted through the 1990s and into the 2000s. For example, one can peruse the pages of the Federal Register in connection with the proposed and final versions of financial regulations and find scant references to quantitative findings by the agency in support of its proposals and final rules or even by interested parties that have commented on the proposals. See also Prasad Krishnamurthy, "Rules, Standards, and Complexity in Capital Regulation," Journal of Legal Studies, 43 (June 2014), pp. S273-S296.

regulations.[199] By contrast, as early as the late 1970s (and possibly earlier), the EPA and other nonfinancial regulatory agencies were regularly trying to quantify outcomes and making estimates of costs and benefits.[200]

This early stage of the application of cost-benefit analysis to financial regulation makes us wary of the requirement that all financial regulations must be accompanied by formal cost-benefit analyses. Such a requirement could entail large commitments of agency resources—at a time when agency budgets are likely to be cut—and thus have the potential to delay substantially or flatly prevent the issuance of new regulations.[201]

To avoid regulatory torpor, then, any requirement for a cost-benefit analysis should be sufficiently flexible to account not only for the cost of regulation but also the cost and difficulties of the *analysis* itself. If a requirement for cost-benefit analysis included an arbitrary evidentiary threshold, then the requirement would block regulation that is likely to be beneficial based on *reasonably* available evidence at the time. Put simply, sometimes even scant

---

[199] For a representative view of these differences of opinions, see the June 2014 (vol. 43) issue of the Journal of Legal Studies and the No. 3, 2015 (vol. 73) issue of Law and Contemporary Problems. It is worth noting that among the authors of these essays, there are skeptics of the social value of much of financial regulation who nevertheless are also skeptical of the practicality and value of requiring formal cost-benefit analyses of financial regulation. See, for example, John H. Cochrane, "Challenges for Cost-Benefit Analysis of Financial Regulation," Journal of Legal Studies, 43 (June 2014), pp. S63-S105. See also Thomas Philippon, "Efficiency and Benefit-Cost Analysis of the Financial System," Journal of Legal Studies, 43 (June 2014), pp. S107-S120; Jeffrey N. Gordon, "The Empty Call for Benefit-Cost Analysis in Financial Regulation," Journal of Legal Studies, 43 (June 2014), pp. S351-S378; and Coates, op. cit.

[200] See, for example, Lawrence J. White, Reforming Regulation: Processes and Problems. Englewood Cliffs, NJ: Prentice Hall, 1981. See also Bubb, op. cit.; and Posner and Weyl, op. cit.

[201] This effect would be exacerbated by the ability of affected parties to challenge in court the agencies' analyses as a means of challenging the regulations themselves.

evidence is sufficient to justify regulation. And as good as cost-benefit analysis is in principle, it is bad policy for the requirement of such analysis to bias the regulatory process against action.

Nevertheless, we believe that an appropriate requirement could encourage the development of cost-benefit analysis by regulators who could choose a relatively small set of financial regulations that do appear to be more amenable to cost-benefit analyses and, for these regulations, engage in relatively intensive investigation.[202] This process would help push the agencies more toward developing methodologies for quantifying costs and benefits and thus help develop an agency culture that regularly considers costs and benefits in the development of new regulations.[203] As part of this process, the parties that are affected by the regulation would be spurred to develop their own estimates of costs and benefits, and there would likely be a beneficial feedback from the agencies to the parties, and back to the agencies, in the development of methodologies and estimates.

Over time, as the new culture takes hold, there would be growth in the list of regulations that would benefit from, and thus require, a fully developed cost-benefit analysis.

Toward this end, Congress should require that the promulgating agency provide what we would call a Cost Effectiveness report in the event that the circumstances do not support a traditional quantifiable cost-benefit analysis. By cost effectiveness, we mean a process whereby the benefits of a regulation are identified, the

---

[202] We suggest the following as potential examples of financial regulation that would be particularly amenable to cost-benefit analyses: the CFPB's proposed "payday lending" regulation; the CFPB's possible restrictions on bank overdraft fees and arrangements; and the DOL's proposal for fiduciary obligations by financial advisers with respect to individuals' retirement accounts. We expect that there are many more examples of such regulations that could be suggested.

[203] A similar belief in encouraging a culture that regularly considers costs and benefits can be found in many of the essays in the two journal volumes that were mentioned in footnote 199.

---

costs of alternative means of achieving a given goal are developed and compared, and an explanation is provided for why a full quantitative analysis is not cost justified.

Throughout the legislative and regulatory process, Congress and the Executive Branch should encourage financial regulators to think in terms of, and to state publicly, the goals (the "output") of specific regulations, ways of measuring that output, the cause-and-effect channels through which the regulation will achieve the goals, and the market failure theory on which the regulatory action is based. The aim should be the provision of a formal a quantitative analysis wherever possible.[204] All of this should be open to review by Congress, the Executive Branch, and the public.

Requiring that Congress approve all major financial regulations

Although the report of the House Committee on Financial Services states that the CHOICE Act would require a "joint resolution" of Congress to effectuate major regulation, the Act provides that such regulation will not become effective unless the joint resolution is "enacted into law", and the report observes that the CHOICE Act adopts the REINS Act, which, according to the CHOICE Act report, "requires Congress to pass, and the President to sign, a joint resolution of approval for all major regulations before they are effective." Or, put differently, one might say that, for important matters, the CHOICE Act is designed to prohibit regulation (as that term is commonly understood).

This proposed significant step back from the administrative state may well be desirable to the drafters of the CHOICE Act, but it is a reversal that we do not endorse. Having Congress and the President deliberate and pass on the details of regulatory minutia is simply a bad use of Congress's time and resources—particularly in the technical, complex, and systemically sensitive area of financial

---

[204] See Cochrane, op. cit., p. S102, for similar ideas.

regulation. In this area, as with others in the general modern structure of governmental administration, Congress should focus on and pass legislation that involves broad policy goals and targets, and then leave the regulatory agencies to fill in the details with suitable specific implementation regulations.

If Congress believes that the regulators have misinterpreted Congressional intent, Congressional committee and subcommittee hearings are an immediate vehicle for encouraging the regulators to re-direct their actions. If hearings, along with other instruments of conveying public opinion, do not succeed in getting regulators to hew to the will of the elected officials, then Congress should consider fine-grained legislation to override and re-direct the regulators' actions. Such legislation should be exceptional, not routine.

There is also a "gaming" issue that may arise: To the extent that regulatory agencies can divide a large—and thereby "major"—regulation into smaller pieces that individually are below whatever threshold is chosen, the goal of this provision will be undermined.

Because we believe a process that requires Congressional joint resolutions and Presidential approval will not improve the quality of financial regulation, we recommend that such a process not be enacted.

Eliminating the "Chevron deference" to regulatory agencies

The Supreme Court's 1984 decision in <u>Chevron v. NRDC</u>, 467 U.S. 837 (1984), directed that lower courts defer to a regulatory agency's interpretations of statute in its promulgation of regulation so long as the relevant provision is ambiguous and the regulation is a reasonable policy choice for the agency to make. Such deference has the advantage of relying on agency expertise and economizing on scarce judicial resources. This process also offers the possibility of a coherent implementation strategy orchestrated by the relevant agency.

Concomitantly with the greater call on judicial resources, an end to Chevron deference would retard the regulatory process, given the greater prospect of success in challenges to promulgated regulation. Rather than throw all regulation into the imbroglio of litigation, where a particular regulation or set of regulations is problematic, it is better for Congress to enact new legislation that better constrains agency discretion. Consequently, we recommend against the elimination of the Chevron deference.

Requiring multi-person governing boards instead of single-heads of agencies

As we noted above, this provision may not be in the "2.0" version of the CHOICE Act. Nevertheless, as a general matter, it is worth discussing. In the "1.0" version of the CHOICE Act, this provision would apply to the CFPB, the OCC, and the FHFA.

Single-headed agency leadership has advantages and disadvantages, as does leadership by a multi-person board that has a mandatory political majority/minority structure. With a single-headed agency, there is clearer direction (and a clearer location of responsibility) and the likelihood of speedier action on regulatory matters. With a multi-person board, there is more opportunity for the exchange of ideas and for the give-and-take that may be important for partisan issues, but at the expense of slower action and a more diffuse location of direction and responsibility. Also, the advantages of a board may be limited if the agency is a member of a multi-agency entity (such as the FSOC) or a multi-agency task force; in such a case, the chair of an agency board is the representative, and other members' views may not be well represented.

Because there are pluses and minuses to both structures, it would seem to us unlikely that a single structure is better suited for all financial regulation in the United States. It appears that the OCC, as a single-headed agency, has had a long-standing (since 1863) record and reputation for successful operation, but so has the FDIC, which has been in existence since 1933 and which is headed by a five-person board.[205]

Whatever the merits of any particular leadership structure for an agency, it is surely the case that the transition from a single-headed agency to an agency that is led by a multi-person board will involve time and disruption—which will slow down regulatory processes. Again, although the drafters of the CHOICE Act may favor impediments to the administrative state as a general matter, we do not.

Further, it is our perception that the drafters of the CHOICE Act are primarily unhappy about the CFPB and its single-headed structure. If this is the case, a provision that was more tightly focused on the CFPB—and that allowed the OCC and the FHFA to remain with their current structures—would better achieve the drafters' goal of improving the structure of the CFPB.

Conclusion

Title VI of the Financial CHOICE Act, which broadly addresses financial regulatory processes and structures, is a reaction to what the drafters perceive as the excesses of the Dodd-Frank Act and the misguided actions of financial regulators both before and since the passage of Dodd-Frank. Although the drafters express a laudable desire to improve the quality of financial regulation (e.g., through cost-benefit analysis), it appears that they also want—implicitly, if

---

[205] Unlike most other multi-person boards, two of the five members of the FDIC's board are currently designated by statute to be the Comptroller of the Currency (i.e., the head of the OCC) and the Director of the CFPB.

not explicitly—generally to slow the processes of regulation and reduce the overall burden of regulation through the broad changes that are encompassed in Title VI.

On this last point, we are concerned that the creation of an institutional bias against regulation will systemically undervalue the benefits of regulation even while limiting its costs. In our view, the goals of better regulation would be better served by a narrower focus on the places where financial regulations are seen to be a special problem, rather than broadly throwing sand in the gears of the regulatory process.

More specifically, with respect to the four areas of Title VI addressed here:

- We favor broad use of cost-benefit analysis but worry that a requirement of such analysis will stand in the way of regulation that would likely be beneficial even if the case for such benefit rests on relatively sparse evidence. Thus, we oppose any arbitrary evidentiary threshold generally applicable to all financial regulation. We encourage searching cost-benefit analysis in specific areas that are most likely to be conducive to such analysis, for its own sake and so as to promote a culture of close analysis within the agencies. We also favor a requirement that the promulgating agency provide a Cost Effectiveness report in the event that the circumstances do not support a traditional quantifiable cost-benefit analysis; such report would explain the agency's process and reasons for the limited nature of its analysis.

- We recommend against the CHOICE Act's requirement that major financial regulations would take effect only if approved by a joint resolution of Congress and by the President. Such a requirement would, in essence, eliminate major regulation and replace it, if at all, through the slower, and more fraught, legislative process. The result would be an impediment not only to detrimental rules, but also to beneficial ones as well, and would not be a good use of Congress's scarce time and resources.

- We recommend that the <u>Chevron</u> deference be retained in judicial review of financial agency regulation. In our view, such deference is a sensible mechanism for economizing on scarce judicial resources and as a means of encouraging an integrated strategy of statutory application.

- Although we take no general position on the wisdom of structuring a financial regulatory agency as a single-headed organization or as an entity that is headed by a multi-person board, we note that the transition from a single-headed to a multi-person-headed organization is likely to be accompanied by organizational disarray, as is the case during any transition. To the extent that the drafters' unhappiness with a single-headed organization is focused on the CFPB, we urge that the board requirement be narrowly applied to the CFPB, so that the OCC and the FHFA be spared the costs of a transition.

It is surely true that the processes and structures of financial regulation can be improved. However, the provisions of Title VI should be restructured and more narrowly focused, so as to achieve those improvements more effectively.

What's *Not* in the CHOICE Act or Dodd-Frank

Streamlining the Regulatory Apparatus

By Kermit L. Schoenholtz

> *"The system for regulating financial institutions in the United States is highly fragmented, outdated and ineffective. A multitude of federal agencies, self-regulatory organizations, and state authorities share oversight of the financial system under a framework riddled with regulatory gaps, loopholes and inefficiencies."* The Volcker Alliance, Reshaping the Financial Regulatory System: Long Delayed, Now Crucial, 2015.

The Great Financial Crisis of 2007-2009, the most severe since the Great Depression, provides stark evidence of a colossal failure of U.S. financial regulation and supervision. In the United States, one of the reasons for that failure is the "complex, incoherent and fragmented regulatory system." This byzantine apparatus made it virtually impossible for an observer—either a market participant, a financial executive, or a regulator—to view the financial system as a whole and to detect its vulnerabilities.

The U.S. regulatory system has been characterized as a "Rube Goldberg regulatory framework that is (fortunately) unique to the United States" (Cecchetti and Schoenholtz, "The Scandal is What's Legal," Money and Banking Blog, February 8, 2016). At the federal level, we have three bank regulators (the Federal Deposit Insurance Corporation, the Federal Reserve, and the Office of the Comptroller of the Currency) and two financial market regulators (the Commodity Futures Trading Commission and the Securities and Exchange Commission), as well as specialized regulators for a range of institutions and activities (including the National Credit Union Administration and the Federal Housing Finance Agency). We also have a college of regulators, the Financial System Oversight Council

(FSOC), along with a Federal Insurance Office (FIO) that monitors that sector, and the Consumer Financial Protection Bureau (CFPB).

But this is only the tip of the regulatory iceberg. *Each state* has its own banking regulator. The states also have sole authority for the regulation and supervision of insurance and have their own state guarantee funds to backstop insurance contracts. State attorneys general also occasionally use state laws to impose structural changes in the financial industry (as in New York's numerous conflict-of-interest suits against securities firms). Finally, on top of the federal and state regulators, there also are the officially authorized self-regulatory organizations, such as the Financial Industry Regulatory Authority and the Municipal Securities Rulemaking Board, along with the numerous finance and real estate industry associations that intensively lobby regulators and legislators alike.

This mix of complexity, loopholes and inefficiency is *not* news. An October 2004 Government Accountability Office report, appropriately titled "Industry Changes Prompt Need to Reconsider U.S. Regulatory Structure," highlighted the challenge both from the perspective of regulators and of the managers of a large, complex intermediary. Taken from that report, the following figure depicts the regulators of the various operations of a hypothetical financial holding company. With each regulator obtaining only a narrow stream of information about its slice of the holding company, no one is properly placed to assess the risks posed by the entire company to the financial system. At the same time, the company executives are unlikely to know precisely who is responsible for regulating each aspect of their enterprise, and may be especially uncertain in a crisis about how its multiple regulators will work (in concert or in opposition) to address the firm's issues. And, this still leaves out the extraordinary challenges facing internationally active intermediaries that also face numerous foreign regulators.

Regulators for a Hypothetical Financial Holding Company

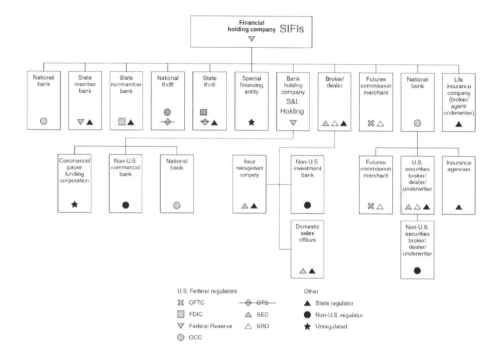

Note: Horizontal hash marks are author's changes highlighting the impact of Dodd-Frank, which eliminated the Treasury Office of Thrift Supervision (OTS), placed thrifts under other regulators, introduced SIFIs, and placed S&L holding companies under the jurisdiction of the Federal Reserve. Source: Government Accountability Office, GAO-05-61, Figure 9, October 2004.

The 2007-2009 crisis revealed key weaknesses of the U.S. regulatory framework. Financial firms had evolved over time in ways that narrowed the differences between their economic functions (say, insurers versus banks), but their regulation remained segmented by their legal form, much as it had been since the 1930s. Above all, despite the vast expansion of *de facto* banking (as opposed to *de jure* banking) over the decades before the crisis, there was little prudential oversight over *de facto* bank activities, and virtually no awareness of the systemic vulnerabilities they created.

Yet, despite the biggest financial crisis since the 1930s, the Dodd-Frank Act did almost nothing to simplify the U.S. regulatory structure. Dodd-Frank eliminated just one federal regulator—the Office of Thrift Supervision (OTS)—which was arguably the most ineffective of the lot. The OTS had supervised AIG (because of a Delaware thrift that it owned), Countrywide, IndyMac, and Washington Mutual, all of which failed (or probably would have failed without federal support) in the 2007-2009 episode. Dodd-Frank added further to the mix by creating the CFPB, the FIO, FSOC, and FSOC's information-gathering and assessment arm, the Office of Financial Research (OFR).

To the extent that there is any coordination at all, it is through the FSOC. But the FSOC's authority over the various federal regulators is quite limited (consider, for example, the Securities and Exchange Commission's resistance to reform of money-market mutual funds, the most bank-like of *de facto* banks). And, the FSOC has no direct influence over the state regulators or attorneys general.

Like Dodd-Frank, the Financial CHOICE Act also fails utterly to simplify this regulatory framework. The only organization that it would fully eliminate is the relatively tiny OFR that focuses on data collection and analysis and has no direct supervisory role. The CHOICE Act's assertion that the OFR is redundant is wrong: While research divisions exist in each federal regulatory organization, they focus primarily on the risks arising either from their direct regulatees or the markets that they supervise. In contrast, the OFR is legally mandated to view the financial system as a whole in order to identify vulnerabilities that the FSOC should consider as potential systemic threats. Indeed, as the 2015 report of The Volcker Alliance has argued, "an appropriately empowered OFR could play the very important role of serving as a check on the agencies involved in financial stability, raising important questions, challenging conventional wisdom, and spurring action when necessary."[206]

Could U.S. regulatory arrangements be radically streamlined, making the system more effective and less wasteful? Undoubtedly. The challenge of doing so is not conceptual, but political. Regardless of which party has majority control, Congress has shown no inclination over time to simplify the system. A Volcker Alliance background report (Elizabeth F. Brown, "Prior Proposals to Consolidate Federal Financial Regulators") details more than a dozen proposals since 1960 for consolidating the U.S. regulatory system. The 2007-2009 financial crisis undermined many of the oft-repeated arguments against consolidation (such as reduced benefits of regulatory competition), leaving mainly the political turf considerations that animate the reluctance of the regulatory agencies themselves and, possibly, the Congressional committees that oversee them.

One recent and useful example of a proposed reform that did not receive serious Congressional consideration is the Treasury Department's Blueprint for a Modernized Financial Regulatory Structure, published in March 2008 under Secretary Henry Paulson. The Blueprint thoughtfully acknowledged the "convergence of the financial services industry" in which intermediaries of different legal forms had evolved to provide services with similar economic functions. Its "optimal regulatory structure" shifted away from "institutionally based" regulation—which it viewed as broadly consistent with a segmented financial structure—to "activities-based" regulation. The key advantage of the latter "approach is that the same set of rules would apply to all institutions performing a particular activity." It foresaw five agencies: a market stability regulator, a prudential financial regulator, a business conduct regulator, a corporate finance regulator, and a Federal Insurance

---

[206] For the purpose of full disclosure, the author serves on the Financial Research Advisory Committee to the OFR.

Guarantee Corporation. Importantly, the prudential regulator would have oversight over any intermediary with a government guarantee (including either a continued state-level, or alternative federal, guarantee for insurers).

The CHOICE Act takes none of the steps—even those far short of the Blueprint's optimal structure—that have been widely viewed as desirable simplification. For example, numerous proposals have called for combining the SEC and CFTC into one capital markets regulator. Similarly, one can easily imagine the creation of a single banking regulator (to replace the FDIC, Federal Reserve and OCC, as well as the state regulators) or a single insurance regulator and a federal guarantee fund (to replace the state-level operations that have become antiquated in a global financial system).

By contrast to the United States, most advanced economies have regulatory systems that are quite simple (see, for example, Elizabeth F. Brown, "Consolidated Financial Regulation: Six National Case Studies and the European Union Experience," the Volcker Alliance). As the economy with one of the world's most competitive financial centers, and one of the world's largest banking sectors relative to its national income, the United Kingdom provides an important and useful regulatory benchmark for the United States. The U.K. regulatory system is composed of only three institutions: the Financial Policy Committee (FPC), the Prudential Regulatory Authority (PRA), and the Financial Conduct Authority (FCA). The FPC and the PRA are housed within the Bank of England (BoE). The FPC is responsible for macroprudential policy, while the PRA implements microprudential oversight over depositories, insurers and major investment firms. The FCA, organized outside of the Bank, sets conduct rules for more than 50,000 financial services firms and acts as the prudential regulator for firms not supervised by the PRA. Importantly, as the diagram below highlights, the BoE's Governor and Deputy Governor for Financial Stability serve on the PRA Board *and* the FPC (as well as the Monetary Policy Committee), encouraging the timely dissemination among policymakers of critical information about institutional and systemic vulnerabilities.

Membership of Bank of England Policy Committees

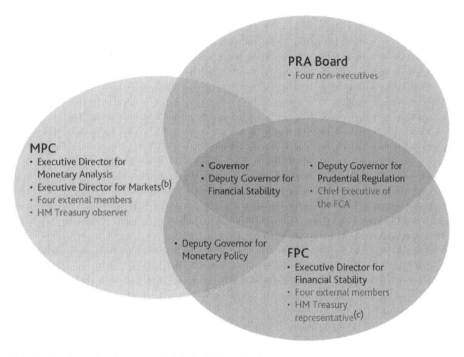

(a) Members shown in red are not part of the Bank's Executive Team.
(b) The Executive Director for Markets will also routinely attend FPC meetings.
(c) Non-voting member of the FPC.

Source: Paul Tucker, Simon Hall, and Aashish Pattani, "Macroprudential policy at the Bank of England," *Quarterly Bulletin* 2013 Q3.

Surely, if U.S. policymakers wished to make the regulatory framework both effective and efficient, the United States is capable of organizing a system just as streamlined as that of the United Kingdom. The failure to do so reduces the nation's attractiveness as a venue for global financial activity and makes it vulnerable to future crises. This problem seems reminiscent of the period prior to the 1913 creation of the Federal Reserve, when the advanced nations of Europe viewed the U.S. banking system as dangerously fragmented and backward, and lacking a mechanism (a central bank acting as lender of last resort) to prevent and mitigate all-too-frequent panics.

The CHOICE Act simply does not address this problem of a byzantine regulatory framework.

De Facto Banking Activities

By Kermit L. Schoenholtz

> *"Important as banking reforms may be, it is worth recalling that the trigger for the acute phase of the financial crisis was the rapid unwinding of large amounts of short-term wholesale funding that had been made available to highly leveraged and/or maturity-transforming financial firms that were not subject to consolidated prudential supervision."* Janet Yellen, Regulatory Landscapes: A U.S. Perspective, June 2, 2013.

In this paper, we have defined *de facto banking* as the transformation of liquidity, maturity and credit by financial intermediaries other than traditional banks. Dodd-Frank focused on the systemic risks associated with *de facto* banking that arise in the largest, most complex, and most interconnected financial institutions. It provided authority to the Financial Stability Oversight Council (FSOC) to designate nonbanks as systemically important financial institutions (SIFIs) and placed them under the stricter supervisory regime of the Federal Reserve. The same applies to certain clearing, payments and settlements firms, which can be designated as financial market utilities (FMUs) and placed under joint supervision of both their traditional regulator and the Federal Reserve. As we have seen, the Financial CHOICE Act revokes the authority of the FSOC to designate SIFIs and FMUs and rescinds prior designations.

Importantly, neither Dodd-Frank nor the CHOICE Act addresses the systemic risks arising from *de facto banking activities* per se. These activities involve transformations of liquidity, maturity, and credit that "take place without direct and explicit access to public sources of liquidity or credit backstops" (see Pozsar, Adrian, Ashcraft, and Boesky, 2013). They are typically financed by systemically important liabilities (SIL) that have no government guarantee or insurance (see Acharya and Öncü, 2013) and that (like uninsured bank deposits) are subject to a run. As examples, SILs include repurchase agreements, securities lending, and asset-backed commercial paper (ABCP).

Following Acharya and Öncü, *de facto* banking becomes a systemic threat when SILs are used to finance systemically important assets (SIA). SIAs are either the SILs of other highly leveraged intermediaries (fueling interconnectedness and systemic vulnerability) or high-risk assets that can become illiquid. The latter includes loans to systemic intermediaries, mortgage-backed securities (MBS)—especially when used as collateral for repo or financed through securities lending—ABCP, and the like.

How substantial is *de facto* banking activity today? Updated estimates provided by the Federal Reserve Bank of New York show gross liabilities of *de facto* banks (including those held by other *de facto* banks) totaled $15.6 trillion as of mid-2016, compared with $19.1 trillion for traditional banks (including chartered depositories, foreign banking offices, and bank holding companies). As the following chart highlights, *de facto* banking liabilities have shrunk from the 2008 peak of $21.6 trillion near the height of the financial crisis. Yet, most of this plunge occurred *prior* to the Dodd-Frank Act (in July 2010), reflecting the demise of the business model of wholesale funding for potentially illiquid, high-risk assets, rather than the impact of regulation.

Traditional and *De Facto* Banking Liabilities (Trillions of U.S. dollars)

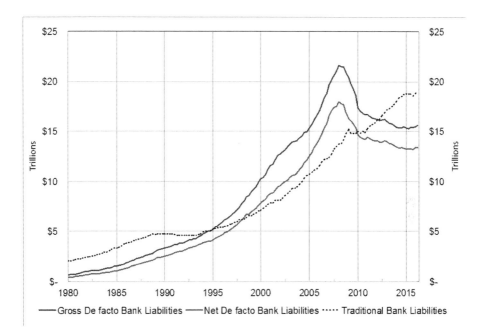

Source: Update courtesy of Federal Reserve Bank of New York; based on Pozsar, Adrian, Ashcraft, and Boesky, Shadow Banking, FRBNY *Economic Policy Review* 19(2) (2013). Underlying data from Financial Accounts of the United States. Shadow banking liabilities include money market mutual funds, open-market paper, agency and GSE-backed securities, mortgages in mortgage pools, asset-backed securities issuers, federal funds and securities repurchase agreements and security RPs of the monetary authority.

Amid the financial crisis of 2007-2009, the Federal Reserve frequently resorted to the use of its emergency facilities to backstop SILs of intermediaries that had paid no *ex ante* premium for this liquidity insurance. For example, the Fed's Commercial Paper Funding Facility (CPFF) provided support for ABCP issuance, while the Primary Dealer Credit Facility (PDCF) effectively supported the tri-party repo funding of broker dealers. As Pozsar et al (2013) note, "upon the complete rollout of the liquidity facilities and guarantee schemes, the shadow banking system was fully embraced by official credit and liquidity puts and became fully backstopped, just like the traditional banking system."

The combination of the government's support in the crisis of 2007-2009 and the failure to address *de facto* banking activities per se in either the Dodd-Frank or CHOICE Acts creates an enormous moral hazard in the U.S. financial system. Intermediaries outside traditional banking will be inclined to issue SILs and to hold SIAs with the understanding that: (a) there remains no *ex ante* fee for imposing such risks on the financial system; and (b) they can expect that emergency liquidity facilities will be provided to sustain *de facto* banking activities in the face of a financial crisis.

Even worse, the necessary and desirable imposition of higher capital and liquidity requirements on traditional bank activities incentivizes the migration of systemic risk-taking to the world of *de facto* banking. To be sure, traditional banking has expanded in recent years, while *de facto* banking has stagnated, but the continued upward ratcheting of bank capital requirements—as favored by this author—could reverse this pattern unless the incentives for risk migration are contained.

One simple and attractive approach is that recently proposed in the Minneapolis Plan to End Too Big to Fail: namely, to impose a broad Pigouvian tax on *de facto* bank liabilities. The Minneapolis Plan estimates that a 15% leverage ratio requirement on the largest, most systemic banks would result in a funding cost increase equivalent to a 1.2% tax on the *de facto* bank liabilities. While that calibration requires careful review, the application of a simple tax on SILs to limit risk migration is consistent with the fundamental principles of effective regulation articulated in an earlier NYU Stern volume, *Regulating Wall Street* (2010). And, just as systemic risk is analogous to pollution—both resulting from externalities and poor incentives—a tax on SILs to limit systemic risk corresponds to a carbon tax, the mechanism that many economists favor as a means of limiting environmental risks (see, for example, Mankiw (2009)).

Alternative approaches also should be considered, including the outright prohibition of some *de facto* bank activities. For example, it may be more effective to forbid the recipient of high-quality collateral in a securities loan to sell that collateral and invest the proceeds in riskier assets. This form of liquidity, maturity and credit transformation can be difficult to observe (and therefore to tax), and it appears to be an important means by which life insurers engage in *de facto* banking (see Foley-Fisher, Narajabad, and Verani, 2016).

To conclude, we believe that the CHOICE Act would increase the systemic threat arising from *de facto* banking by revoking the FSOC's SIFI authority and by failing to introduce any means to prevent risk migration from the traditional bank sector.

What to Do about the GSEs?

By Matthew P. Richardson, Stijn van Nieuwerburgh and Lawrence J. White

Introduction

Fannie Mae and Freddie Mac—the two large "Government-Sponsored Enterprises" (GSEs) that are at the center of U.S. residential mortgage finance[207]—remain the "elephants in the room" that are being ignored as part of broad-brush financial sector reform. Neither the Dodd-Frank Act nor the proposed Financial CHOICE Act have addressed the reform of the GSEs' structures—even though the GSEs were placed in government conservatorships in early September 2008 and have remained in that state since then.

Nevertheless, as we argue in this section, their reform is essential for a more efficient housing finance system.

Accordingly, there are two central issues for financial reform with respect to the GSEs: first, the immediate issue of what should be done with/about the GSEs; and second, the larger issues of how residential mortgages should be financed and how U.S. public policy toward housing finance and toward housing, more generally, should be structured.

---

[207] There is one additional large GSE—the Federal Home Loan Bank System (FHLBS)—that will not be addressed in this section. The FHLBS is a group of 11 large wholesale banks that collectively borrow in the capital markets and provide wholesale financing for banks and other depository institutions. As of year-end 2015, the FHLBS had $969 billion in assets. Any legislative reform of Fannie Mae and Freddie Mac would likely—and should—include the reform of the FHLBS. More detail on the FHLBS can be found in Frame and White (2011). For the remainder of this section, references to "GSEs" will mean only Fannie Mae and Freddie Mac, unless otherwise indicated.

What the GSEs Do[208]

Fannie Mae and Freddie Mac are large financial institutions that operate in the secondary mortgage market. They buy residential mortgages[209] from mortgage originators—banks[210] and mortgage companies[211]—and bundle the mortgages into pass-through mortgage-backed securities (MBS) that are sold in the capital markets. Those MBS carry the GSEs' guarantees to the MBS investors against losses due to credit risks on the underlying mortgages.[212] They charge a small fee to the mortgage originators for this guarantee and, at least in the past, were required to hold $0.45 of capital for every $100 of mortgage face value guaranteed.

In addition, both banks and the GSEs keep some of the mortgages on their own balance sheets, financing these retained mortgages

---

[208] More detail on Fannie Mae and Freddie Mac can be found in Frame and White (2005), and Acharya, Richardson, Van Nieuwerburgh, and White (2011); see also Jaffee, Richardson, Van Nieuwerburgh, White and Wright (2009) and Acharya, Oncu, Richardson, Van Nieuwerburgh, and White (2011).

[209] The mortgages that they buy must conform to specified standards and are thus described as "conforming loans:" There are limits on the value/size of the mortgage that can be bought; and the mortgage borrowers are expected to make a 20% down payment (unless they obtain mortgage insurance or there is some other support for the mortgage) and to have credit scores that make them good credit risks.

[210] Unless otherwise indicated, by "banks" we mean commercial banks and other depository institutions, such as savings institutions and credit unions.

[211] These are companies that originate mortgages and immediately sell them in the secondary market; they are sometimes described as "mortgage banks."

[212] The GSEs charge an annual "guarantee fee" ("g-fee") for that credit-risk guarantee. Elenev, Landvoigt, and Van Nieuwerburgh (2016) argue that this guarantee fee was substantially underpriced prior to the crisis. This led to a system with too much mortgage credit extension, more risky mortgages, a more levered financial system, and artificially inflated house prices. A radical increase in g-fees would crowd in the private sector and remedy these issues.

with deposits (for banks) and debt (for the GSEs).[213] During the financial crisis, banks and GSEs purchased large amounts of both prime and nonprime (Alt-A and subprime) mortgage-backed securities. While the GSEs were required to hold just $2.50 for every $100, banks were required to hold an even smaller amount, i.e., $1.60, if the MBS were guaranteed by the GSEs. Coupled with the aforementioned $0.45 capital requirement for GSE guarantees, the total capital required in the system was then a paltry $2.05. This is approximately half the $4.00 per $100 of mortgage assets that banks were required to hold on their balance sheets for the *exact same mortgage loans* without involvement of the GSEs.

Only Washington D.C. could dream up such a system.[214] Given both the implicit guarantee of the U.S. Government (resulting in a below-market cost for debt financing) and favorable capital requirements, the GSEs grew unencumbered for decades. From the last major GSE legislation in 1992, for example, Fannie Mae and Freddie Mac combined went from holding $153 billion in mortgages and guaranteeing the credit risk of another $714 billion to holding $1.4 trillion and guaranteeing $3.5 trillion, respectively, by the end of 2007.

The GSEs still play a major role in housing finance. During 2015, the GSEs' mortgage purchases accounted for approximately 45% of all single-family mortgage originations; and as of October 2016, their outstanding MBS guarantees plus the mortgages that they held on

---

[213] The GSEs financed these asset purchases by issuing debt (so-called "agency" debt). Because of the implicit government guarantee (which has now become an explicit guarantee), the GSEs are able to borrow at below-market interest rates: below what an otherwise-similar company (but without the guarantee) would have to pay.

[214] David Frum, a former speechwriter for President George W. Bush, writes in the National Post, July 11, 2008: "The shapers of the American mortgage finance system hoped to achieve the security of government ownership, the integrity of local banking and the ingenuity of Wall Street. Instead they got the ingenuity of government, the security of local banking and the integrity of Wall Street."

their respective balance sheets accounted for 49% of all single-family residential mortgages.[215]

To understand how this happened, note that, as GSEs, they are hybrid organizations: They each have corporate structures, with private shareholders and boards of directors. But their charters come from Congressional legislation (and not, for example, from the state of Delaware); the President had the power to appoint five of the 18 directors on their respective boards; and they have had special access to U.S. Treasury financing and other special government-related privileges. Hence, they are described as "government-sponsored enterprises." The problem with the GSEs is that capital markets have always treated them as special—with the strong expectation that the Federal Government would support their creditors if the GSEs had financial difficulties; and thus (as mentioned above), the GSEs were able to finance themselves at a lower cost than their financial structures would otherwise have warranted.

The Conservatorships

Although the GSEs had had a history of conservative operation and substantial profitability, that discipline broke down in the early 2000s: The "private-label" (i.e., non-GSE) MBS (PLMBS) sector grew rapidly; and, to protect their market shares, the GSEs expanded their operations into buying and securitizing more risky mortgages than had previously been true. However, the aforementioned levels

---

[215] The GSEs operate also in the secondary mortgage market for multi-family housing, but that is a far less important part of their operations; the mortgage market for multi-family housing is about a tenth of the size of the single-family mortgage market. In addition to the GSEs, Ginnie Mae (which is an agency within the U.S. Department of Housing and Urban Development) securitizes mortgages that are insured by the Federal Housing Administration (FHA), the Department of Veterans Affairs (VA), and U.S. Department of Agriculture. And banks hold some residential mortgages—typically those that exceed the conforming loan value limit and/or that don't meet the documentation or other criteria of the GSEs—on their own balance sheets.

of equity financing that they were required to maintain—only 0.45% against their MBS credit-risk guarantees, and 2.5% against the mortgages that they held on their balance sheets—were not sufficient to protect them against the potential credit losses of these more risky mortgages.

The GSEs' profitability fell in 2006, and they ran losses in 2007 and the first half of 2008. By the late summer of 2008, they were approaching insolvency; and on September 6, 2008, they were placed into government conservatorships.[216] In essence, they were placed under the direct control of their regulator—the Federal Housing Finance Agency (FHFA)—where they remain today.

The capital markets' expectations that the GSEs' creditors would remain whole in the event of financial difficulties proved to be accurate: The direct creditors (bondholders) to the GSEs—including subordinated debt holders—have not suffered losses as a consequence of the conservatorships, and the GSEs' guarantees to their MBS investors have been honored as well.[217]

Important Changes during the Conservatorships

Prior to the conservatorships, the GSEs' critics worried that their on-balance sheet holdings of mortgages had ballooned because of their favorable financing from the capital markets (due to their GSE status) and because their equity-financing requirement for these mortgages was only 2.5%. In essence, they worried that the GSEs

---

[216] A discussion of the conservatorship decision and processes can be found in Frame, Fuster, Tracy, and Vickery (2015). See also Sorkin (2009), Poulson (2010), Morgenson and Rosner (2011), Hagerty (2012), Howard (2014), and McLean (2015).

[217] However, the common equity shareholders were wiped out, and the preferred shareholders were diluted—with the U.S. Treasury acquiring a 79.9% ownership—but not eliminated. The preferred shareholders—which are now largely hedge funds and private equity funds—are currently suing the Federal Government over the legality of the continued conservatorships and the Treasury's absorption of all of the current operating profits of the GSEs.

had become very large, highly leveraged, and (possibly) maturity-mismatched "hedge funds" for the benefit of their shareholders. Subsequent to the conservatorship, there was the realization that their credit-risk guarantees on their MBS also posed a risk to the Federal Government—again, because of the GSEs' special status and the beliefs of the capital markets that the Federal Government would cover the GSEs' losses at a time of financial difficulties, as had actually happened in 2008 and would likely happen again.

The FHFA has taken actions to address both of these concerns: First, the size of the GSEs' balance sheets has shrunk. Whereas at year-end 2008 (shortly after the onset of the conservatorships) Fannie Mae had on-balance sheet mortgage holdings of $768 billion and Freddie Mac had on-balance sheet mortgage holdings of $749 billion, as of the third quarter of 2016, their on-balance sheet mortgage holdings were $307 billion and $308 billion, respectively.

With regard to the second issue, the GSEs have been reducing the credit risks on the mortgages that they own and have guaranteed through two mechanisms: a) They have been buying insurance against credit losses on the mortgages; and b) they have issued the rough equivalent of "catastrophe bonds," whereby the bond buyer is repaid less principal in the event of credit losses on the underlying mortgages.[218] In essence, the GSEs have privatized some of these credit risks through these "front-end" (insurance) and "back-end" (CRT) transactions. As of November 2016, the risks on 23.7% of Fannie Mae's guarantees and 34.9% of Freddie Mac's guarantees had been privatized in this way. In addition, the annual guarantee fees on the GSEs' MBS—which had been in the range of 20-25 basis points—have more than doubled to a range of 50-60 basis points. In conjunction with the privatization of some of the GSEs' risks (which, as we discuss below, we strongly endorse), the higher g-fees have meant that the GSEs appear to be earning more

---

[218] These bonds are frequently described as "credit risk transfer" (CRT) transactions.

in compensation for default risk than they have been paying for insurance and to the investors in the catastrophe bonds.

The GSEs: What Dodd-Frank Did and the CHOICE Act Proposes to Do

As mentioned earlier, Dodd-Frank did nothing substantive with respect to the GSEs. Section 1074 of Dodd-Frank mandated a report by the Treasury on what should be done about the GSEs. The Obama Administration delivered its report in February 2011. That report provided a range of choices as to possible actions, but did not indicate what course of action the Obama Administration endorsed.[219]

The proposed CHOICE Act similarly avoids any substantive actions with respect to the GSEs. Like Dodd-Frank, it requires the Treasury to report to the Congress; however, the CHOICE Act requires annual reports (Section 336) rather than the single report specified in Dodd-Frank.

Why Have the GSEs Been the "Elephants in the Room?"

Before we offer our recommendations for the disposition of the GSEs and for housing finance and housing policy more generally, it is worth considering why the GSEs were ignored by Dodd-Frank and seem likely to be ignored by the proposed CHOICE Act.

First, the crisis that precipitated the conservatorships for the GSEs has passed. The GSEs are not currently engaging in the kinds of risky activities that brought them to the brink of insolvency in 2008. Although the GSEs in conservatorships jointly had to draw on the Treasury for $188 billion to avoid insolvency, they have

---

[219] Dodd-Frank devoted a considerable amount of attention to regulation with respect to residential mortgages, which have some indirect consequences—often favorable—for the GSEs.

subsequently produced positive earnings and have made payments to the Treasury totaling $250 billion.[220] That the GSEs are currently making positive contributions to the Treasury is no small thing when the overall Federal budget continues to run substantial annual deficits.

In addition, as discussed above, the FHFA has required the GSEs to take actions—shrink their balance sheets, offload some of their risks to the private sector, double their annual guarantee fees—that have reduced the Federal Government's exposure to the downside risks of the GSEs' actions. Again, the crisis has passed.

Second, broadly encouraging and subsidizing home ownership (and also rental housing, which the GSEs also finance) has been a politically popular activity. It is even more popular when the subsidy is implicit and off-budget, as has been true because of the special GSE status of the two organizations. Any proposed reform of the GSEs would likely reduce the extent of government backing for them and thereby raise mortgage costs for their future borrowers. A substantial fraction of the Congress would immediately object.

Third, any proposals to reform Fannie Mae and Freddie Mac would raise the question of whether the other large GSE, the FHLBS, should also be reformed. That prospect adds an extra set of issues and controversies.

---

[220] This fact deserves two comments. First, these are nominal sums and do not take into account the time value of money. Whether one believes that the GSEs have completely "paid back" their original draws on the Federal Government depends on what one thinks the appropriate interest rate on the government investment in the GSEs should be. It is worth recalling that at the time of the conservatorships the GSEs were unable to raise funds in the capital markets—i.e., private investors were unwilling to lend to them. Second, these earnings do not incorporate potential losses from future mortgage defaults that may arise if another widespread housing collapse occurs. Since the financial crisis of 2007-2009, housing prices have mostly recovered, and therefore there have been far fewer defaults. Extensive defaults take place only during periods when housing prices fall, so earnings of the GSEs will tend to be asymmetric.

In recognition of all of this, in addition to the silence of Dodd-Frank and the CHOICE Act with respect to the reform of the GSEs, there have been very few specific legislative proposals aimed at addressing the GSEs. During 2013-2014, there were a few exceptions—such as the Corker-Warner Act, the Johnson-Crapo Act, and the Protecting American Taxpayers and Homeowners (PATH) Act[221]—that gained some media attention but then lost momentum without being passed by the Congress. We comment on these proposals in a later section.

What Should Be Done?

The goal of reforming housing finance should be to ensure an efficient mortgage market, both in primary (origination) as well as in secondary mortgage markets. We have in mind a housing finance system that incorporates the following:

- Corrects any market failures if they exist—notably, in this case: (i) unpriced government guarantees that destroy market discipline and lead to below-market borrowing rates, encouraging excess leverage and risk taking; and (ii) the externality from undertaking too much credit and interest rate risk, as this risk is inherently systemic in nature;

- Maintains a level playing field between the different financial players in the mortgage market to limit a concentrated buildup of systemic risk;

- Does not engender moral hazard issues in mortgage origination and securitization; and

---

[221] See http://www.housingwire.com/ext/resources/files/Editorial/GSELegislativeProp osalsComparison.pdf for detailed summaries of all three bills.

- Does not inject public housing policy into the mortgage finance system.

As a result of what we learned from the financial crisis, the mortgage finance system should be one that is primarily private in nature, involving the securitization of mortgages that conform to reasonable credit quality and are standardized with the underlying credit risk being borne by investors, perhaps with some support from private guarantors—in other words, with few guarantees (if any) from the government. We see no reason why the system cannot be capital-market based (i.e., relying on securitization), compared to bank-based. The institutions involved in this endeavor should not be housed in government, and, to the extent securitization requires government guarantees of tail credit risk, these guarantees must be priced by the market.

Housing Finance and Private Securitization

The question is how does one effectively get to this private system given the current state of mortgage finance? We call this the "genie in the bottle" problem. A quarter century ago, the proverbial "genie" was let out of the bottle when mortgage markets were exposed to wider market forces, yet the government guarantees and special treatment of Fannie Mae and Freddie Mac were left in place. Capital markets over the past 25 years have come to rely on these guarantees. To wean the system off these guarantees—to put the "genie back in the bottle"—we need to transition away from a government-backed system to a private-based one. The problem is that the transitional process will only succeed if private markets are not crowded out, regulatory capital arbitrage by private guarantors is averted, and the systemic risk that is inherent in mortgage credit and interest rate risks is managed.

There has been some limited success at moving in this direction. Even though the GSEs remain front and center of the mortgage market, they have been shrinking their portfolio of mortgages, effectively reducing their footprint. Also, the GSEs' guarantee fees were increased after the crisis, thus reducing the market subsidy and, in theory, increasing market discipline. Moreover, a 2015 report by the FHFA argued that the guarantee fees were consistent with the pricing implied by the GSEs' credit-risk transfer (CRT) transactions.[222] Nevertheless, on the downside, these GSE reforms do not seem to have led to a significant re-emergence of PLMBS.

In the aftermath of the 2006 housing market collapse and the concomitant collapse of the PLMBS market, there has been no revival of significant PLMBS activity. The reasons for this absence aren't entirely clear. Among the possibilities: fears of a renewal of the moral hazard behavior by mortgage originators and securities packagers; continued uncertainty over the legal liabilities of private issuers and originators (with respect to their representations and warranties); distrust of the credit rating agencies' ratings for PLMBS; continued favorable capital treatment (a 1.6% equity financing requirement) that applies to the GSEs' MBS when they are bought by banks; and a lack of comfort and familiarity by insurance companies and pension funds (who would be the natural buyers of long-lived MBS that are based on 30-year fixed-rate mortgages) for PLMBS.

It is often argued that mortgage finance necessarily requires heavy government involvement, in particular, guarantees of mortgage defaults. This is clearly untrue. The cross-section of mortgage funding models across various developed countries shows that few countries have any entities that resemble Fannie Mae or Freddie Mac. The majority of countries rely on a deposit-based system in which the mortgage lender retains the mortgage loans on their books. These institutions are subject to prudential regulation just like any other bank. And the argument cannot be that this has a major impact on homeownership rates. Of the 25 most developed

---

[222] See, for example, https://www.fhfa.gov/Media/PublicAffairs/Pages/Results-of-Fannie-Mae-and-Freddie-Mac-Guarantee-Fee-Review.aspx.

countries, the U.S. ranks 17th. What is unique about U.S. mortgage finance is that almost two thirds of all mortgages are securitized, whereas abroad, for the next largest securitizers—Australia and Canada—it's only around 20%.[223]

In the mortgage finance systems abroad, lenders retain the risk of mortgages ("skin in the game"). Yet there are reasonable economic grounds for preferring the U.S. mortgage finance system of securitization. Securitization truly can turn "lead into gold:" Securitization takes illiquid mortgage loans and pools them to form liquid MBS that trade on the secondary market. Because illiquidity commands a risk premium, the more liquid mortgage assets from securitization command better prices and thus a reduced mortgage rate. An additional benefit is that the credit risk gets transferred out of the systemically risky banking sector to the capital market at large. In other words, if securitization works the way it is supposed to, the banking sector can better share its mortgage risks with rest of the economy. Finally, MBS provide banks with access to investors worldwide, which diversifies their funding base.

However, since mortgage default guarantees were an essential element of the development and liquidity of the mortgage securitization market, it seems likely that investors would continue to demand mortgage default insurance in some form or another (at least in the short term).[224] The problem is that the private sector cannot be the sole provider, as this insurance is systemic due to its dependence on macroeconomic events, resulting in mispriced negative externalities. Yet because there is no accountability (let

---

[223] Denmark's mortgage market relies for 90% of financing on covered bonds, which are a close cousin of mortgage-backed securities, but which provide investors with full recourse not only to the mortgage loans but also to the bank's capital. Several other European countries, such as Germany, the U.K., and Spain, have substantial covered bond market shares.

[224] This statement is controversial. There are other parts of the capital market, albeit smaller and less liquid, that function just fine without guarantees of the underlying credit risk. Two examples include corporate bonds and commercial MBS.

---

alone political considerations) and the incentive structure is not right, the public sector cannot step into the breach.

In Acharya, Richardson, Van Nieuwerburgh and White (2011), we argue for a public-private partnership in which the private sector prices the mortgage guarantees and insures a small X% fraction, while the government is a silent partner, insuring the majority (100-X%) of the remainder and receiving the corresponding premiums.[225] Market pricing of the guarantees will ensure that: (i) a competing private sector mortgage market (without guarantees) will not be crowded out; and (ii) market discipline will return to the mortgage market. Interestingly, a similar proposal—*The Partnership to Strengthen Homeownership Act*—was offered in 2014 by Congressmen John Carney, John Delaney and Jim Himes, along with a number of bipartisan cosponsors.[226]

Thus, we envision that the initial phase of a transition to a new mortgage finance system would preserve mortgage default insurance via the aforementioned public-private partnership, primarily because such guarantees have been essential for the way that the securitization market for mortgages has developed. This way, the private sector would be encouraged to shrug off any regulatory uncertainty and allowed to flourish. Financial innovation in these markets could return. New investors that are focused on the credit risk of mortgage pools would emerge. Mortgages would become more standardized, and underwriting standards would improve.

---

[225] The private sector firm/subsidiaries would be "well-capitalized" and, if large enough, would be subject to the nonbank "systemically important financial institution" (SIFI) designation. An example of one such private-public program is given by the Terrorism Risk Insurance Act (TRIA) of 2007. Note that, given the aforementioned development of the market for mortgage credit risk sold off by the GSEs, it is possible that the public-private partnership is only required for tail or catastrophe risk.

[226] For a text of the bill, see https://delaney.house.gov/sites/delaney.house.gov/files/Partnership%20to%20Strengthen%20Homeownership.pdf.

Transitioning the GSEs

To help the transition process, reliance on the GSEs' guarantees should be mandated to end and their mortgage portfolios should continue to shrink. One example of such a mandate would be a gradual reduction of the size limit for conforming mortgages; another would be an increase in the fees that the GSEs charge for their guarantees (as was done post financial crisis).[227] Keeping the GSEs in conservatorships and thereby as wards of the Federal Government serves no good purpose. If there are efficiency gains and/or innovation possibilities that would accompany their operation as private for-profit companies, these advantages are foreclosed by their continued operation as government wards.

Further, their continued operation as government wards makes them prime candidates for "mission creep" and the diversion of their revenues and activities to other purposes. For example, within the past few years, 4.2 basis points of their annual guarantee fees has been earmarked for an affordable housing fund, and ten basis points has been earmarked for transfers to the Social Security Trust Fund to offset reduced payroll taxes. In addition, affordable housing goals for their securitization activities remain likely.[228]

A reasonable question is whether the two GSEs have significant going-concern value—e.g., that their brand names have worth and/or their organizations and technologies have value if kept intact. It may be a waste, therefore, to shutter them, and instead

---

[227] From 2006-2016, the conforming loan limit for most parts of the U.S. was $417,000, with higher amounts allowed in "high" housing price areas. For 2017, however, the conforming loan limit will be raised to $424,100—which is the opposite direction from what we believe is appropriate.

[228] Of course, even before the conservatorships, the GSEs (starting in 1992) were subject to explicit (and rising) affordable housing goals; and commercial banks and savings institutions have been subject to obligations to support their local communities by the Community Reinvestment Act of 1977. Nevertheless, the temptations and likelihoods of mission creep and diversions are surely greater when an organization is the direct ward of the government.

the GSEs should be privatized. Indeed, given that they currently securitize large chunks of the mortgage market, guarantee the mortgage payments, and sell off an increasing fraction of the credit risk to private investors, the GSEs might be good candidate firms to handle the residual "catastrophe risk" guarantees of the aforementioned public-private partnership.

If this is the case, then the Federal Government's 79.9% stake in the companies should be sold to the public in an initial public offering (IPO), and the companies should be structured (to the greatest extent possible) as normal companies (i.e., not as GSEs) with normal charters (e.g., from the state of Delaware) and normal bylaws, etc. The Federal Government's IPO of Conrail in 1987 could serve as an example. In the IPO of the GSEs, however, the Federal Government should be clear that the resulting private-sector entities will be required to be well financed with equity and that they (along with other residential mortgage securitizers) would be subject to bank-like rigorous prudential regulation, so that the likelihood that they would (again) require bailouts from the Federal Government would be quite small.

If the two GSEs are privatized—or even if they are wound down and replaced by other securitizers—it is clear that the maintenance of adequate levels of equity financing for private residential mortgage securitizers (relative to the risks of the mortgages that are securitized) is a key feature. It was clear in 2008 that the two GSEs were systemic and could not be allowed simply to fail and cause their creditors to suffer losses. The same would continue to be true if the two organizations are privatized and maintain roughly their current sizes, or even if they are wound down and replaced by somewhat smaller organizations.

For such systemic organizations, any *ex ante* government statements about refusals to bail out the organizations (or, in reality, their creditors) are likely to lack credibility *ex post* at times of financial difficulties.[229] It follows, then, that to reduce the likelihood of such situations arising, the organizations should be required to maintain adequate levels of equity financing relative to the risk characteristics of the mortgages that they are securitizing. They would therefore have adequate loss-absorbing capacities (i.e., equity) that will allow them to continue to operate and (until the equity is wholly depleted) avoid the disruptions and uncertainties of insolvency.[230] In the determination of appropriate levels of equity financing for these organizations, the same kinds of stress testing that is conducted for banks should be applied to these organizations, as well.

In addition, their prudential regulator should have clear powers of receivership in the event of insolvency, as is true for bank regulators. One of the important features of a receivership is that it eliminates the existing shareholder-owners—which was not true of the conservatorships of the GSEs. Receivership need not imply liquidation of the insolvent entity: As is true for banks, if there is sufficient going-concern value (which would disappear in a liquidation), the receiver can try to find new owners quickly, or even operate the entity for an interim period while finding those new owners.

GSEs aside, even if PLMBS returns to pre-crisis levels, given that the tranching/subordination structure was supposed to—but didn't—provide safety for the holders of the "safe" PLMBS tranches, the provision of guarantees (similar to those that have been offered by

---

[229] It is worth recalling that all of the GSE debt securities explicitly stated that these were not obligations of the U.S. Government; nevertheless, in September 2008, those securities did become obligations of the U.S. Government.

[230] Equivalently, adequate equity financing will mean that the equity holders/owners of these organizations will bear most of the losses, as well as enjoy all of the gains. The pre-2008 GSE structure, with inadequate equity financing, meant that the GSEs' gains were privatized, while their losses were socialized. "Never again" is an appropriate phrase for this outcome.

the GSEs) may be necessary.[231] Whether those guarantees are offered by the securitizers themselves (as was true for the GSEs) or by a set of third-party guarantors seems less important than the issue of who will back up the guarantors.

Rigorous prudential regulation of the guarantors is surely part of the answer. But the provision of a government backstop for the guarantors—in essence, government coverage of "catastrophic risk," much like the role that government-provided deposit insurance plays for bank depositors—may be important as well.[232] But the pricing of the risk to which the government is thereby exposed is a difficult problem by itself; there will always be intense political pressures to underprice that risk and thereby provide an implicit subsidy for mortgage finance.

To address these problems, we propose a system of side-by-side guarantees, whereby the Federal Government would provide PLMBS guarantees that would stand *pari passu* with those of private guarantors. The Federal Government could thereby price its guarantees on a par with the pricing of the private guarantors. Given the dearth of PLMBS activity since 2008, we continue to believe that such a system deserves serious consideration.

Other Proposals

Despite the absence of successful legislation—or, perhaps, *because* of that absence—there have been a plethora of policy papers and blueprints for GSE reform and/or more general reform of the residential mortgage finance system that have been offered by individuals and policy think tanks. For a recent effort under the auspices of the Urban Institute that offers a diversity of proposals,

---

[231] Indeed, if privatization of the GSEs occurs along the lines that we have described above, then their MBS ought to be considered as PLMBS.

[232] Once the government enters the role of a backstop for the guarantors, then the system of prudential regulation can be seen as a protection for the government (and ultimately taxpayers).

see: http://www.urban.org/policy-centers/housing-finance-policy-center/projects/housing-finance-reform-incubator. The NYU Center for Real Estate Finance Research hosted a discussion of recent reform proposals, a summary of which can be found here: http://www.stern.nyu.edu/experience-stern/about/departments-centers-initiatives/centers-of-research/center-real-estate-finance-research/research/gse-reform-will-it-happen-and-what-form-will-it-take.

Most of these proposals describe specific mechanisms whereby the government catastrophic risk insurance is provided in conjunction with the securitization and first-loss private-sector guarantee processes. Regardless of the details of these proposals, along with the previously mentioned legislative proposals, we reiterate that rigorous prudential regulation of the securitizers and guarantors—with adequate levels of equity financing, so as to provide private-sector first-loss and second-loss capacity that will protect the ultimate government (and thus taxpayer) guarantor—is an essential first step for any such plan.

Housing Finance Reform in General

Any discussion of the reform of the GSEs should acknowledge the larger policy context in which the GSEs are embedded: Public policy in the U.S. broadly favors housing—encouraging the construction, financing, and consumption of housing—through a broad range of explicit and (all too often) implicit policy tools at all levels of government. In addition to the GSEs,[233] the FHA, VA, and USDA provide government-backed mortgage insurance; and the mortgages that are insured by these three agencies are securitized by another government agency: Ginnie Mae. With respect to

---

[233] Also, the FHLBS was established in 1932 as a wholesale bank for savings institutions, which at that time were focused almost entirely on making residential mortgages. Although the FHLBS has broadened in terms of its institutional members and the kinds of lending that it supports, the support of residential mortgage lending is still an important part of its mission.

personal income taxes, the Federal Government and the states encourage housing through the mortgage interest deduction and the exemption of most capital gains on housing from reported income; the Federal Government also allows deductions for the state and local property taxes that home owners pay. The Federal Government and the states provide subsidies to builders to build multi-family housing; the Federal Government provides rental vouchers to low-income households; and "public housing" continues to be provided to low-income households by various levels of government.

"Too much is never enough" is a reasonable overall description of U.S. public policy toward housing. In that context, then, along with the above suggestions for reforming the GSEs, we discuss changes in mortgage finance and housing policy more generally.

Subsidies for Home Ownership Should Not Be Done Through a Revived PLMBS Market.

Whether the GSEs survive and are privatized—or are wound down and replaced—the resulting PLMBS market should not be the vehicle for subsidies for home ownership and/or for income redistribution that favors lower-income households:

First, any subsidies should be transparent, explicit, and on-budget; none of those characteristics apply to the cross-subsidies that would occur through a distorted PLMBS market. The FHA and Ginnie Mae, as on-budget entities of the Federal Government, are better vehicles for such subsidies.

Next, we believe that home ownership is an overvalued feature of U.S. housing policy. A house is a large, illiquid asset, with large transactions costs for buying and selling. Home ownership, and the accompanying mortgage finance, is not for everyone; it requires a relatively steady (and adequate) income and budgetary discipline on the part of the owning household. Those large transactions costs can impede job mobility when better employment opportunities would require moving to a different community. And, given the experience of the steep decline in house prices after the 2006 peak, by now the idea that home ownership is a sure road to building household wealth should have been dispelled.[234]

Any de-emphasis of home ownership should include a de-emphasis of the importance of national home ownership rates. In essence, renting should be promoted in respectability.

Finally, trying to do income redistribution through housing policy—whether explicit (e.g., through rent vouchers) or implicit (e.g., through the GSEs)—is a distinctly inferior method compared with direct income transfers (e.g., through refundable tax credits for low-income households).[235]

There may well be some modest positive externalities from home ownership and from encouraging low-income households to move to better neighborhoods through vouchers.[236] But, again, these goals should be pursued through transparent, explicit, on-budget means and vehicles.

---

[234] To the extent that the paying off of mortgage principal is a form of forced saving for a household, there may be some wealth building. But, again, the transactions costs of buying and selling are large; and the variance in house prices can also wipe out the forced saving.

[235] If one thinks of the GSEs as providing a subsidy for borrowing, they encourage greater leverage by home-owning households. And, to the extent that lower-income households are more leveraged, there may be income-distribution consequences from the termination of subsidies through the GSEs. See Gete and Zecchetto (2016). As they point out—and as we discuss below—a ready offset would be the termination of the income tax deduction for residential mortgage interest.

[236] See Sodini, Van Nieuwerburgh, Vestman, and von Lilienfeld-Toal (2016) for a recent study on the benefits from home ownership, and the references therein.

Reforming Housing Policies More Generally.

We believe that U.S. public policy has encouraged too much investment in housing. Concomitantly, other forms of investment—whether in physical production capital, such as plant and machinery; in community capital, such as schools, hospitals, roads, airports, etc.; or in human capital, such as more and better education and skill development for children and adults alike—have been neglected. Similarly, U.S. Gross Domestic Product (GDP) has suffered. Along the way, the specific tools that are used to encourage investment in housing are often inefficient and have perverse consequences for income distribution.

The personal income tax deduction for mortgage interest is a prime example. Notionally, it is intended to encourage home ownership by reducing the personal cost of a mortgage that is used to purchase a house. But it is explicitly a subsidy for borrowing, which encourages households to become more leveraged than would otherwise be the case. Next, it is far more likely to provide benefits to high-income households, who are more likely to itemize on their income tax filing and who are far more likely to take out a larger mortgage on a more expensive house and thereby get a larger deduction, than to low-income households.[237] Since high-income households are more likely to buy even in the absence of a mortgage subsidy, the mortgage interest deduction largely encourages those who would buy anyway primarily to buy a larger and better-appointed house. We fail to see the social value of such outcomes. And, finally, we question the goal of broadly encouraging home ownership—even if the mortgage interest deduction was effective in doing so, which it largely is not.

In sum, we believe that the American economy would be better served by a general "dialing back" of subsidies to housing. But where a good case can be made for correcting a substantial market

---

[237] See, for example, Poterba and Sinai (2008).

failure, we urge that the relevant housing program be focused on that specific problem and that it be conducted in an explicit, transparent, and on-budget fashion.

Better Ways to Reduce the Cost of Housing

There are better ways to reduce the cost of housing. They involve attacking the issue from the supply side, instead of (through subsidies) through the demand side.[238] There are at least three such ways:

First, the Federal and state governments should limit the ability of local (suburban) communities to restrict the supply of land for rental housing and for smaller houses (that tend to be on smaller lots) through those communities' restrictive zoning ordinances. Second, the Federal Government should undo protectionist trade measures that have limited the supplies of building materials, such as cement and lumber. And third, the Federal and state governments should limit the ability of local communities generally to impose local building codes that raise costs without providing commensurate benefits. In sum, there are ways of reducing the cost of housing that are consistent with improved efficiency—and with improved social equity.

Conclusion

It has been more than eight years since Fannie Mae and Freddie Mac were put into government conservatorships. The Dodd-Frank Act largely ignored them. The Financial CHOICE Act does the same. And thus, the GSEs remain in those conservatorships.

---

[238] Builder subsidies for multi-family housing appear to be the sole existing policy that operates through the supply side.

The U.S. system of financing residential housing is badly in need of reform. Keeping the GSEs in conservatorships is surely not an element of any sensible reform.

In this chapter, we have laid out our ideas for moving the system of financing residential housing in the direction of greater efficiency and greater equity. Since the CHOICE Act is still at the stage of proposed legislation, there is plenty of time for its drafters to address the GSEs and develop a blueprint for a better financial system for residential housing. We hope that this analysis can be useful in that process.

References

Acharya, Viral V., T. Sabri Oncu, Matthew Richardson, Stijn Van Nieuwerburgh, and Lawrence J. White, "The Government-Sponsored Enterprises," in Viral V. Acharya, Thomas F. Cooley, Matthew Richardson, and Ingo Walter, eds., Regulating Wall Street: The Dodd-Frank Act and the New Architecture of Global Finance. Wiley, 2011, pp. 429-442.

Acharya, Viral V., Matthew Richardson, Stijn Van Nieuwerburgh, and Lawrence J. White, Guaranteed to Fail: Fannie Mae, Freddie Mac and the Debacle of Mortgage Finance. Princeton University Press, 2011.

Elenev, Vadim, Tim Landvoigt, and Stijn Van Nieuwerburgh, "Phasing out the GSEs," Journal of Monetary Economics, vol. 81, August 2016, pp. 111-132.

Frame, W. Scott, Andreas Fuster, Joseph Tracy, and James Vickery, "The Rescue of Fannie Mae and Freddie Mac," Journal of Economic Perspectives, 29 (Spring 2015), pp. 25-52.

Frame, W. Scott and Lawrence J. White, "Fussing and Fuming at Fannie and Freddie: How Much Smoke, How Much Fire?" Journal of Economic Perspectives, 19 (Spring 2005), pp. 159-184.

Frame, W. Scott and Lawrence J. White, "The Federal Home Loan Bank System: Current Issues in Perspective," in Vivek Ghosal, ed., Reforming Rules and Regulations. MIT Press, 2011, pp. 255-275.

Gete, Pedro and Franco Zecchetto, "Distributional Implications of Government Guarantees in Mortgage Markets," Working Paper, October 2016.

Hagerty, James R., The Fateful History of Fannie Mae: New Deal Birth to Mortgage Crisis Fall. History Press, 2012.

Howard, Timothy, The Mortgage Wars. McGraw-Hill, 2014.

Jaffee, Dwight, Matthew Richardson, Stijn Van Nieuwerburgh, Lawrence J. White, and Robert Wright, "What to Do about the Government Sponsored Enterprises?" in Viral V. Acharya and Matthew Richardson, eds., Restoring Financial Stability: How to Repair a Failed System, Wiley, 2009, pp. 131-137.

McLean, Bethany, Shaky Ground: The Strange Saga of the U.S. Mortgage Giants. Columbia Global Reports, 2015.

Morgenson, Gretchen and Joshua Rosner, Reckless Endangerment: How Outsized Ambition, Greed, and Corruption Created the Worst Financial Crisis of Our Time. Times Books, 2011.

Poterba, James and Todd Sinai, "Tax Expenditures for Owner-Occupied Housing: Deductions for Property Taxes and Mortgage Interest and the Exclusion of Imputed Rental Income," American Economic Review, 98 (May 2008), pp. 84-89.

Paulson, Henry M., Jr., On the Brink: Inside the Race to Stop the Collapse of the Global Financial System. Hachette, 2010.

Sodini, Paolo, Stijn Van Nieuwerburgh, Roine Vestman, and Ulf von Lilienfeld-Toal, "Identifying the Benefits from Home Ownership: A Swedish Experiment," Working Paper, December 2016.

Sorkin, Andrew Ross, Too Big to Fail: The Inside Story of How Wall Street and Washington Fought to Save the Financial System--and Themselves. Viking Penguin, 2009.

There's Still Time

CHOICE Act vs. Dodd-Frank

Conclusions

By Thomas F. Cooley, Matthew P. Richardson,
Kermit L. Schoenholtz, Bruce Tuckman, and Lawrence J. White

The Dodd-Frank Act was not the perfect remedy for all of the problems of the U.S. financial sector that came together to form the "perfect storm" of the financial crisis of 2007-2009. Many faculty authors at Stern have previously criticized the shortcomings of Dodd-Frank, and in this White Paper, we again criticize many of these shortcomings with the advantage of a few more years of experience. But, to its credit, Dodd-Frank did recognize the importance and pernicious nature of systemic risk in the U.S. financial system and created prudential regulatory institutions and procedures to address and lessen that risk. Again, those institutions and procedures are far from perfect and could surely be made better. But, on net, Dodd-Frank represented a positive step in lessening the risk in our financial system.

The Financial CHOICE Act espouses some principles that we heartily endorse. Chief among them is that the more well-capitalized institutions are, the less of a threat they pose to financial stability. And we endorse removing many inefficient parts of Dodd-Frank. But at the end of the day, the CHOICE Act is fatally flawed by a failure to recognize systemic risk and to understand the dangers that it poses for the financial system—and thus for the healthy functioning of the U.S. economy. Because of this failure, the CHOICE Act represents a step backward in the establishment of a prudential regulatory system that would ensure a safer and better functioning financial sector for the U.S. economy.

Because the Financial CHOICE Act is still at the stage of proposed legislation, there is still adequate time and opportunity for its drafters to reach a better understanding of these issues. We hope that the chapters in this White Paper will help in that process.

41544695R00150

Made in the USA
Middletown, DE
16 March 2017